CW00519388

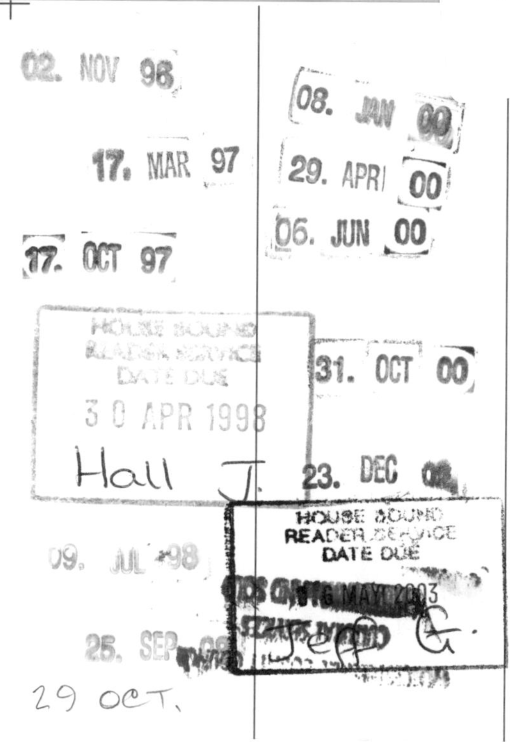
02. NOV 96
17. MAR 97
17. OCT 97
HOUSE BOUND
READER SERVICE
DATE DUE
30 APR 1998
Hall J.
09. JUL 98
25. SEP
29 OCT.
08. JAN 00
29. APRI 00
06. JUN 00
31. OCT 00
23. DEC
HOUSE BOUND
READER SERVICE
DATE DUE
16 MAY 2003
Jeff G.

70001377130 6

KINGSTONE

KINGSTONE

'Blanched Pence and One Hawk'

The story of a Herefordshire Village
from Domesday to the present time

Delphine Coleman

Delphine Coleman

LAPRIDGE PUBLICATIONS
1996

First published in 1996 by
Lapridge Publications
25 Church Street
Hereford HR1 2LR

ISBN 1 899290 00 1

Printed in Great Britain by
Biddles Ltd. of Guildford

For Eric with all my love

CONTENTS

Acknowledgments

I would like to express my thanks to all those people who have helped me in so many different ways:

Mr. George Clive for allowing me access to the archives of the Whitfield Estate, without which this history would be much the poorer, and for his kindness in writing the foreword; Miss M. Jancey, Mrs. M. Roberts and Miss J. Williams for their courtesy and patience in dealing with Hereford Cathedral Library matters and Mr. M. James for providing information from Llandaff Cathedral records; Miss S. Hubbard and the staff of the Hereford Record Office for their willing help and advice at all times and Mr. D.J.H. Smith and the staff of Gloucester Record Office for assistance relating to Newent Priory.

The National Library of Wales, Aberystwyth, for access to the Mynde Collection; Mr. R. Hill and the staff of the reference section of Hereford Library for never failing to produce just what was required; the Reverend David H. Williams for generously allowing me to quote freely from his researches on the Cistercian order; Mr. K. Lawton of Madley Communications Centre who found the time to conduct me round the site and explain its work; Dr. F. and Mrs. C. Thorn for assistance with the intricacies of the Domesday Book; Mr. S.D. Coates for allowing me to reproduce his photographs of the mills at Kingstone and Eaton Bishop; Mr. R.G. Berkeley and the trustees of the Grimthorpe and Drummond Castle Trust Ltd. for permission to reproduce the portraits of Lord Hunsdon and Lady Philadelphia Wharton.

The Public Record Office, London; the Methodist Archive, Manchester; Royal Air Force Museum, Hendon; Courtauld Institute of Art; National Portrait Gallery; National Monuments Record; Royal Commission on Historical Monuments, England; Kingstone Parish Council.

And to all the following persons who contributed greatly to the Kingstone story by producing photographs, deeds, records, maps and, above all, their reminiscences: Miss G. Addis, Miss M. Ballard, Mr. J. Bethell, Mrs. C. Bevan, Mr. M. Bride and the staff, past and present, of Kingstone High School, Dr. & Mrs. D.A. Chandler, Mr. Ted Colcombe, the late Mr. K. Cruse and Mrs. Cruse, Mrs. A. Ellis, the Rev. B. Gillett, Mr. A. Griffiths, Mr. E. Griffiths, Mrs. E. Hayter, Mr. E. Hughes, Mr. & Mrs. J. James, Miss S. Jay, Miss M. Johnson, Mrs. R. Meats, Mrs. D. Meek, the late Mr. & Mrs. G. Parry, Mr. & Mrs. M. Phillips, Mrs. A. Pitcher, Mr. C. Powell, Mr. & Mrs. R. Powell, Mr. J. Pullen, Mr. J. Reed, Mr. & Mrs. E. Sayce, Mr. & Mrs. T. Stevens, Mr. W. Stone, Mr. R. Vincent, Mr. Bill Watkins, Mr. & Mrs. Brian Watkins, Mr. Cecil Watkins, Mrs. D. Watkins, Mr. John Watkins, Mrs. J. Watson, Mr H.J. Waugh, Mrs. E. Wilding, Mr. & Mrs. G. Williams, Mr. & Mrs. K. Winney and Mr. & Mrs. N. Winney.

FOREWORD

by George Clive

Anyone who has been lucky enough to read Delphine Coleman's history of Orcop will know that she is a quite exceptional local historian. The present history of Kingstone confirms this. Here it is; from before the Norman Conquest to the present day, the fruit of years of tireless research, with graphic detail never submerged in the mass of material, and the story of Kingstone and its people always vividly told.

It is all here - the mediaeval manors, the church, the story of the Kingstone schools, right up to the RAF in the second World War and British Telecom in recent times. All this is told with a wonderful feel for the countryside - the changing field patterns, the features that have stayed like the oaks at Kingstone Grange and those that have disappeared, like the Barrow Pool.

It is tempting to call it a definitive history, but the attraction of local history is that it never can be completely definitive; there are always leads to other parishes and to other sources that those enthused by this book can follow. For all of us who know and love this beautiful part of England this book is an inspiration.

Whitfield
March 1996

Crown Copyright. Photo reproduced by permission.

Above: Great and Little Domesday books on the chest in which they were stored in the seventeenth and eighteenth centuries. Completed in 1087, they have been re-bound seven times, most recently in 1985.

Below: The original Kingstone entry in Exchequer Domesday Book.

Rex ten' ~~Chingestone~~. Rex. E. tenuit. Ibi .iiii. hidę.
In dnio sunt .ii. hidę una v min'. 7 ibi. e una car. 7 alia
posset. ee. 7 .vi. uilli cu ppósito 7 .iii. bord 7 .ii. fab. Int oms
hnt .vi. car. Ibi Silua noe Triueline. nulla reddes csu
etudine nisi uenatione. Villi T.R.E. ibi manentes. portab
uenatione ad hereford. nec aliud seruitiu facieb. ut scira dicit.
Hui m decima tota ten ~~[illegible]~~ de cormelius. 7 .ii. uill cu .i. virg
terrae. Ilbod. f. turoldi ten de hoc m .ii. hidas. p uno m.
huic m pertineb T.R.E. una pars tre ~~cheweshope~~. 7 csue
tudo de ea ptineb in Chingestone. Roger de Laci ten de rege.
Ad hoc m apposuit uicecom Tpr W. comitis ~~Waplefort~~.
hoc m tenuit Aluuin. 7 poterat ire ad que dnm uolebat.
Ibi .i. hida. Tra .ii. car. Ibi sunt .ii. uilli cu .i. car. firm.
Tot hoc ita cgregat. redd regi. L. sol de candid den. 7 .ii. accipi

INTRODUCTION

One cannot understand the English landscape, town or country, apprehend all its wonderful variety, without going back to the history that lies behind it.

W. G. Hoskins

Kingstone is situated some seven miles south west of the city of Hereford. The heart of the village lies on either side of the road from Ross-on-Wye to the border town of Hay-on-Wye, while the modern extension which emerged after the departure of the R.A.F. Training Establishment at the end of World War II, sits comfortably beside the main Hereford to Hay road. It is a pleasant amalgam of buildings of all shapes, sizes and ages, interspersed with open spaces, school playing fields, tarmac roads, country lanes, footpaths, ancient bridle ways and farm tracks. It has a degree of local employment, is well served with necessary amenities, is in the country, yet within easy reach of town.

It is a typical caring village community, carrying on its daily tasks at its own pace and, although rubbing shoulders with the gems of nearby Dore Abbey, Kilpeck Church and medieval glass of Eaton Bishop, it does not feature in county tourist itineraries. Approached from Hereford on the main road it merits little attention other than the massive dish aerials of the British Telecom Communications Centre situated on its boundaries with Madley.

My first glimpse of Kingstone was in 1952 when I accompanied my husband who was appointed on that visit as Rural Science master of the Secondary Modern School. We were to live there for twenty-five years interspersed with thirteen years teaching at Orcop and Much Dewchurch, not far away, returning when he was appointed head teacher of Kingstone Primary School. Much has changed since then, in great part due to the fact that Kingstone was designated a key village when long term planning for South Herefordshire was finalised. This has resulted in excellent health and educational facilities, a village shop, post office and a regular bus service.

It is a complete reversal when compared with the village of Orcop about which I wrote some years ago. Orcop village in the 1850s had a population double that of Kingstone, while today Kingstone has a population threefold that of Orcop, which has no surgery, school, shop, post office and only a very minimal bus service. Orcop is beginning to flourish again after a steady decline but its topography, which is so much more isolated than Kingstone, has set the pattern for the future. This is what makes local history so absorbing; all parishes are different since it is mainly outside influences that fashion their development.

The greater part of the material I have used is from primary sources, namely hand-written manuscripts, letters, documents, wills and court rolls, parish records, accounts and magazines, together with reputable books of reference, not forgetting shanks's pony! Spellings may vary at times, particularly with regard to places, but when quoting from documents the original spelling is retained.

I am very grateful to the many people named in the foregoing acknowledgments and trust that everyone has been remembered. Please accept my apologies if anyone has been inadvertently omitted. My husband, who prepared the diagrams and maps and has patiently coped with being left for hours on end when particularly obscure points cropped up, deserves a very special mention. Also Paul Latcham whose kind advice and painstaking attention to detail has made the final hurdle of publication a pleasurable experience.

Inevitably, there are questions that still remain to be answered and, no doubt, documents will continue to come to light which may help future historians who wish to pursue the trail. For this reason source references and bibliography have been included.

1 GEOGRAPHICAL LOCATION

Kingstone was well established by the time of the writing of the Domesday Book in 1086. Possibly its proximity to Hereford and the main route from the city into Brecknockshire would have been contributory factors. The name derives from the Old English or Anglo-Saxon name, meaning the 'tun' or town of the King.

1086	CHINGESTUNE	Domesday Book
1249	KINGESTON	Charter Rolls
1291	KYNGESTON	Taxatio Ecclesiastica

Many of the villages and hamlets in the vicinity have the same suffix, e.g. Dorstone, Brampton and Tyberton, indicating Anglo-Saxon settlement whereas those retaining Welsh names tend to be in the area embracing the hundreds of Ewias and Archenfield. The entry in Domesday indicates that it was 'ancient demesne', that is to say, land known before the coming of William the Conqueror. The Manor of Kingstone was known as 'Land of the King', the monarch in question being Edward the Confessor, who reigned from 1042 to 1066.

Herefordshire, in common with other counties in ancient times, was divided into areas named hundreds, and Kingstone was situated in the southern hundred of Stretford, which was bordered by the Golden Valley or Straddle hundred on the west, Dinedor and Wormelow hundreds on the east, and the hundred of Archenfield to the south. By the year 1316 Stretford and Dinedor had been amalgamated into the hundred of Webtree, and so it remains to this day.[1] Its boundaries stretch north to Madley, east to Allensmore and Thruxton, west to Abbeydore, and south to Treville. Its northernmost tip runs alongside the Roman road of Stone Street, and to reach that one traverses the centuries old Coldstone Common adjacent to the twentieth century Madley Post Office Satellite Earth Station, known since privatisation as Madley Communications Centre. Although in the hundred of Stretford at the time of Domesday, the Welsh region which embraced the hundreds of Ewias and Archenfield was very close, and the area was subject to much border skirmishing between the Normans and the Welsh.

Ancient earthworks, barrow tombs, and an iron-age fort are recorded at Abbeydore, Kerry's Gate, Dorstone and Eaton Bishop[2] but the only suggestion of pre-historic monuments in Kingstone itself is that of slight earthworks on land adjacent to Arkstone Court apparent in aerial photographs.[3] There is no trace of Roman occupation in the Kingstone area but Stone Street, which they built from Kenchester west of

HEREFORDSHIRE
MAP SHEWING DIVISION OF COUNTY INTO HUNDREDS
SHROPSHIRE
RADNORSHIRE
WORCESTERSHIRE
MONMOUTHSHIRE
GLOUCESTERSHIRE
WIGMORE
WOLPHY
STRETFORD
HUNTINGTON
BROXASH
GRIMSWORTH
EWYAS
LACY
WEBTREE
RADLOW
GREYTREE
WORMELOW
LEOMINSTER
KINGTON
HEREFORD
BROMYARD
LEDBURY
ROSS
Leintwardine
Downton
Brampton Brian
Elton
Wigmore
Lingen
Little Hereford
Aymestry
Croft
Orleton
Kinsham
Middleton on the Hill
Eye
Shobden
Eyton
Kimbolton
Titley
Staunton
Kingsland
Pudleston
Thornbury
Wolferlow
Pembridge
Monkland
Stoke Prior
Docklow
Tedstone Delamere
Huntington
Lyonshall
Dilwyn
Marston
Bredenbury
Almeley
Weobley
Hope under Dinmore
Kinnersley
Little Cowarne
Stanford Bishop
Brilley
Eardisley
Dinmore
Bodenham
Stoke Lacy
Canon Pyon
Norton Canon
Felton
Bishops Frome
Amberley
Great Cowarne
Clifford
Moreton on Lugg
Cradley
Bredwardine
Staunton on Wye
Mansell Lacy
Castle Frome
Moccas
Burghill
Withington
Westhide
Cusop
Dorstone
Holmer
Bosbury
Blakemere
Canon Frome
Weston Beggard
Yarkhill
Colwall
Peterchurch
Eaton Bishop
Stoke Edith
Craswall
Madley
Turnastone
Lower Bullingham
Mordiford
Pixley
Kingstone
Allensmore
Woolhope
St Margarets
Bacton
Aconbury
Fownhope
Much Dewchurch
Ballingham
Much Marcle
Abbey Dore
Kilpeck
Much Birch
Ewyas Harold
Clodock
Rowlstone
Kentchurch
Orcop
Hentland
Sellack
Upton Bishop
Walterstone
St Weonards
Bridstow
Brampton Abbots
Linton
Tretire
Garway
Weston
Llangarren
Marstow
Walford
Welsh Newton
Goodrich
Whitchurch
RIVER WYE
Scale of Miles

Hereford, runs close to Coldwell and over Brampton Hill in the parish. From there it runs via Kerry's Gate to join a probable Roman road along the Golden Valley from Dorstone to Pontrilas.

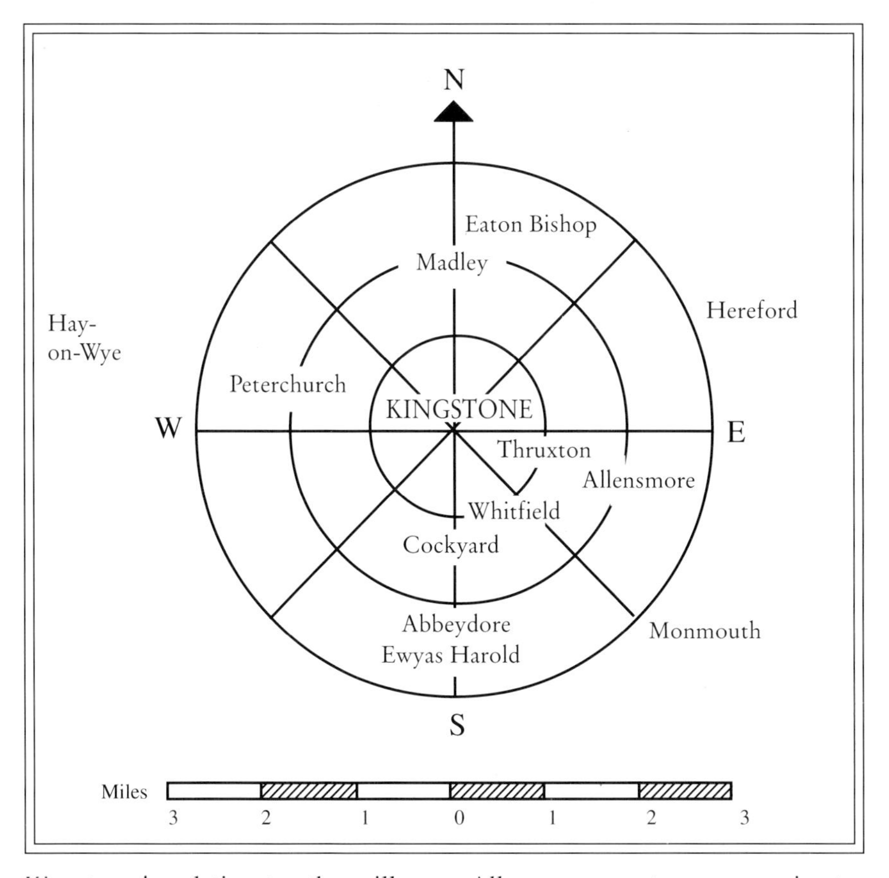

Kingstone in relation to other villages. All measurements are approximate.

The Roman road passes close to the old Madley airfield and it was near here, close to the line of the road, that a Dubonic gold stater was found in 1981. This ancient coin dates from 30 BC to AD 10 and, as can be seen from the photographs, is in very good condition. The design on the reverse side depicts a six-jointed triple-tailed horse to the right, with a wheel, bell and other ornaments. The obverse shows an ear of corn.[4]

There are motte and bailey castle sites in the surrounding villages of Madley, Bacton, St. Devereux, Kilpeck and Ewyas Harold and, while it is not improbable that there could have been one in Kingstone, the only reference is to be found in the name of Castle Field on Kingstone Grange land. At nearby Thruxton, close to the church, there is a tumulus or mound of unknown origin but no documentary or archaelogical evidence has yet been found to link the two. The mound at Thruxton has been excavated but remains unclassified according to the National Monuments Record.

The Dubonic gold stater found on Stone Street, Madley.

Copyright Hereford Archaeological Unit

REFERENCES

[1] *Domesday Book: Herefordshire.* Edited by F. and C. Thorn. Phillimore, 1983.

[2] *Herefordshire Register of Countryside Treasures.* H. & W.C.C., 1981.

[3] University of Cambridge. Comm. for Aerial Photography. O.S. map ref. SP.434362.

[4] National Monuments Record, Swindon. Transactions of the Woolhope Naturalists Field Club, 1979-81, R. Shoesmith.

2 THE COMING OF THE NORMANS

When William, Duke of Normandy, decided to press his claim to the English throne in 1066, he commanded a formidable fleet of some 690 large ships supported by many smaller vessels equipped with arms, stores and horses. Most important of all, he had mustered a large force of some 12,000 foot soldiers led by knights who were quick to seize the chance of increasing their estates in Normandy by the acquisition of land in England. William had promised rich pickings to those who would serve him well. The expedition was financed from the treasuries of Caen and Rouen.

He embarked from the shores of Normandy at Dives-sur-Mer, not so many miles away from the D-Day landing beaches of 1944. Today, Dives is a small seaside resort with a fine medieval market hall dating back to the twelfth century, lying much in the shadow of its sophisticated and illustrious neighbour, Deauville, with its race course, yacht marinas and expensive housing nestling in the hills behind the coast. In the church of Notre Dame de Dives can be seen the memorial erected in 1862 which bears the names, written both in French and English, of the men who were to become so influential in the cities, towns and villages of England.

Could the de Laci knights, from Lassy in Normandy, have foreseen that they would be involved with the founding of Llanthony Abbey in the mountains of Wales, with the building of St. Peter's Church in Hereford, and have manors and villages named after them in Herefordshire, not to mention huge estates elsewhere in the kingdom? Did Bernard of Neuf-Marché envisage that he would conquer countless stretches of the Welsh Marches, and build himself a castle in Brecon? He certainly could not have known when he landed on the beach at Pevensey, in the company of his half-brother Duke William, that he would one day be possessed of a great lordship, known as the Honour of Brecknock. This was to make his daughter and heiress, Sibyl, a much sought after lady in the marriage market. She married Milo FitzWalter, later to become Earl of Hereford in addition to holding office as Sheriff of Gloucester.[1]

Certainly Bernard and Sybil Neuf-Marché played a part in the Kingstone story, since Kingstone was part of the possessions of the Honour of Brecknock, albeit a very small part, and the knight who was termed Lord of Kingstone was, in effect, a tenant. He was allotted the lordship on payment of a money rent and, what was more important in those days of self-seeking and treachery, had to swear an oath of fidelity or allegiance in addition to providing knight service in event of war. It depended very much on the amount of land granted as to whether it was the tenant himself who followed his liege lord to war, or whether he was wealthy enough to provide a fully equipped knight in his stead.

William landed at Pevensey on the 28th September 1066, constructed fortifications at Hastings, won his memorable battle on 14th October, and was eventually crowned in Westminster Abbey on Christmas Day. Duke William of Normandy had become William I of England, more commonly known as William the Conqueror.

The Normans were now firmly established, adding greatly in numbers to the few who had settled here in the time of Edward the Confessor. There was to be much bloodshed when various uprisings, notably in the north and at Exeter, were ruthlessly dealt with. Vast tracts of land were laid waste if Norman authority was challenged; the rule was to be absolute. The Normans were improvers rather than innovators, and the twenty-one years of William's reign (1066-1087) were to see much ecclesiastical re-organisation together with the building of abbeys, cathedrals and the many village churches with their rounded arches, square towers and dog-tooth patterning on columns and doorways.

Kingstone parish church is regarded as a well preserved unadorned late Norman/early English edifice dating from circa 1150. The organisation of urban and rural communities was already in being prior to the coming of the Normans but administration was centralised and made more efficient under them.

Powerful lords were entrusted to rule large areas or regions, often with the authority to sub-infeudate (sub-let) to lesser knights but, at the end of the day, they were under no illusions as to their ultimate responsibility. They held their positions of trust directly from the King in Chief. There were some so high in the King's esteem that they held their lands and position by oath of fealty alone, with no other commitments. An interesting example of this is Meer Court (a small part of which is in Kingstone parish) which, at one time, was held from the Honour of Weobley by service of a rose at midsummer.

Such a lord was Bernard of Neuf-Marché who outlived William I. Another with whom Kingstone had a direct link was William FitzOsbern who was entrusted with the mammoth task of subduing any opposition on the southern end of the Welsh Marches. He had supplied sixty ships for the invasion fleet, was a very able administrator and soldier, and one of William's staunchest followers. He rose to prominence earlier than Bernard, was created Earl of Hereford soon after the Conquest, and in the five years from then until his death in 1071, whilst fighting in Normandy, was responsible for the building of castles at Clifford, Wigmore, Chepstow and Monmouth.

William FitzOsbern founded two Benedictine Abbeys in Normandy, one at Lyre where his wife was buried, and one at Cormeilles where he himself was buried. The trust shown in him by King William is evidenced by the fact that FitzOsbern granted the tithes of many of his manors to these two communities. The tithes of Kingstone were granted to the Abbey of Cormeilles, and such was the importance of both, that their respective abbots were represented by canons and vicars in the Church of St.Mary and St.Ethelbert (Hereford Cathedral) before FitzOsbern's death in 1071.

View of the Rue de l'Abbaye, Cormeilles where the Benedictine Abbey of St. Mary was situated.

Cormeilles is a quiet little village south of Le Havre and north-east of Liseux. It has several ancient houses with typical Norman brown and white timbering and plaster, and a small square from which one can see the parish church towering above the rooftops. The abbey has long since disappeared although one street still bears the name Rue de l'Abbaye. When I went there some years ago the parish priest told me he had visited the parish church of St.Mary in Chepstow since it too had belonged to the abbey at the time of the Domesday Survey. Chepstow is twinned with Cormeilles. All the churches attached to Cormeilles were dedicated to St. Mary but Kingstone church was not built when the tithes were originally given, probably between 1066 and 1071.

The connection between Kingstone and Cormeilles is clear enough as regards its original intention, but it becomes increasingly difficult to follow as time goes on. This is most likely due to the fact that when

William FitzOsbern died his son Roger did not have the same loyalty as his father and rebelled against the King, was soon dealt with and forfeited his right to lands and title. For some while the King left the matter in abeyance. Not to be wondered at perhaps!

Kingstone was a settled community prior to the coming of William the Conqueror and, by the time of the Domesday Book in 1086, there existed a village that had links with the Cathedral Church of Hereford, the Norman Abbey of St. Mary of Cormeilles and the Earldom of Hereford.

REFERENCES

[1] 'The Honours of the Earls of Hereford in the Twelfth Century', by D.G. Walker, in Transactions of the Bristol and Gloucestershire Archaeological Society, vol. 79-80 (1960), pp. 174-211.

3 DOMESDAY BOOK

Domesday Book, the starting point for studying the history of so many hamlets, villages, towns and cities throughout the land, has a sizeable entry relating to Kingstone. In fact, it appears on the very early pages of Herefordshire, after the account of the customs of Herefordshire and of Archenfield. William, Duke of Normandy, having conquered England in 1066, seems to have decided in 1085 that it was high time he found out exactly what he could expect by way of service and money from his new subjects.

So we find him spending midwinter at Gloucester and, as the Anglo-Saxon Chronicle states:

'the King had deep speech with his counsellors...and sent men all over England to each shire...to find out....what or how much each landholder held...in land and livestock, and what it was worth. The returns were brought to him'.

This historic meeting took place in the Chapter House of the Abbey of St. Peter, later to become Gloucester Cathedral. There is little doubt that William who, since his landing in 1066, had shown no mercy to anyone who opposed him, while rewarding those who served him faithfully, would have made it quite clear that nothing was to be overlooked. Robert Losinga, Bishop of Hereford at that time, stated that William, in order to discourage any form of corruption, took the added precaution of sending out different clerks to districts unfamiliar to them, to check on the statements.

One cannot help but wonder what other plans William had in mind when ordering this work to be carried out. Domesday is acknowledged to be the finest piece of socio-economic analysis available until the compilation of the first official census in 1801. William did not live long afterwards to benefit from its data. He had embarked from the shores of his kingdom of Normandy in 1066 and it was to Normandy he returned in 1086 to put down insurrection there. When his horse stumbled on some hot cinders, he was thrown and suffered severe internal injuries from which he died after much suffering.

It seems that questions were sent to tenants, to the representatives of each vill (which might contain several manors and tenants), and to the hundreds (which were made up of several vills). The commissioners, or different groups of commissioners, had to travel to each shire town to hear on oath the evidence of each vill and hundred at a meeting of the shire moot (county court). They set out the answers to their questions in a very orderly fashion and in the finished work, Great Domesday Book, chapters were numbered, capital letters were used to denote and show up place names and important facts and, all in all, one feels that the seeds of today's civil service were already flourishing very nicely some 900 years ago.

The same searching questions were put to a cross-section from the most powerful and influential to the most humble:

What is the name of your village?
Who owned it before our Liege Lord, King William?
How many mills are there in the village?
How many ploughs have you?
How much is all this worth now, and how much was it worth before our Lord the King came to these shores?
How many villagers live here, how many own their own land and are free men?
How much land is woodland, meadow land and pasture land?
How much land belongs to your Lord and how much to the rest of you?

And so it went on. The enquiry took account of village gossip and events of the past when land had changed hands, sometimes perhaps wrongfully. Did John of the Green and William the Smith wonder what the outcome would be? Perhaps they were so accustomed to being quizzed about village doings by the steward of their lord in readiness for the regular manorial courts that they just took it in their stride, shrugged their shoulders, and trudged back home when it was all over. One thing was reasonably certain, they must have guessed it meant more money to be found from those who had very little to give. It probably made a change to see some different faces, and they must have marvelled at the skill of those diligent, clever, but ordinary men who were able to transfer their speech on to parchment with considerable speed. Could any of them ever have hazarded the slightest guess that they had been participating in an undertaking that would be translated, analysed, discussed, printed, photographed and agonised over by their descendents to the extent that it has been ever since? It was probably a nine-days wonder that was soon forgotten.

The answers the commissioners received to their questions would have come from the whole spectrum of the community who had to swear on oath before giving their evidence; the barons, sheriffs, clerics, reeves (manorial bailiffs) and six inhabitants from each village, both French and English

The customs of the city of Hereford are mentioned first in the survey. We learn that 103 men dwelt there, of whom six were blacksmiths each paying one penny for his forge, and that each made 120 horseshoes from the King's iron. They were paid a customary three pence and exempted from any other service. The first district dealt with was Archenfield, an area incorporated into England by King Edward. The survey recounts that when the army advanced on the enemy, the Welshmen of Archenfield formed the vanguard and, on their return, the rearguard. These archers were regarded as the finest in England and it seems a fitting tribute that they are commemorated today in Herefordshire's worldwide industrial export of cider, Strongbow.

The Kingstone entry in the survey is as follows, according to the most recent translation.[1]

> KINGSTONE King Edward held it. 4 hides. In lordship 2 hides less 1 virgate. 1 plough there, another would be possible. 6 villagers with a reeve; 3 smallholders and a smith. Between them they have 6 ploughs.
>
> A wood named Treville which pays no customary dues except hunting rights. The villagers who lived there before 1066 carried (the produce of) the hunt to Hereford and did no other service, as the Shire states.
>
> St. Mary's of Cormeilles holds the whole tithe of this manor, and 1 villager with 1 virgate of land.
>
> Ilbert son of Thorold holds 2 hides of this manor as 1 manor.
>
> Before 1066, 1 parcel of land, Cusop, belonged to this manor; its customary dues went to Kingstone. Roger of Lacy holds from the King.
>
> The Sheriff placed Wapleford in this manor in Earl William's time. Alwin held this manor; he could go to whichever lord he would. 1 hide there. Land for 2 ploughs. 2 villagers with 1 plough.
>
> The whole of this, added together thus, pays the King 50s. of blanched pence and 1 hawk.

To summarise this as briefly as possible, King Edward was Edward the Confessor who reigned before the conquest, indicating that the village was in being well before the Norman invasion, and subject to ancient laws and customs. The villagers were likely to have been quite vocal about this as evidenced by the recorded fact that they carried the proceeds of the hunt from the forest of Treville, a royal forest (adjacent to Kingstone), to Hereford and, put bluntly, that was their lot. It was very clearly put; they 'did no other service'.

The reference to four hides is the acreage of arable land. A hide varied in different parts of the country but is generally thought to be about 120 acres, although by King Edward's time a hide was also a measure of taxation. The fact that the land was calculated in hides is indicative of long English settlement. Welsh settlement was usually measured as ploughlands or carucates.

The Lord of the Manor's land or demesne, the Home Farm, consisted perhaps of some 240 acres less one virgate. A virgate was in the region of thirty acres, or a quarter of a hide, so he had about 200 acres which were his own to farm. There was enough arable land for one plough, possibly sufficient for another plough.

With regard to population, the manor had six villein or tenant farmers, plus three smallholders or cottagers, a reeve, a smith and one more villager working on land held by the Abbey of Cormeilles. This totals twelve males who, with their families, would yield a population of at least fifty persons, probably more. The recorded rural population of Herefordshire according to the Domesday Survey was about 4500, and the average number of recorded persons per populated vill was sixteen.[2]

The tenant farmers were small farmers who farmed the lord's land, paying a money rent and giving so many days a year service for planting and harvesting. The manor house table would be replete with poultry, eggs, and other items which were part of their lease. In return the tenants had a settled way of life, and were protected in their holdings by their lord. The smallholders or cottagers likewise had the same obligations, but would have had very little land, possibly about four acres.

All this brought a new language, Norman French, to their daily lives which still, in the twentieth century, is part of our own daily lives. The Anglo-Saxon villager might have felt aggrieved hearing such name changes as cow-boeuf-beef; sheep-mouton-mutton; chicken-poulet-pullet; pig-porc-pork. Nowadays we take these words for granted

The mention of a reeve may indicate that the lord had appointed one villager to act as a bailiff or farm manager to administer the working of the land, which included the day to day managing of the strips in the fields and ensuring that all the manorial customs were adhered to.

The smith too was considered worthy of special mention. He was a craftsman whose maintenance of all implements of husbandry together with the shoeing of oxen and horses made him a valued member of the village community. The smith was often allotted a strip of land in the common field, and a share in the plough in recognition of his skills.

Treville was a parish in its own right. King John later hunted in the forest of Treville and spent several weeks in the area visiting Kilpeck and Grosmont shortly before his death in 1216.[3] He is buried in Worcester Cathedral.

There is no mention of a priest or a church but the tithes went to the Abbey of St. Mary of Cormeilles which also had about thirty acres of land together with a tenant to work it. The abbey's daughter house in England was the Priory of St. Mary at Newent which was in the diocese of Hereford until the Diocese of Gloucester was created in 1541.

There are problems in attempting to sum up the Domesday entry for Kingstone. It is hard to visualise the piecemeal nature of the land, parcelled out to various high-ranking barons and knights, who in their turn had their own sub-tenants, the lesser knights, when compared with villages today, with their clearly defined parish boundaries. This border region had seen, and would still see, regular skirmishing with the Welsh, and much of the land was waste. Scrubland, common and wood were all under the jurisdiction of the manor, but unless it was worthy of paying tax, it was not recorded.

A manor could be a whole vill, it could be just one large farm, or the village itself could contain several manors. The entry states that the manor of Kingstone was four hides. At the time of the survey there were:

- One manor of two hides held by Ilbert, carved out of Kingstone.
- Another manor, Wapleford, amounting to one hide had been added, and it had been held by Alwin.

Added to these two manors and the strange earlier addition of Cusop, which seems rather remote from Kingstone (near the Welsh border at Hay-on-Wye), was the Treville wood. So the Manor of Kingstone, as recorded in Domesday, was not a complete entity as it might have been in 1066; it had already been partially split up, sub-infeudated, which makes tracing its history a complex task.

However, there exists a later manuscript known as the Herefordshire Domesday, written circa 1160-1170, which reproduces and updates the original Domesday survey.[4] It is thought to have been the work of Thomas Brown, who worked for the Exchequer and had connections with Herefordshire. It is from this later survey that one can see how so many manors came to be split up and farmed out to aspiring lesser knights who had to pledge homage and service to the King in times of war. They got their feet on the manorial ladder, the sovereign was able to call on his barons for men and arms and they, in turn, provided these from their sub-tenants.

Herefordshire Domesday is a remarkable document. It identifies and places Ilbert's manor of two hides at Hungerstone on the eastern boundary of Kingstone as it is today. It was also associated at that time with Mawfield, a farm and small hamlet in Allensmore. Many Kingstone documents refer to Kingstone in Mawfield, so presumably in 1086 this land was considered to be part of Kingstone manor. There was another manor named Kingstone in the parish of Weston-under-Penyard, Herefordshire. It too was part of the possessions of St. Mary of Cormeilles, so there would have been a need for specific identification.

The other land named Wapleford is re-named in Herefordshire Domesday as 'terra laur in Kingest'. This is no more helpful than Wapleford, but it is open to conjecture whether 'terra laur' could have been corrupted to the Trelough known today. The local pronunciation can be 'tre-law' or 'tre-loo'. It is situated close to the Treville wood, which is part of the Kingstone manor entry. Alwin, the lesser knight who had been given this small manor, was allowed to go to any lord or protector in time of trouble.

Although the Great Domesday entry is not a straightforward one to unravel, it marks the first steps by which Kingstone treads through the centuries and provides the basis and points the way for us to follow. So far as William the Conqueror was concerned the important fact was in the final sentence:

> 'The whole of this, added together thus, pays the King 50 shillings of blanched pence and one hawk'.

Blanched pence indicated coin that had been tested for base metal. Which farmer or cottager reared the hawk, one wonders, and did King William ever hunt with it in his enclosure of Treville?

REFERENCES

[1] *Domesday Book: Herefordshire.* Edited by F. and C. Thorn. Phillimore, 1983.

[2] 'Evolution of Rural Settlements in Herefordshire'. C.W. Atkins.

[3] *History of Ewias Harold.* A.J. Bannister. Hereford, 1902.

[4] *Herefordshire Domesday.* Edited by V.H. Galbraith and J. Tait. Pipe Roll Society, London, 1950.

4 THE MANORS OF KINGSTONE

The word manor is derived from the ancient French *manoir* meaning a freehold estate given by the sovereign to a follower in return for certain services, usually military service. Its origins are still the subject of much debate, but it is thought to have been in existence in England by A.D. 700 and certainly in Western Europe before A.D. 1000. Kingstone is recorded in Domesday Book as a Royal manor held by the King and was regarded as ancient demesne, since it was held by Edward the Confessor before the Norman Conquest. The area was thus steeped in antiquity and subject to a way of life that carried various laws, written and unwritten, which were known to its inhabitants, to quote an oft used and most poetic phrase, 'from time immemorial'.

A village could consist of more than one manor and Domesday tells us that this was certainly the case with regard to Kingstone. There are sufficient primary sources to indicate that Arkstone and Meer Court were manors in their own right. The court rolls for Kingstone and Allensmore in the cathedral library of Hereford indicate that the rents from both villages were collected for the dean and chapter.[1] Meer Court is mentioned as a manor in Inquisitions Post Mortem from 1350 onwards.[2] Later on it is recorded as belonging to Sir Richard Symons of the Mynde at Much Dewchurch and, still later, to Sir Hungerford Hoskyns at Harewood End.[3] Meer Court was not mentioned in Domesday Book but there are extracts from court rolls in the National Library of Wales with lists of chief rents due to the manor from freeholders. A small acreage of Meer Court was in Kingstone parish and had to pay tithe to Kingstone together with a small percentage of wool and lambs. This was by consent of the dean and chapter and the respective vicars in 1672.[4] A terrier made in 1775 stated that fifty acres in Meer Court paid tithe to Kingstone, while the 1840 Allensmore tithe map mentions '17 acres in Meer Court lying in Mawfield to pay £1.16.0. in lieu of two thirds of Corn of Great Tithe'.[5]

Arkstone belonged at one time to the Cathedral of Llandaff[6], later to the Morgan and Parry families and, when the estate was sold in 1825, it was advertised in the Hereford Journal and other papers as carrying with it the lordships of Arkstone, Mawfield and Hungerstone. It was in the hands of the Martin family by 1841, and continued so for a century until the death of James Hamilton Martin in 1940. The estate, which by then included Meer Court and the 'reputed lordships or manors of Arkstone, Hungerstone, Mawfield and Meer Court', was bought by Guy's Hospital. They eventually sold it to Mr. Charles Clore in 1961 from whence it passed to the Prudential Assurance Company. Arkstone and Meer Court have now been separated and are owned by Mr. John Watkins and Dr. R.

Aldridge. I have been unable to trace any court rolls for Arkstone to date but, on an inventory taken when one of the Parrys died, there is the following remark under money due:

> 'arrears of Chief Rents due but not known what it will amount to until a Cort be kept'.[7]

So, throughout the centuries the manors of Kingstone were tossed back and forth amongst many feudal lords. The very earliest was Bernard de Neuf-Marché and, by the mid-1100s, the de Bohun family, Earls of Hereford for many generations, were the overlords. These powerful barons probably knew very little of Kingstone other than as a possession which would yield a rental and knight service when the raising of arms was necessary. It is their tenants or underlords who emerge more often from the mists of time when giving gifts of Kingstone land or rentals to the church.

The best documented of the Kingstone manors is that referred to as Kingston Furches or Kingston Forges, the title originating from the family who were lords of Kingstone for well over a century. The Furches family were to be found in Shropshire and Herefordshire by the twelfth century. In 1085 the Holme Lacy Charter lists a Herbert de Furches in Herefordshire as a follower of the de Lacy family, while the Domesday entry for Bodenham records that 'Herbert holds from Roger de Lacy'. One of the Bodenham manors was named Bodenham Furches, most likely as in the case of Kingstone, to distinguish it from other manors within the village boundaries.

The first half of the thirteenth century records William de Furches witnessing 'a grant of land in Kingest' made by Walter de Haia to the Church of St. Mary and St. Ethelbert in Hereford (the cathedral).[8] The land was granted in frank-almoign of sixpence, a form of tenure whereby the clergy would pray for the soul of the donor. It is worth noting that Walter de Haia was at one time prior of Llantony Prima in Wales and that one of the first known clerics at Kingstone, presented by a William de Furches prior to 1281, was a Master Henry de Llanton.[9] Llantony Prima was of the Augustinian order (the Austin Canons) and land in Kingstone numbered 50 on the one and only Enclosure Act of 1812 was owned by the cathedral of Hereford and named 'Austin's field meadow'. Today the two fields nearby are referred to as Great and Little Horston, which must surely be an oral corruption of Austin. They are part of Kingstone Grange.

Another grant from William de Furches to the almshouses of St. Ethelbert in Hereford was of 'pasture for seven kine in his pasture in the moor which runs between Kingstun and Madeleia, with a right of way through his land to the said pasture'. This was witnessed by two of his brothers, yet another William and Robert.[10] The tithe map of 1842 shows a field of eight acres, number 240, named Lord's Meadow which runs right up to the Madley parish boundary. This was part of the land bought by the Post Office for the Communications Centre but until 1874 it formed part of the manor lands.

The Furches family were the lesser Lords of Kingstone for several generations and, prior to 1300, William de Furches gave an important concession to the monks of Dore, who had established a grange near his own demesne farm of Dunswater. Kingstone Grange grew from land given to the Abbey circa 1170[11] and, at some time after that, he gave the monks a way on his demesne passing through the garden of their grange leading to the 'kings way', allowing them to enclose it and ditch it.[12] This ancient way existed for several centuries and is referred to in the manor rolls of 1594. It runs out of the 'king's way', now the main B.4348 road past Dunswater, entering Dunswater 'Old lands', then proceeds along the 'New house field' through 'Thornfield' into 'Twelve acres' where it meets with the grange lands. These field names are all to be found on the tithe map. This way runs parallel to the Kingstone/Abbeydore road and is marked as a footpath on Ordnance Survey maps. In medieval times it was used for wains and carriages and would certainly have been far less taxing for users than the present Cockyard road.

The Furches family line in Kingstone appears to end with the marriage of the heiress to a son of Sir William Lucy of Charlecote in Warwickshire[13], the Lucy family retaining their Kingstone connection until the 1580s when, after passing through various hands, the manor of Kingstone Furches or Forges was acquired by Sir Thomas Coningsby of Hampton Court, Herefordshire, late sixteenth/early seventeenth century. His great grandson, Sir Thomas Coningsby, and his second wife, Frances, had two daughters, Lady Margaret, created Countess of Coningsby in 1717, and Lady Frances, who married Sir Charles Hanbury Williams of Coldbrook, Monmouth. The title became extinct on the death of Margaret in 1761, prior to which time she appears on the court rolls of the hundred and manor of Kingstone as lady of the manor. Her only child died an infant and in later court rolls Lady Frances was named as lady of the manor until 1767 when they appear to cease. The manor, mansion house, estate and farm of Dunswater was advertised for sale in the Hereford Journal on 30th December 1773. The tenant at that time was Richard Russell, who died in 1778. Lady Frances died in 1781. Her daughter and son-in-law inherited Hampton Court.

Many fresh documents, including leases of land and property in Kingstone, have been deposited with the Hereford Record Office recently.

These show that the manor of Kingstone Forges and Dunswater estate were being leased and mortgaged before the death of Sir Thomas Coningsby in 1729 and during the lifetime of his two daughters, who were still being regarded and recorded as respective ladies of the manor. Richard Russell was a tenant of Dunswater for many years before his death. His lease was for his own and another life which would account for his son-in-law being noted as the proprietor in the land tax records of the late 1700s.

There were more leases and mortgages prior to 1812 when William Croome, a Cirencester banker, eventually became the owner of the whole manor and Dunswater estate. Counsel's opinion was needed on the inheritance of the estate from 1703 to 1809 and, in 1774, only two-thirds could be leased since the other third had been leased previously. Some names involved in the transactions are those of descendants from Sir Thomas Coningsby's first marriage so, no doubt, there was a legal wrangle which rumbled through Chancery for many decades before it was resolved.[14] Lady Frances's husband, Sir Charles Hanbury Williams, was a prominent ironmaster in Pontypool. She was buried in Westminster Abbey on the 31st December 1781.

William Croome was to be an absentee landlord residing in a lovely mansion in the Cotswold village of Bagendon, near Cirencester. He gave the land for the old school in Kingstone in 1845. His name features very often in subscription lists for church repairs and like projects. It was through his descendant that the chance for the Parochial Church Council to acquire the old school came about. The Croome family retained ownership until 1874 when the Clive family of Whitfield, Allensmore bought the manor and lands. The Whitfield Estate still owns the ancient farms of Dunswater, Hanley Court and Kingstone Grange, but the title of lord of the manor, although listed in trade directories of the 1930s as remaining with the Clives, is not acknowledged any more.

A fascinating document in the Mynde Collection at the National Library of Wales reinforces the fact that the tenants of the manor were bound by oath to their lord but, no doubt, as time went on the link between lord and tenant became weaker. After the Black Death in 1348 agricultural workers were so few in number, and the need for them so great, that services were commuted into wages, wages began to increase, and the men on the land began to realise that their labour had far more value than hitherto. There occurred a gradual increase in the number of tenants holding their land by lease or copyhold, that is by a document signed by their lord, which was re-negotiated on death. Quite often the lease covered the family for several lives, and services or duties which had been regarded as normal and routine became less so. Tenants had more

North Cerney House, near Cirencester. Home of William Croome, Lord of Kingstone Forges Manor. He was buried in the nearby parish church.

freedom and probably resented too much interference from the manorial hierarchy. To put it into modern day parlance, they wanted to be their own men.

The document referred to is entitled 'Notes of an address of the Lord to his Suitors, Manor of Mear Court' and is seventeenth century. It is to be found with extracts from court rolls dated 1528-1641 which suggests that the address was to have been given sometime after 1641. Since there are also notes of rent arrears from 1649 to 1661, which covered the time of the Commonwealth when many estates were confiscated, the restoration of Charles II to the throne in 1660 probably gave impetus to the need for returning to normality.[15]

Part of the document was obviously copied from ancient court rolls, some in Norman French, so the writer was possibly not conversant with the full import. It is quite likely that the address was to be delivered by the steward of the manor on behalf of his master and that a court had not been held for a long time. Perhaps the manor was in new hands, and the owner had to show his authority and tighten up the administration. This could well have been undermined during the Commonwealth period. The military tenancies granted to the great barons on condition that they provided knights when required were abolished in 1660 having been in abeyance for the preceding twenty years. Tenancies were granted by straightforward documentation and, no doubt, people quickly became aware that they were not always subject to the same feudal dictates as had previously obtained.

The address commences:

> 'Gentlemen, I hope I need not insist much in informing your sounder understandings of the sollemne obligation you have laid upon your conscience by the oath you have taken and the dangerous hazards that may attend to yourselves, and also consequente to others by breach of it, the reward of trueth and the punishment of lying beeing so frequently manifested to you in holy writt'.

This stern warning is followed by another.

> 'Because you possibly gave the leste respect to your oaths being administered unto you but by a meane person and in an Inferior Court, yet lett mee tell you that Court is a Court that hath a power by the Comon Law and the Stuard an officer to whom the law has allowed a power to administer an oath, which oath is to all intents and purposes as binding to your consciences as if administered by the highest minister of state.....'

The writer then goes on to quote the laws of King Alfred and other ancient kings, that they had in demesne all the lands of the realm, that they kept the greater manor, and gave the rest to the barons for 'ye defence of ye realme' and afterwards the lords gave these lands to the 'severall tenants, binding them by oath and service'.

This seems to convey that the tenants had fealty or loyalty to the sovereign through oaths sworn in the courts of the greater barons, and also to the lesser manor court of their lord.

It becomes apparent in the next part of the document there had been trouble in the manor.

> 'Itt may bee feared that some of you may (partly out of kindness to your neighbours, partly out of feare lest they should requite you) for bear to present the truth of your knowledge...........but I hope you have learned ye good maxime of morallity, that honesty is the best pollicy'.

Then follows an ominous threat.

> 'If you have not, I doubt not by the Grace of God but I shall have so

much tyme and by the leave of Your Lord soe much power as to make your owne experience teach it to you'.

He then says he will go though all the articles or happenings which should be brought to the court, and will also produce the past court rolls which prove that this was the ancient custom, how they can put things right, and if they do not:

'Doe not hope for any advantage by it for I shall refuse your presentment and impannell another Jury to enquire into your neglect which being found I shall not spare your fines, but I hope I need not use these courses and severity...'

In the final few sentences, hoping no doubt, to sweeten the pill and win over the recalcitrant tenants, he softens the tone somewhat:

'...I hope you will not abuse but cheerfully serve him who give you trouble soe seldome. You know it is not unusual with other Lords to expect services from their tenants which are not reserved.....then pray do not think it much to serve him being your duty, who will bee more willing to serve you and his cuntry in such manner as befitts him ....he too requires this just service from you which by your Tenure you are bound to performe'.

This intriguing document goes on to list successions of tenants into free land which meant that a heriot (fine payable on the death of a tenant) of the best beast, usually an ox or cow, had to be paid as well as a sum of money, known as a chief rent, as opposed to the rental from a tenant who held his land by copy or lease. Very often a man farmed both his own free land plus a copyhold but it was custom that these tenancies had to be approved, together with the various services expected, at the manor court in the presence of a jury of local worthies.

It was usual that tenants held their holdings by service to their lord (labour given at harvest, etc.), suit of court (attendance at the courts), heriot (as above), reliefs (cash sum), merchet (permission to marry) and fealty (oath to serve). I am inclined to think that there was a 'conspiracy of silence' amongst the locals against a new lord of the manor, and that they thought there was strength in unity which might enable them to live without so many manorial dictates.

The list of tenants and changes together with what was due, or in arrear, was accompanied by the date in the margin which in one case went back over a century to prove the established pattern. Then other points regarding the use of wasteland and commons for grazing, the breaking of the pound and so on were presumably read to the tenants. The village pound was a small enclosed area set aside for confining stray animals, also sometimes referred to as a pinfold.

The manorial tenants of Meer Court were left in no doubt that failure to report any breach of ancient custom to the manor court would be dealt with severely. They were still answerable to their lord, however much it was resented.

Meer Court, Allensmore in 1927. *RCHME Crown Copyright*

REFERENCES

[1] Kingstone and Allensmore Court Rolls. R.1122 and R.1123. Hereford Cathedral Library.

[2] Inquisitions Post Mortem. Hereford Record Office.

[3] Mynde Collection, National Library of Wales.

[4] Allensmore Terrier. Hereford Record Office.

[5] Kingstone Glebe Terrier. Allensmore Tithe Map. Hereford Record Office.

[6] *Description of the Cathedral Church of Llandaff.* Browne Willis. 1718.

[7] Deanery Wills and Inventories, book 1. John Parry. 1689. Hereford Record Off.

[8] Muniments Book III, no. 1269. Hereford Cathedral Library.

[9] Muniments Book III, no. 1498.

[10] Muniments Book III, no. 2030.

[11] *White Monks in Gwent and the Border.* David H. Williams. 1976.

[12] ibid.

[13] *Antiquities of Shropshire.* R.W. Eyton. Part V, pp. 48-49. 1854-60. Also 'Hereford Gold Part II' by Joe Hillaby, ref. 294, in Transactions of the Woolhope Naturalists Field Club, vol. 45, 1985.

[14] Whitfield Estate Archives. Hereford Record Office.

[15] Mynde Collection, nos. 299, 5134, 5155-6, 5135.

5 LIFE ON THE MANOR

Life within the manor was lived in accordance with the dictates of the Manor Court, certainly with regard to the way in which ploughing, sowing and harvesting was to be conducted. It is fortunate that the manorial history of Kingstone Furches was recorded on court rolls which also comprised the manors of Bodenham, Burghill, Much Cowarne and Stretford. They were known as the Five Hundreds.

The court rolls in Hereford Record Office are to be found in the Coningsby collection and date from circa 1590 to 1767. The earlier ones are recorded on thin sheets of paper, approximating to A4, and are sewn together, while the later ones are inscribed on thick parchment and were truly rolled.

They are headed with the names of the essoins (absentees), followed by the names of the grand inquisition or jury. There are marginal notes denoting to which of the five hundreds the business dealt with relates. Attendance at the manor court was expected and absentees were amerced (fined) according to their station, namely teamholders sixpence each and labourers one penny each. The proceedings were recorded, not unlike our minutes of meetings of today, and signed by two or three tenants who had to serve as afferatores, the manorial officers who assessed the fines or pains, as they were often called.

The various items to be dealt with were known as presentments of which Kingstone had a wide range. They make fascinating reading and vary from general directives involving everyone to work to be carried out in specified areas by certain people.

In 1594 twenty-two inhabitants were fined twopence each for 'cloth caps'. This would seem to be a somewhat strange offence until we discover that Queen Elizabeth I, in her endeavour to stimulate the wool trade, had an Act passed in 1571 which insisted that woollen caps must be worn on Sundays. Presumably the Kingstone men presented were stubborn, uninformed or did not possess woollen caps. That good old Herefordshire expression 'plain ognel' covers it all.

All inhabitants were to 'make their butts [boundaries] before the Feast of the Purification on pain of 3s.4d.' It was agreed that warning should be given in church and a day announced for the making of the butts. The boundaries between strips in the common fields were very carefully regulated and, while there is no indication of how this was done, the building up with turf is the likely method.

The depasturing of the common land was also clearly laid down by a court of 1767 when the bailiff had to give notice that the land lying fallow should not be grazed by more than three sheep to every one acre owned.

It was also the practice that pigs should be yoked and ringed within a week of notice being given and that cattle or horses should not be turned into any of the common roads or lanes before the 24th August, or 'such times as the fields are ridd'.

The need to mete out punishment within the parish was also part of the court's prerogative and, circa 1590, a pain was put on all inhabitants to 'devise and make a cucking stoole and set him up in place before the next court upon payne of twenty shillings'. A cucking, or ducking, stool was often used to punish 'scolds' (nagging women) or those foolish or wily enough to defraud by way of short weight or measure. The manuscript did not say just where 'him' should be set up. Another delightful instance of local dialect. There were several pools in the village. Maybe the Barrow Pool which used to lie between the church and the common fields of Kipperley and Cristfield was its location. A fine example of a ducking stool can be seen in Leominster Priory Church.

The village had a whipping post and stocks which were often presented as being in need of repair, together with the village pound. The latter was certainly in use in 1736 when one David Jones de la Coldstone broke it open to regain one of his cows which had caused damage on the lands of a village notable, Francis Clarke. David had done this against the will of Francis and in open court he asked pardon of the lady of the manor, the Lady Margaret Coningsby, and of Mr. Clarke, paying him the sum of five shillings which seemed to be a satisfactory settlement.

The court was against anyone who engaged in illicit games such as cards or dice. It did not approve of quarter dancing or of villagers acting as pedlars. The latter might prove a form of competition for existing shopkeepers. Cases of ill neighbourliness, referred to as 'an affray and clamour', were also presentable.

Men 'breaking the park' were fined, giving food for further thought. The land around the old grange of the monks of Dore, the Kingstone Grange of today, was referred to as Baskerville's Park or Kingstone's Park in ancient leases, and in a perambulation of the lordship of Abbeydore.[1] The Baskerville family were in occupation of the Grange for some while after the dissolution of Dore Abbey circa 1536, and the siting of many beautiful oak trees on the Grange lands lends credence to this having, indeed, been parkland at one time. Alternatively, on the Arkstone Court estate there were fields named Upper, Little and Great Park but, since practically all court presentments deal with the area up to the brook which divides Arkstone Court from Kingstone village, it is most likely that this referred to the Grange and not to Arkstone.

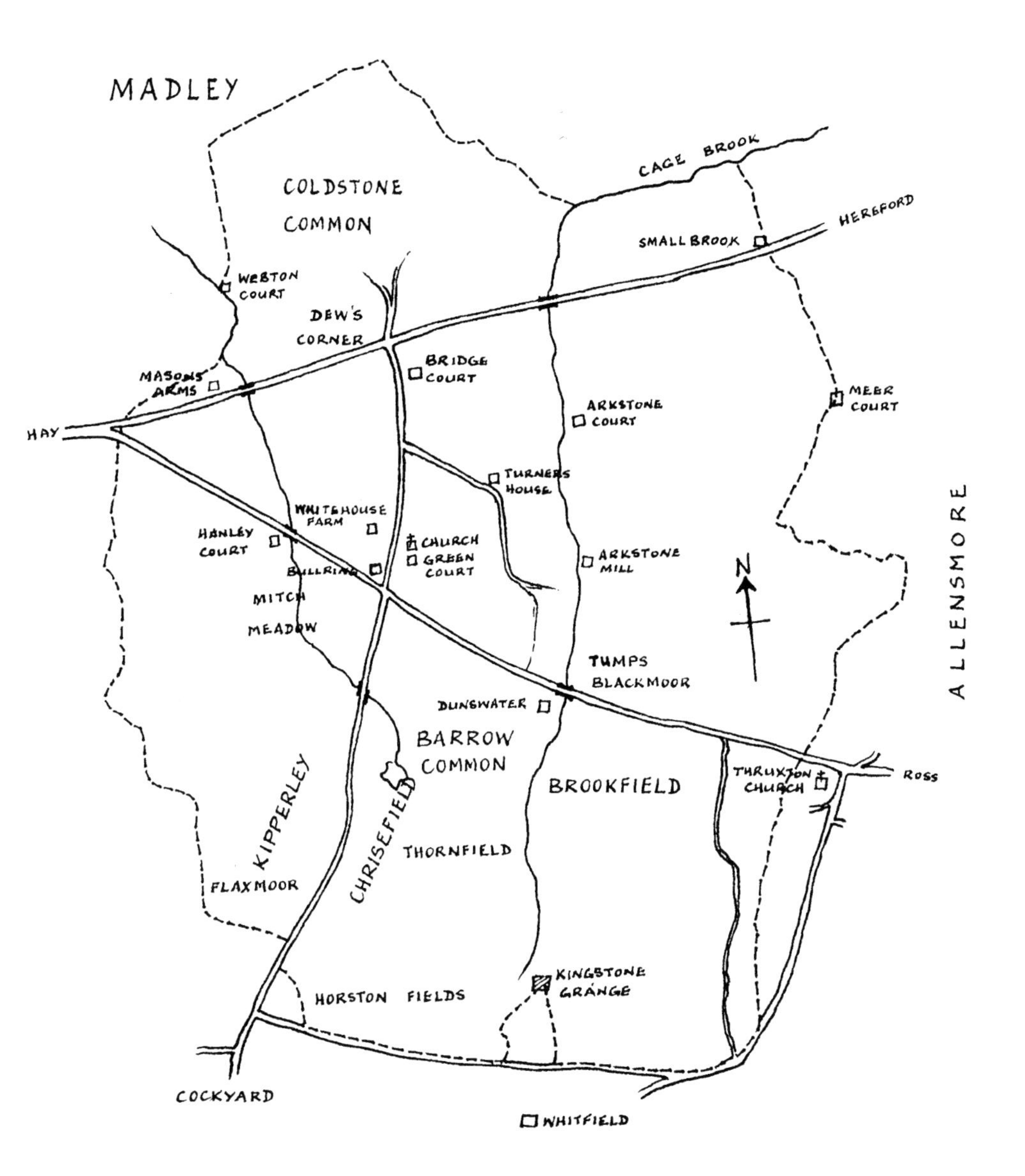

Kingstone in the past. The map is not to scale but will aid location of areas mentioned in the text.

WELLS, DITCHES AND HIGHWAYS

The maintenance of these was a source of regular complaint and the following entries provide a representative selection.

> 'A payne is put upon William Tomkins,Richard Lowe and Harry Marshe that they shall well and sufficiently cleanse and make clear one well in the hiyhe waye when they fetch water before the Feast of Symon and Jude next.'
> 'A payne is put..........that they shall make a good and sufficient bucket and rope and hang the same in the same well before the Feast of Saint Thomas the Apostle....'
> 'A payne is put upon Leonard Thomas to remove all his timber out of the highway before Midsummer next'.
> 'A payne is put that noe man or person shall water hemp or flax in the brook between Arkston and Kingeston'.

The inference in the last item is that the retting process would foul the water and block the brook. It also indicates that the boundary brook divided Kingstone Manor from Arkstone Manor. Part of the dean's glebe in 1587 consisted of some acres named Flaxmear. This can still be traced on the tithe map as numbers 41 and 42, Flaxmoor.

THE COMMON OR OPEN FIELDS

H. L. Gray stated that he thought Kingstone had a three-field system, and that the fields in question were Brookfield, Christfield and Kipperley.[2] The basis of this supposition was the Enclosure Act of 1812 which showed these areas to be those where most land remained to be enclosed. Brookfield and Christfield were similar in acreage but Kipperley was smaller since much of it had been enclosed at an earlier date. Glebe terriers and estate maps show that these three areas right up to the end of the eighteenth century were still farmed in strips and on a three-field rotation of two years cropping and one year fallow.

There were other common fields in Kingstone, namely Lower Field to the west and Mill Field to the east which, by the time of the tithe map, had been parcelled into many small fields, the names of which are indicative of enclosure from a common field, e.g. Six Acres, Four Acres, Part of Eleven Acres, Bridge Court Common Field, Horston Common Field, and so on. Towards the northernmost end of the parish, a map relating to Meer Court, recording exchanges of land mid-eighteenth century, mentions Smallbrook Common Field which the tithe map records as the Inclosure and Far Inclosure.

CHRISTFIELD The name Christfield is unknown today. There have been several corruptions, namely, Chrisefield, Grisefield and Groosefield. It was part of the open fields bordering on the Kingstone-Abbeydore road or the Cockyard, as it is called. It is recorded by name on the tithe map, numbers 115, 117, 118, etc. and bordered on to the Thornfield which was on the demesne land. The name is of long standing, being recorded in a list of the Dean of Hereford's glebe in 1587 which indicates that it was church land. The strips in Christfield ran up to the boundary hedge of Thornfield. The court rolls contain directives that 'every inhabitant against his owne land shall well and sufficiently repair and amend their hedge between Christfield and Thornfield' and that 'every inhabitant shall well and sufficiently make his hedges about the lent field now sowed'. This indicated the importance of all the villagers carrying out their obligations to ensure that there was no danger of their animals breaking out of the land in the field lying fallow into the arable field sown with lent grain.

Apart from the maintenance of hedges, ditches and watercourses, by the sixteenth century private enclosures were in evidence in the village, and there was often a need to remind one's neighbour of the fact. Richard Marshe asked that John Symons 'shall hang two gates in the Thornfield at a place there lately enclosed out of the same before Whitsuntide upon payne of twenty shillings'. John Symons wasted no time in passing the message on. He asked for 'a payne to be put upon

Dunswater. Dating from early 1600, referred to as the Mansion House in old documents.

William Kinge to hang a good and sufficient gate being one of the gates between the Horston field and the Thornfield'. The Horston fields were part of Kingstone Grange. The Thornfield was part of Dunswater demesne (manor) lands, and the field adjoining and leading to the Horston field is called the Twelve Acres, again suggestive of enclosure.

The ancient way given by William de Furches to the monks of Kingstone Grange was to cause disputes when the possessions of Dore Abbey came to be split up after its dissolution. The jury of the manor court decided 'that all such persons as have used and accustomed to pass with their wains and carriages from Kingeston along the Thorne field to Cocket Field [Cockyard Field], that they shall still pass the usual way without interruption'. The new tenants were apparently making life difficult for those who traversed the way they had followed for many years.

KIPPERLEY FIELD Kipperley was located on the opposite side of the Kingstone-Abbeydore road from Christfield and was more adjacent to the Barrow Common area of the village. The name is of very ancient origin, being mentioned in Dugdale's *Monasticon* as part of the land given to the abbey of Dore in December 1232, 'groveland from Kiperlegh'.[3] At the time of the 1812 Enclosure Act only fifteen acres remained. The dean and the custos and vicars of the cathedral held another ten acres between them which was of long standing. Land above Kipperley called the Adder Pits is mentioned in the will of farmer William Popkin in 1605. He wills 'my part of the acres of oates and pease' to be divided between his brother and brother-in-law indicating strip tenancies.

It appears that the area around Kipperley, as it was at the time of the Enclosure Act, had long been parcelled into enclosures. An estate map prepared for Sir George Cornewall in 1791 of the land he had recently purchased shows strips in several areas bordering, and close to, the remaining land known as Kipperley.

Kipperley is mentioned in the court rolls when Roger Crosse put a pain upon John Tomkins to enclose and make a good hedge 'between Kipperley and the pinfold at the lower ende'. The land adjoining is known today as Mitch Meadow. The same Roger put pains on several villagers that 'they should kepe the right path in the meadow called Mitch meadow at the times when they shall passe through the same meadow' indicating that, although it was planted, there was a footpath or bridle way through it to the common field area of Kipperley. Another entry refers to the 'grete ditch meadow' giving rise to the question as to which name is the corruption. There is a great ditch running through Mitch Meadow. The name of Mitchell, which has been given to the wood at the furthermost end, is unknown in any records.

The Barrow Common area of today is variously named Barrow Ground and Barrow Meadow in the Enclosure Act. Here again there were strips in 1791. The area roundabout is also described as 'Old Crisefield' which again indicates that this was the main area of open fields and communal farming. There have been suggestions that the name Barrow derives from ancient burial chambers but there is no trace of such earthworks. There was, however, a Richard de la Barewe, named as holding one and a half acres in the village in the thirteenth century and there was a family named Barrow living there in 1605. Old leases often make mention of the Barrow farm. Just where it was and how much land was attached to it remains unsolved. The old Ordnance Survey maps show a pond there as a small feature but there are a few people today who remember it as being quite sizeable. In the sixteenth century it was referred to as 'Barrows Poole' when three worthy locals were told to 'well and sufficiently scoure one ditche from Barrows Poole to the Stonyhe'. This ditch is still liable to flood today and has caused much aggravation to those living close by. Although the pool has disappeared and the cottage named the Stonyhe was rebuilt in 1986, the owner has retained its original name since he was born in Kingstone and has a great interest in its past.

BROOKFIELD The Brookfield was the other large area of open field mentioned many times in court rolls. It still retains its name today, is signposted as such, and marks the boundary between Kingstone and Thruxton. The Brookfield lane runs southwards from the B.4348 to an area called Grithill, known as Great Hill in early manuscripts. This was the largest allotment area in the Enclosure Act, namely 112 acres, which was allocated amongst the lord of the manor, the dean and chapter, and the custos and vicars of the cathedral. The Brookfield is mentioned in the will of David Morgan of Arkstone in 1524. The dean possessed seven acres of it in 1587. It was a large area which had to be sufficiently hedged and gated to prevent damage to crops while, at the same time, providing entries for ploughing teams. There are numerous fines put on the inhabitants to 'make and hang a good and sufficient gate into Brocke Field next Druxton'. Apart from the foregoing references to areas adjacent, there were many other presentments made regarding areas which did not appear in the Enclosure Act.

THE AREA AROUND ARKSTONE AND BRIDGE COURT

'A payne is put upon all the inhabitants of this lordship and the lordship of Arxton to repair and amend sufficiently one bridge called Bridge Brook before Midsummer next upon pain of forty shillings'. This is the bridge on the B.4349 main Hereford-Hay road which would have been widely used and is still subject to flooding. The size of the fine emphasizes the priority of the task.

'A payne is put upon William Greenwich, Clerk, and John Tomkins that they shall well and sufficiently escoure one ditch from the over end [upper] of the Longe Flingyett to the lower end of the Marshe Leasow...' The latter is still named Marsh Leasow.

'A payne is put upon John Tomkins that he shall well and sufficiently scour one ditch between his leasow called the Chauntray Leasow and the Marshe...' This refers to the meadow which borders on the Far and Hither Marshes. The ditch passes under the Bridge Brook and the reference to the Chantrey Leasow is linked to the will of David Morgan and his chantry chapel which is mentioned later. The Watkins family, who have farmed Arkstone for three generations, have always referred to this field as 'the Stevens'. This could be an abbreviation of the name Stephen's Meadow on the tithe map or an oral tradition spanning centuries since the chantry chapel was dedicated to St. Stephen.

COLDSTONE CROSS, COLDSTONE COMMON

This area of the parish was part common field, part common and part marsh. There is mention of the need for severe fines of £1 19s 11d to be put upon 'any inhabitant within the hundred and manor who shall turn in or depasture any cattle in a certain common field called Coldstone common after notice given to him by the bailiff'. There was an established path from the common to Kingstone Church. William Madox was presented and fined in 1767 for 'tinding up and obstructing a church way leading from Coleston and Bridge Court to Kingstone church'. The marsh area was a source of trouble to those farming adjacent to it since Richard Russell, Thomas Symons, William Dew and Nicholas Tucker were frequently presented for 'not cleansing their ditches and keeping their ditches in repair adjoining the Jack marshes'. Jacks land was land largely unused or unusable in a common field; possibly this referred to similar marshy ground. Today, 200 years on, the name Dew is still commemorated. The road out of Coldstone Common where it meets up with the main Hay-Hereford road is known as Dews Corner. There was a family named Dew living there early this century.

In the late fifteenth century John Prosser was told to 'make a good hedge at the end of the land out of Cowleston to Marshe meadow, and every man that should pass through the said glat [gap] for his necessary use of, or with his cattell must make the same sufficient to save his neighbours harmeless', a nice example of local dialect.

Where the courts were held was seldom mentioned. 'At the same place' was the usual description. But a court held on 19th October 1767 mentions 'at the house of James Evans at ye Buldring' so the Bull Ring public house may have become the meeting place by then. I have come across one lone reference to 'the meadow court' in a deed of title which relates to the parsonage glebe.[4] It is numbered 425 on the tithe map and by that time was named Mill Meadow.

REFERENCES

[1] Perambulation of the Parish of Doore. Hereford Record Office. R.70/1.
[2] *English Field Systems.* H.L. Gray. London, 1959.
[3] *Monasticon Anglicanum*, V. W. Dugdale. 1849 ed.
[4] Accessions Sequence. Solicitors Collection. A.43/1-7. Hereford Record Office.

Coningsby Collection. Court Rolls. Hereford Record Office.

A True List of ye Names of those Incited To this Court at Kingstone Heath at ye Dwelling House of James Evans at ye Buldring October ye 19: 1767 Under ye Right Hon: Lady Frances Coningsby Presented To ye Stewards and Attorneys at Law By William Meek Baylif For This Mannor —

Richard Russell Esqr.
Nicholas Tucker Gent
William Hopkins Gent ap
James Walthen — ap
William Gulloy
William Dew
John Prichard —
James Elliott — ap
Robert [illegible] ap
James Fisher — ess
William Maddox — ess
Morgan Phillips — ess
John Herring —
William Baugh — ap
William Crump — ess
Thomas Prichard
Henry Baynham
Thomas Symmonds
James Crump — ess
Thomas Griffiths — ess
John Baggley — ess
John Hergest —
James Jones
James Williams Labourer [illegible]
John Williams — ess
William Hampton — ess
Thomas Price
William Preece — ap
Thomas Jones — ess
John Arnold — ess
John Preece ess
William Williams ap
James Evans — ap
Walter Jones — ess
Isaack Roberts
David Roberts — ess
James Williams farmer ap
James Morgan
Mrs Mary Walthan ess
William Coock ap
William Probert — ess
James Davis — ess

Benjamin Crump ap
William Burgam ap
Thomas Lowls —
William Shuter ess
William Davis — ess
Benjamin Jones ess
Mrs Mary Hill ess
Walter Gunter
James Dickins ess
Thomas Coock
Ann Baugh — ess
Elizabeth Jones —
Ann Prichard — ess
Martha Crump — ap
Martha Hughs — ess

List of names of those called to the court held at 'ye Dwelling House of James Evans at ye Buldring October ye 19, 1767.' Those attending are indicated by 'ap', those absent by 'ess', short for *essoin*, a type of apology for absence. Non-attenders were fined; 4d for those who had a team of oxen or horses for ploughing, 1d for labourers.

6 THE PARISH CHURCH

The parish church of Kingstone, St. Michael and all Angels, is described by Nikolaus Pevsner as an interesting church. It has no great architectural features but is considered a relatively unspoiled Early English building. On entering it one feels it has a comfortable and welcoming atmosphere, due in great part to the loyal band of dedicated worshippers who work tirelessly to keep it well maintained.

The church probably started life as a simple building with no aisle, early 1100 to 1150. The south door with its unmoulded Norman arch is the oldest remaining feature. Around 1160-1170 the floor level was lowered (hence the steps down into the church) in order to add the north aisle. An arcade of two bays was inserted in the north wall of the nave. About fifty years later another bay was inserted, followed by the addition of the north chapel and rebuilding of the chancel.[1] The north aisle has a thirteenth or fourteenth century recess, possibly a tomb for someone of importance. In St. Luke's Chapel there is a small slab of the same age with a cross and a heart which may commemorate a knight who had been to the Crusades. A book of charters in Hereford Cathedral library notes that around 1218 a Hugh de Kingston sold to the chapter a rent charge of half a mark (6s 8d) in Tyberton together with a tenant for seven marks towards the cost of a pilgrimage to Jerusalem. However, there is nothing to connect him with the tomb or memorial slab.[2] The two earlier arches in the arcade differ from the later addition in the choice of stone used, the style of base and the patterning on the capitals.

The tower was added in the latter part of the thirteenth century. Finally the nave was extended to meet up with the west wall of the tower and the north aisle was widened. The nave extension necessitated the blocking up of the original tower window in the south wall. From the interior it is possible to see the solid, deeply recessed, blocked window that originally looked out across the churchyard. The south wall of the chancel was rebuilt in 1762, the date being commemorated on a small stone which can be viewed from the churchyard.

There was once a gallery running across the nave at the west end, directly above the west door with steps in the south west corner, which required repair in 1835 costing £1 16s 0d The very old seats that remain near the west door may have been made from 60ft. of timber purchased in 1741 for that purpose.[3] However, records of the same date tell of 'halling ye three pews from Blackmore'. There is a Blackmoor Farm in Abbeydore, not far from Dore Abbey, so it could be that after the Dissolution items that were no longer required were taken from there. Another possibility is that Blackmore refers to Blackmoor or Hackmoor, a field on the

Dunswater estate, adjacent to the field named the Tumps, east of the church, which was mentioned by one incumbent as the possible site of a chantry chapel.

Kingstone church at the beginning of the century. The pinnacles added in 1852 were removed in 1975 as being unsafe.

The parish officers were responsible for levying a church rate and a poor rate on parishioners and, if required, additional rates could be asked for. This happened when church repairs were likely to be excessive, as in the case of the tower. Over the centuries it was to prove very costly since there was a steeple which, most likely, was partly of wood. Mention is made in a visitation return of 'singling part of our steeple', which indicates wooden tiles (shingles), in 1735 and in 1741. In 1781, four tons of 7 ft. lengths of timber were bought for the steeple from Lady Catherine Stanhope of the nearby Whitfield Estate. At the same time work on the weathercock was dealt with as instanced by an item for 'painting and sodering the cock 5/-'. The cost of timber was £8 6s 0d. Some thirty years later in 1811, after an inspection of the tower costing half a guinea (10s 6d), it was decided to spend '£313.11.0. to take down the spire and makeing a tower of the same and all other repairs agread on'. This expenditure, unfortunately, did not solve the problem since the years 1842-47 saw well over £200 laid out for buttressing, stonework and drains.

The local farmers hauled hogsheads of water (54 gallons), bricks, sand, barrels of lime, and cinders, while stone was procured from Hereford Cathedral which had a surplus due to its collapsed tower. Finally, between 1848 and 1851, the tower was completely rebuilt at a cost of £561. It must have been a considerable undertaking; there was sixteen and a half day's work involved in removing soil round the church, a further nine and a half day's work on drainage and buttressing. One man was taken from mowing barley to sink foundations. Old mortar was sold together with 8 yards of stone out of the rubbish. One poor woman, Ann Williams, earned a shilling for cleaning the churchyard. It must have been hard work but possibly the money was a windfall to her.

As treasurer for many years to Kingstone Parochial Church Council I well know how difficult it always was to raise money to meet repairs even at a time of a much larger population and a greater variety of outlets for fundraising. Whatever must it have been like for our forebears to have had these large sums of money to find for essential repairs? Certainly the church had a far greater meaning for everyone then; there were fewer worldly distractions to woo them from their joint responsibility to preserve it for their descendants.

Alongside the problem of the tower came care of the churchyard which in those far off days was surrounded by green and common, liable to be invaded by grazing animals and foraging poultry. The magazines in the early 1900s often contained appeals for people not to drop paper or allow fowls and dogs in and banned children from playing there. Gates and fencing were frequently renewed, likewise windows often required glazing and leading, while 'mending the dial plate' indicated work done to the sundial to the right of the porch.

A county council survey of the area points out that the detour round the churchyard made by the road suggests that there was originally a smaller churchyard, namely the eastern part behind the church, with a straight village street running past it. This would have passed the west door and Yew Tree House continuing down to the Bull Ring Inn. An item for hauling stones for churchyard steps in 1833 indicates that the churchyard had been extended by then, but since there are few memorial stones before 1800, it is difficult to be definite. It is quite likely that Kingstone did not have its own consecrated burial ground for some while after the church was built since it was to be in the charge of the dean and chapter from 1281 which meant it was known as a Dean's Peculiar. Burials from such parishes were only allowed in burial grounds very close to the cathedral. Mortuary fees were not payable to the vicar but to the dean and chapter. This was the subject of a long running dispute with the parish of Allensmore from 1318 to 1348, which was eventually resolved when ground there was finally consecrated by the bishop. The bishops registers state that very poor people were buried at home since they could not afford the journey to Hereford. The cathedral had suffered loss of fees. There are several instances of burials being permitted in the church itself provided the cost of a set of new bell ropes was paid for the privilege. This was in the 1700s and, since the registers commenced in 1659, there is no record of what went on before that.

As late as 1865 a wooden pulpit, with a clerk's desk below, was adjacent to the main aisle of the nave near the south walls, some few yards from the present pulpit.[4] The original was mentioned in the accounts as far back as 1666, 'Paid John Jones for moving ye pulpit 2/6d.' In 1777 the pulpit and pew were moved again at a cost of one shilling. The present pulpit, together with the altar, was made by a Mr. R. Clark of Hereford at the time of the full-scale 1890 restoration.

In 1793 John Bartram, who lived in nearby Church House and was the clerk for some years, provided material for 'Ye pulpit cloth £2.8.10. and 2/6d. for making same'. The village meeting in 1750 passed the following resolution:

> 'Agreed that chancel on south side of church before the Communion table shall be rayled in at the expense of the parishioners. Also agreed that Thomas Prichard should have seven shilling each yard for rayling in the chancel, he finding timber and carpenter work fitt for the same and he doth agree that the same shall be dun by Easter'.

In 1836 kneeling benches for the communion rails were purchased. The sacrament of Holy Communion was only administered four times a year and in the 1700s it would appear that the linen was washed the same number of times at a cost of ten shillings. At Christmas 1746, three pints of wine were required and another entry mentions 'One Pottel of wine [4 pints] and one Manchet [small loaf], and washing linnen and cleaning plate the same time 2/6d'.

The surplice was parish property and was mended for sixpence on one occasion, but 12_ yards of fine Irish cloth was purchased in 1766 to have a new one made; the cloth cost £2 10s 0d and the making 12s, while both a communion cloth and a bier cloth were procured for £6 in 1801.

One of the proudest possesions of the church is the thirteenth century dug-out chest with coped lid divided in two, each hung on two iron hinges and strengthened with ornamental work. Locks were renewed on this several times, costing two shillings in 1746, and two shillings and fourpence in 1814, so prices were more stable then than they are today.

The wagon roof of the nave is largely unrestored, possibly fourteenth or fifteenth century, but in 1790 the whole ceiling area was plastered over which gives an insight into materials used.

Sam Payne for ceiling the Church.		£30.12.0.
Eleanor Bethell 16 bags Moss	4d. a bag.	5.4.
100 ft.Timber	10d.	4. 3.4.
72 ft.Timber	1/-	3.12.0.
84 ft.Quarton	2d.	14.0.
394 of Boards	30/- per 100	5.18.0.

Tiles, slabs, lath, oak boards and lime were also bought. The church was frequently limewashed, while moss and hair were used for plastering and pointing the stonework.

Thirteenth century dug-out chest in Kingstone church.

RCHME Crown Copyright

By the middle 1800s different priorities were noted in the accounts. A new porch was built by John Seal whose family were prominent in the village as carpenter, innkeepers and small farmers. One of John's sisters donated a memorial window in 1895 as a tribute to him and another sister. A stove was installed in 1860 which must have given plenty of heat since sixteen years later new piping and overhauling was required. In place of the expenditure for candles came seven Hesperus Burner lamps in 1886, and in 1897 a new system of 'warming' was installed for £80.

Two beautifully carved chairs and alms dishes were made for the church by the Rev. Edward Jacson, rector of Thruxton and Kingstone from 1858 to 1870 and an excellent craftsman.

The church was in a poor state by the late 1870s and the arrival of a new vicar, the Rev. Reginald Hereford Bird, saw a move towards a full restoration so beloved of the Victorians. The architect described the general condition thus, 'miserably comfortless pews, very dilapidated, of all shapes and sizes, facing in contrary directions, choke up the body of the church, the floors of which are decayed and redolent of damp and mildew'.

It must have been a cheerless atmosphere to worship in. The floor consisted of stone slabs laid upon bare soil while the roof leaked, so the worshippers were enveloped in damp air. The mention of pews facing in contrary directions is especially interesting since I had come across a document dated 1st March 1759 in Hereford Cathedral library which was naming a seat to be rented to a Kingstone inhabitant.[5]

> '1 seat south side of the North Isle containing 6'6" and of breadth 3'3" having N. Isle on the N part, an old seat or bench and pillar of said Church on the west, a seat belonging to Mr.James Clark on the East, and the seat belonging to Thomas Maddox on south side, between Moore Green, owner and proprietor of Smallbrook, and Thomas Wathan of Grithill, to sit, stand or kneel....'

I spent some time in the church talking myself through these directions until it occurred to me that the pews must have been placed in no particular order. The architect's report seems to confirm this.

The ceiling of the church, which had cost so much to repair a century before, was stripped to expose the original timbers which required much renewal. New open pews were installed while a few of the old ones already referred to were kept. The renovation took six months during which time services were held in the nearby school. On April 17th 1890 the bishop attended the reopening ceremony. Reports in the Hereford Times and the church magazine tell of a great crowd present on this occasion. All available spaces, including land adjacent to the Bull Ring, today's car park, were filled with the carriages of visitors. The final cost of the restoration was £1800, two-thirds of which had been collected by subscriptions and donations from the parishioners.

With the church now in such good condition it was necessary to increase the insurance premium from £1500 to £3000, and this would involve a payment of £2 5s per year by the Parochial Church Council which was stated to be 'a very heavy item on church funds'.[6]

There are several interesting floor and wall memorials to members of the Russell, Wathan (sometimes Wathen), Hill and Parry families who were all well-to-do yeoman farmers occupying the farms of Arkstone, Dunswater, Green Court, Bridge Court, Meer Court and Hanley Court in the eighteenth and nineteenth centuries. These will be referred to in greater detail elsewhere.

There are two memorials of more recent years which commemorate lives of dedicated service to the village. They are those of Dr. Oliver John Goode Cotton, who died suddenly of a heart attack in the bitter winter of 1963 after battling through snow to complete his rounds, and Mr. Allan Colcombe who died in 1974. Dr. Cotton came to the village in 1931 and was a strong supporter of village life, serving as manager of the old church school, and was ahead of his time in his insistence that all the ancient footpaths were walked every year in order to preserve their being. Allan Colcombe was born in Kingstone and was a fount of local knowledge. He served the church for most of his life as clerk, sexton and bellringer.

The font was originally situated in the north-west corner of the north aisle. It is a font of what is known as the plum pudding variety due to its irregular circular bowl-like shape. It is mounted on a short moulded stem, possibly a re-used capital of thirteenth century origin, on a modern step and is very similar to the font at Kilpeck.

The organ, a two manual instrument, was built by Nicholson of Worcester about 1870. It was a condition of the appointment of Mr. Charles Bullock as headmaster of the school in 1885 that he played the organ at services. An earlier entry in the records states that Miss F. Polkinghorne was paid £2 2s 0d 'for 42 weeks playing the organ', a rate of a shilling per week. The boy who pumped the instrument received seven shillings. Miss Polkinghorne also taught at the school. The parish is fortunate that there has always been someone to fill the vacancy, very often on an honorary basis, when organists have retired.

When it was decided to refurbish the north chapel to its original use in 1983, transferring the vestry to the tower, the organ, which had been on the south wall of the chancel, was transferred to the north aisle. This involved considerable expense made possible by a generous donation in memory of William Lewis, who had lived at Barrow Common, by his widow, Mrs. E. Lewis, and Mrs. E. Kenney, one of the church's past organists. A plate can be found attached to the organ. It is a pleasing thought that Nicholsons carried out the work on the organ they had supplied over a century before.

The tower now houses the vestry which is separated from the church by a fine screen of oak and glass made by Clive George of Young & George of Hereford. The tower has a new bell-ringing platform made by John Arnold which was completed in 1983 together with newly designed cupboards to house choir robes. The cupboards were constructed with timber from the old partition by Keith Brackley of Ballingham. The work and cost involved was considerable. A brass plate records that the creation of the vestry and installation of of the bellringing platform was made possible by the handsome endowment of William George Lewis in memory of his parents. Mr. W. G. Lewis left the area many years ago to farm in Australia. The vestry cupboards were donated by the late B.A. Williams, headmaster of the primary school for many years and a choir member, in memory of his wife Gwenllion. These changes were re-dedicated on 28th April 1985.

The church clock, housed above the vestry, was erected in 1931 due to the efforts of Miss Annie Catherine Wathen together with donations from relatives, friends and parishioners. She died shortly afterwards at the age of 73.

The north chapel houses wall monuments and memorial stones to the Parry family of Arkstone. Notes made over a hundred years ago refer to it as the Arkstone Chapel recording that a thirteenth century coffin lid with the seventeenth century inscription to John Parry of Arkstone was lying above the pavement there. This stone and several others were moved at the time of the 1890 restoration, the Parry stone being adjacent to the tower for upwards of the last hundred years.

Since there was some doubt about the name of the chapel it was decided to re-dedicate it to St. Luke. This was done at a service in April 1985 when new seats were purchased with donations given in memory of Russell (Russ) Watkins of Dunswater, while altar kneelers, rails and electrical work were added by his widow, Mrs.Doris Watkins, and brother William (Bill) Watkins whose family have farmed at Arkstone and Dunswater for many years.

It is possible that the oak communion table in the chapel could be the original from the chancel, moved there in 1890. It has turned legs with moulded rails and edge to top and is late seventeenth century.

A new ciborium was purchased and dedicated to the memory of the Rev. Vaughan Warner, vicar of Kingstone from 1959 to 1978, while a new Bible presented in October 1975 was dedicated to the memory of Miss Irene Lee Warner. They were not related. Vaughan Warner was appointed first vicar of Kingstone when it was made a separate parish from adjacent Thruxton and he set the parish on a firm spiritual and financial basis while remaining a very approachable person. Irene Lee Warner devoted herself to the young all her life, running the Guides for many years.

From the foregoing it can be seen that the church, like many another throughout the land, has had a great many changes in its layout. Come day, go day, there have always been people who have worked hard and given generously to ensure its survival. Those who enjoy worshipping there today have much for which to thank those shadows of the past. Some of them we know of from their memorials, others we shall never know but they were all there once.

REFERENCES

[1] Royal Commission on Historical Monuments. Herefordshire, south west.
[2] Cape's Charters. Hereford Cathedral Library.
[3] Parish Records. Hereford Record Office.
[4] Notes on Kingstone and Thruxton by Reverend E. Jacson. Hereford Record Office.
[5] Manuscript 4202. Hereford Cathedral Library.
[6] Kingstone and Thruxton Almanacs.

All references to church expenditure from Parish Records which include Churchwardens' account books, Vestry Minutes, Overseers' accounts, etc.

7 THE DEVELOPMENT OF THE PARISH CHURCH

The Domesday Book entry for Kingstone makes no mention of a church and the present building dates from some fifty years afterwards, between 1100 and 1150. As already mentioned, the Norman Abbey of Cormeilles had been given the tithes of Kingstone and some land there with a villager to work it.

At this time, tithes were a tenth part of all grains and livestock. In later times great and lesser tithes were introduced; the great tithe comprising cereals and lesser tithes being livestock and cottage garden produce. This led to the distinction between the title of rector and vicar. A rector received the great tithes and a vicar the lesser tithes. The rector of a living was not always a priest. He could be a layman who did not minister to the parish but employed a priest to carry out parish duties. The word vicar is from the Latin *vicarius* meaning substitute, while the word rector applied to the incumbent of a parish which had been appropriated (taken over by a religious foundation) as was the case with Kingstone. Today there is no difference with regard to spiritual duties and tithes are a thing of the past.

Hereford Cathedral was known as a cathedral of the old foundation of which there were nine, amongst them York, Salisbury and Wells. They were known as secular cathedrals since they were administered by canons who were allowed to hold estates which were also known as prebends (from the Latin *praebenda*, provender) hence their other title of prebendary. They were allowed to share in the distribution of a common fund derived from money or rentals of land donated to the church, and when they assisted at memorial or obituary services for cathedral benefactors. The other ten cathedrals were served by regular clergy, most of them Benedictine monks, who had no outside commitments. These were refounded after the dissolution of the monasteries under Henry VIII and known as cathedrals of the new foundation.

As a result of Earl William FitzOsbern's wealth and influence there were four canons with separate estates representing the Norman abbeys of Lyre and Cormeilles in the cathedral church of Hereford by the time of his death in 1070/71. The canons were responsible for the music and chanting of prayers and were allowed to present their own vicars who had to be proficient in singing and musical ability to take over their duties.

The Reverend Custos W.D.V. Duncombe suggests that this is the way the first vicarages came into being, since the canons were permitted to hold their own estates and train their own vicars.[1]

It seems reasonable to assume that the tithes from Kingstone were part of the prebend of the canons of Cormeilles and that the vicarage of Kingstone was endowed from this revenue. Bearing in mind the date of 1070 or thereabouts, it can be seen that the origin of Kingstone as a vicarage is very ancient indeed. It is rather perplexing that Kingstone was a vicarage and yet did not have a vicar in the parish, as we understand it, and there is no mention of a church at that time.

Land bequeathed for the benefit of the common fund was often leased to the resident canons, who paid a fixed rent or 'farm' to the cathedral chapter and had any profit for themselves. These were referred to as farms, thus by the seventeenth century the land in Kingstone belonging to the cathedral was referred to as the Kingstone Farm.

These secular canons did not have the same strict monastic regime as that followed by monks; they could live where they wished provided it was within a six mile radius of the cathedral in order to perform their duties satisfactorily. It was not until the consecration of Bishop Reynelme in 1107 that a more orderly rule of life was instituted when the prebendaries and their vicars were required to live in the confines of, or adjacent to, the cathedral in the area which today is Castle Street. In 1140 Bishop Robert de Bethune, a former Prior of Llantony Abbey, completed the cathedral church and established the dean and chapter. This was to be very important with regard to the church in Kingstone.

Prior to this organisation, the vicars who were required to read and sing masses on behalf of their canon or prebendary came to be known as vicars choral. In 1396 Richard II, by charter, created them a College of Custos and Vicars with a common seal.

In a document dated 1327 the vicars were given permanent status as *vicarii perpetui* and they were to be in constant attendance for services. There were only six at that time, the vicar of St. Michael's or Kingstone being one of them.

One can only assume that originally the parish was served by a priest vicar from the cathedral. There could have been a small chantry or field chapel endowed by the abbey in Kingstone or there could have been one in the cathedral itself. The notes of a vicar of the 1850s mention that at one time there was reputed to be a chapel in the field named the Tumps behind the church.[2] This was due to a clearly defined mound of earth there but constant ploughing over the years has levelled the area. I have discovered a reference to a decayed Kingstone vicarage chapel in the cathedral records but it is just one reference dating back nearly 500 years.[3]

The next milestone must have been the building of St. Michael's as seen today. There is nothing to tell us how this came about but it must be remembered that, although the Abbey of Cormeilles was in possession of the tithes with a virgate of land, the manor belonged to the King.

By the time the church was built, the Kingstone manor was in the possession of the Lacy family, who had sub-let it to a William de Furches, named in a document of circa 1165 as having land in Kingstone.[4] The Furches family were to be lords of Kingstone for several generations. They were also in possession of a manor at Bodenham in Herefordshire, called Bodenham Furches or Forges. The first church register for Kingstone has the title Kingstone Forges written on its cover which must surely have been to distinguish it from other manors held by that family.

It seems likely that the Lacy influence on the church was considerable. Walter de Lacy had come to England with William the Conqueror. His son, Hugh, was a great benefactor to many religious foundations and had helped to complete the building of Llantony Abbey. He had also granted two parts of the tithe of Arkstone, a large farm in Kingstone and a manor in its own right, to the prior and monks of St.Guthlac in Hereford and to the Abbey of Gloucester, which became Gloucester Cathedral.[5]

At a later date a Walter de Furches is cited as having the right to present to the living of Kingstone so the surmise that Kingstone church was built under the auspices of the Furches family seems logical.[6] A cathedral book of obituaries records the death of a William Furches, knight, and of a Roberti de Furches and his wife Edith, who gave land to the cathedral church of Hereford and four shillings to keep a lamp perpetually burning before the great altar.

The church interior early 1900s.

The first mention of clergy comes in a document dated 1239 when the rector of Kingstone, William Rufus, was in dispute with the monks of Dore Abbey over tithes due from land around Kingstone Grange.[7] A Canon William Rufus left money for regular obituary services to be said for his soul yearly on the 11th April in the cathedral. Was he perhaps a Cormeilles Canon? Cathedral archives mention a William and a Philip Rufus living in the first half of the thirteenth century, both of whom founded chantries and were connected with Kingstone. It has not been possible to trace whether they were one and the same but certainly it was Philip Rufus who founded a perpetual vicarage, originally as a chantry for masses for his soul, which was financed or endowed out of the living of Kingstone. This is mentioned in a lease from the dean and chapter in 1556 which tells of 'their lands lying at Kyngston withyn the countie of Hereford called grene lands belongyng to a Vycarege funded in the quere of the syd cathedral church called Philyppe Ruffs Vycarege'.[8]

It appears there was some agreement that Cormeilles, through the vicars choral, still had the tithes but the lord of the manor had the right to appoint to the living which was a vicarage.

Things really started to move when prior to 1281 the living of Kingstone was vacant. The dean of Hereford stated that a William de Furchis, who had the right of presentation, had presented a Master Henry of Llantony, who had either died or resigned. Since no one else had been presented within a given time, the dean claimed the right to appropriate the church to further endow the decanal office.[9]

This was confirmed when a charter of Bishop Thomas Cantilupe was inspected in 1281 at Prestbury, near Cheltenham but a portion of the endowment was allowed to the Prior of Newent. This again shows the connection with Cormeilles since Newent Priory was the mother church of the Norman abbey in the area. The Abbey of Cormeilles still had considerable estates in England and by 1274 eight of its thirty monks were resident here.[10] The taxation for the Hereford diocese in 1294 shows that Kingstone was assessed at ten marks (£6 13s 4d), the total for the whole of the Hereford deanery being £3881 15s 4d.[11] It mentions the word *porcio* (portion) which might indicate this was a separated benefice or that it had been appropriated.

A similar situation existed in the parish of Diddlebury which had its revenues split between the Abbey of Shrewsbury, the Abbey of Sees in Normandy and the Bishop of Hereford. This was due to grants being made by various wealthy lords over a lengthy period. The parish is in Hereford diocese and there were Diddlebury vicars in the vicars choral, possibly representing the Abbey of Sees.

The appropriation by the dean, sanctioned in 1281, might have been expected to give the church stability, or so one would have thought. No, not a bit of it. By 1368, the Earldom of Hereford was in the hands of the powerful de Bohun family. Humphrey de Bohun decided that, since he was the overlord of Kingstone, he should have the right of presentation and not the dean. He took his case to the King's Court and stated that he had 'suffered injury to the value of one thousand pounds'. There is a wonderful document in the cathedral library, complete with a huge seal, which recounts the succession of those sub-tenants, including William de Furches, who had the right to present to the living, mentioning the Lucy family who became lords of the manor when a Furches heiress married one of the Lucy heirs. Since the grant had been confirmed once again by Edward II, the dean won the case.[12]

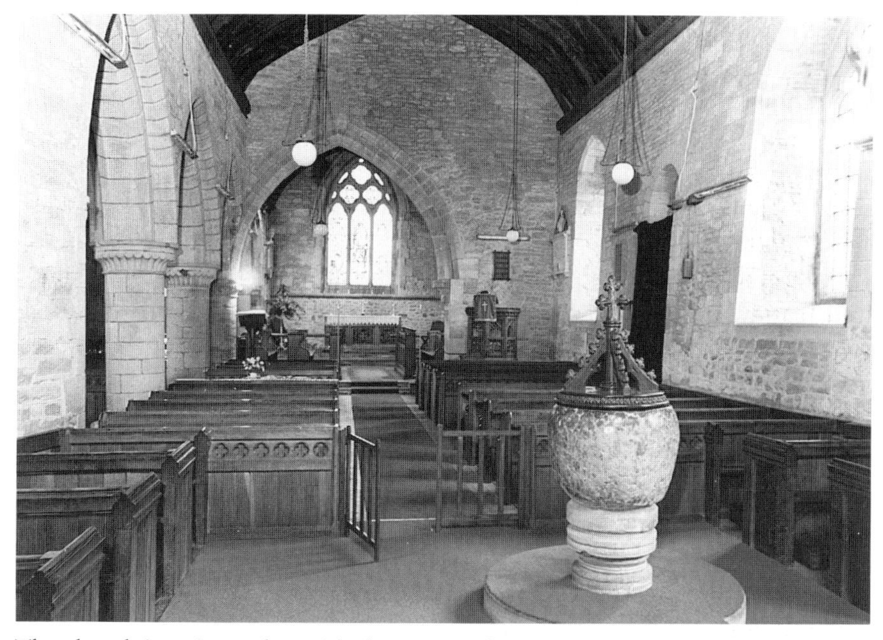

The church interior today with the ancient font.

The Dean of Hereford who took over the church to endow the decanal office was a Frenchman, John de Aquablanca from Burgundy, who was very unpopular with his fellow clergy. His lengthy will dated 1320 mentions four churches, Kingstone, Allensmore, Clehonger and Withington.[13] Amongst other bequests the churches were to buy 120 lbs of wax for his funeral, half of which was to remain in the cathedral. The other half was to provide two candles each for the four churches together with a request that the poor parishioners of Kingstone be given one seam of wheat and one seam of peas. A seam was a horse load. He might not have been popular with his fellows but maybe Kingstonians would have viewed him in a more mellow light.

The fact that the church was appropriated by the dean gave it the title of a Dean's Peculiar. This made it practically exempt from the jurisdiction of the bishop and his officers, having its own court with the power to prove wills. It was only the Dean's Peculiars which were in receipt of the Canon's Dole, a charity which consisted of so many loaves being delivered from the cathedral bakehouse to the parishes twice a year, at Christmas and Candlemas. Kingstone received forty loaves each time in the 1830s. The total distribution was 4360 loaves to thirty-three churches, some to prisoners in gaol, and to certain persons in the cathedral.[14] The bakehouse was situated in Quay Street.

Throughout the fourteenth century there are many references in the bishops registers of priests, deacons and acolites connected with Kingstone. The names of John Hancockes de Kingstone, Johannes le Erle de Kyngestone and so on appear but, since the dean had the right of presentation from 1281, the parish was probably served by a succession of monks. Several of those mentioned were from the abbeys of Dore, Llantony and Grace Dieu (near Monmouth), all of which had links with the cathedral church.

The connection with Cormeilles was finally severed during the Hundred Years War with France which commenced in 1338. Edward III seized the Priory of Newent together with other alien priories for his own use. However, since Newent was in Hereford diocese until the creation of Gloucester diocese in 1541, this would account for the portion of income allowed to Newent.

The bishops register relates that Kingstone church was unable to pay its dues around 1406 due to the devastation wrought in the area by the marauding army of Owen Glendower. It mentions once again that there was a portion due to Newent of £1 5s 0d together with a payment of five shillings to St. Guthlac's.[15]

It will be remembered that a small part of the tithes of Arkstone had been given by Hugh de Lacy to St. Guthlac's, originally a chapel within the castle of Hereford. Later it was merged with the church of St. Peter which had been built by Hugh's father, Walter de Lacy, and a new church named St. Peter, Paul and Guthlac was built outside the city of Hereford. This was to be granted to the monks of St. Peter of Gloucester, later to become Gloucester Cathedral.

This would explain why the income from Kingstone was split amongst three different foundations and why a small portion of tithe was paid to Gloucester at one time. Since land in Kingstone parish, given over the centuries to the church, was parcelled out as belonging to the custos and vicars of the cathedral church (the old vicars choral) and the dean of the cathedral church, I have felt it was necessary to give the background to these endowments. There will be much that can never be fully explained, since one is delving back so many centuries. Links in the chain have disappeared, however hard one endeavours to find them.

One illuminating piece of information comes to light through the Rev. H. Knight, rector of Thruxton and Kingstone from 1905 to 1917, who found a document dated 1586 showing that the Dean of Hereford had sold the right of presentation to a Christopher Hyggins, whose executor had presented a priest named Henry Barwarde. This is an example of a lay rector who would have received the great tithe, while the vicar, Henry Barwarde, received the lesser tithes and possibly a pittance to carry out his parish duties. In later years it became common practice to let the Kingstone 'farm' lands, the glebe and the tithe, for periods of up to twenty-one years to yeoman farmers who in turn sub-let parts of the land to under-tenants. Echoes of the feudal system being applied to agriculture. It seems a sensible arrangement since the College of Vicars Choral and the dean between them were relieved of overseeing the farming and of dealing with any problems.

The first Kingstone register dates from 1659 and has the title Register of Kingstone Forges, a reminder of the Furches family of long ago. There are very few entries which indicate who was in charge of the parish and the registers of institutions from 1530 to 1900 have little information to give. The first instance of a priest in charge for any length of time comes from 1670 when the name of Christopher Whiting appears, although he was not instituted to the living until 1680 when he was made vicar of Thruxton. From then on the parishes of Thruxton and Kingstone seem to have been in the care of one priest. The presentation was, at different times, in the gift of the Bishop of Hereford, the Bishop of Llandaff and the Dean of Hereford.

This uncertain state of affairs stablilised in 1804 when the Rev. Henry Wetherell became Rector of Thruxton and Vicar of Kingstone. There are numerous entries in the bishops registers relating to stipendary curates being licensed to serve the two parishes and to live in glebe houses owned by Mr. Wetherell, some in Kingstone and others in Thruxton. The houses varied in distance from one mile to 200 yards from Kingstone, Green Court being the only one mentioned by name. Well into the 1900s the pattern continued with the rector of Thruxton living in Thruxton rectory, the curate by this time being allowed to live elsewhere, often outside the parish. It was not until the building of a vicarage at Kingstone in 1959 that the parish became a separate entity.

It is unfortunate that the succession of clergy throughout the ages

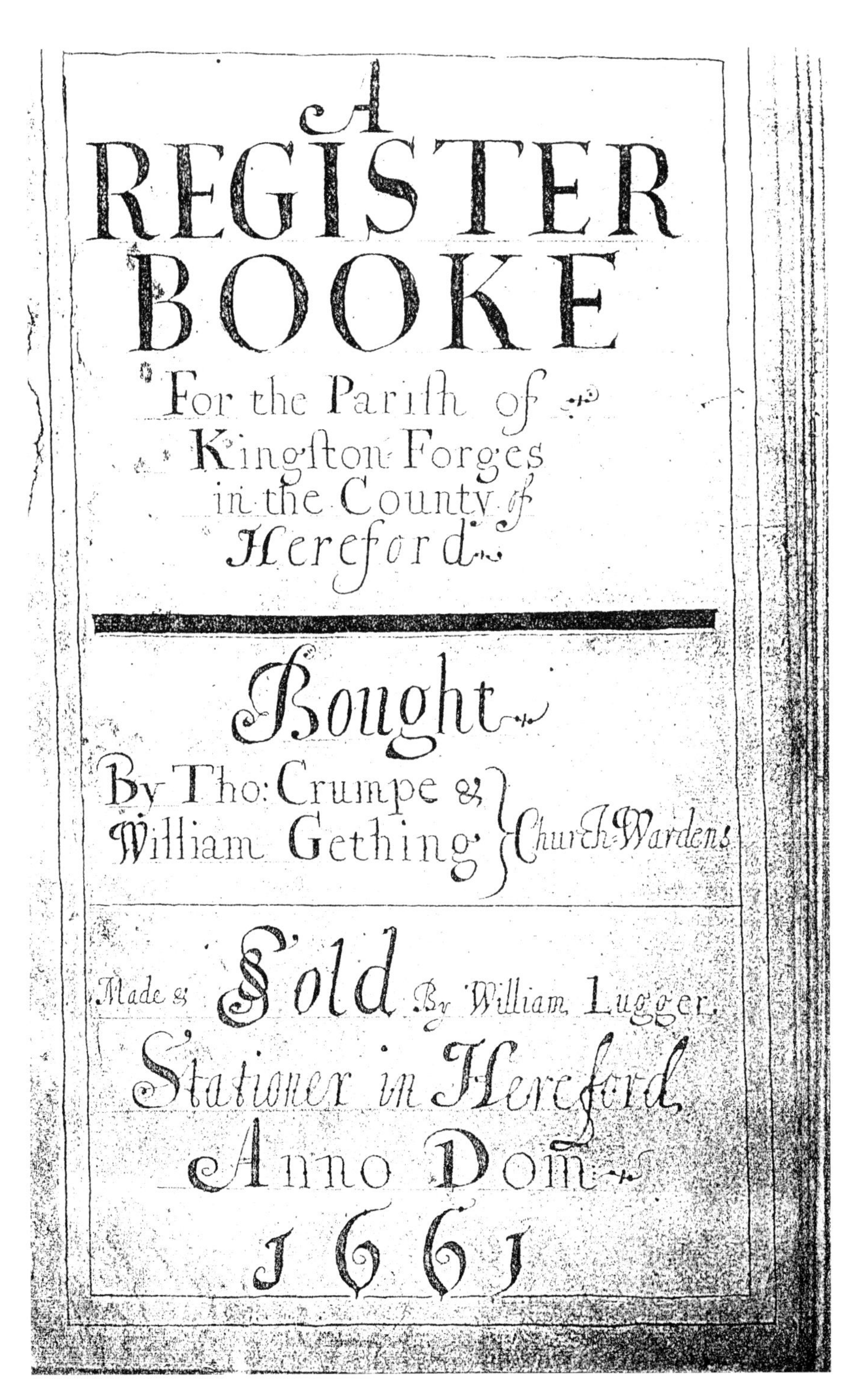

A
REGISTER
BOOKE
For the Pariſh of
Kingſton Forges
in the County of
Hereford

Bought
By Tho: Crumpe &
William Gething } Church Wardens

Made & Sold By William Lugger
Stationer in Hereford
Anno Dom
1661

The titlepage of Kingstone Parish Register.

cannot be set down clearly, but there were so many religious foundations with a finger in the parochial pie that one feels the possible sources are potentially too numerous to pursue here.

REFERENCES

[1] 'Sketch of the History of the College of Vicars Choral, Hereford' by Reverend Custos W.D.V. Duncombe in *Memorials of Old Herefordshire*, edited by Compton Reade, 1904

[2] Notes on Kingstone and Thruxton by Reverend E. Jacson. Hereford Record Office.

[3] Dean and Chapter Act Book, 1512-1566, p.11, no. 106.

[4] *Antiquities of Shropshire*, pp. 22 and 48. R.W. Eyton.

[5] Calendar of Cathedral Muniments. Book 1, 2178. Hereford Cathedral Library.

[6] Calendar of Cathedral Muniments. Book 3, 1498.

[7] *White Monks in Gwent and the Border*. David H. Williams. Also Perambulation of the Parish of Doore. R.70/1. Hereford Record Office.

[8] Lease, ref. 3354. 28.12.1556. Hereford Cathedral archives.

[9] Cape's Charters and Records of Hereford Cathedral, p.144.

[10] *The Cathedral Church of Hereford*. A.T. Bannister.

[11] *Antiquities of the Cathedral Church of Hereford*, p.147.

[12] As 5 above.

[13] Extracts from Cathedral Registers 1275-1535. Cantilupe Society.

[14] Report of the Commissioners for Inquiring Concerning Charities (City of Hereford), 1838.

[15] Register of Bishop Mascall. Cantilupe Society. p.20

8 THE ANCIENT CHURCH BELLS

The original ancient peal of bells in the church comprised four bells and no history of the church would be complete without reference to them. The earliest mention comes from the report compiled by Royal Commissioners appointed by Edward VI (1547-1553) to make inventories of the quantity and value of goods owned by the churches and to forbid these being sold or misappropriated.

Any plate, jewels and money considered to be surplus were to be given over to the King's use. These inventories were compiled following the dissolution of the monasteries and chantry chapels in the reign of Edward's father, Henry VIII, when it was felt that rich vestments and statuary were unecessary in places of worship.

Further instructions were given that 'all parcels and pieces of metall except the metall of great bell or saunce in every of the said churches or chapels' should be sold. In the Middle Ages the term great bells meant those forming part of a ring as distinct from the smaller sanctus bells. The real intention was that broken bells and odd pieces of metal should be sold.

Unlike most other parts of England, Herefordshire gave the dimensions of its bells. The Kingstone bells were described thus

> iiii belles whereof the least of xxviii ynches
> the second of xxxiii ynches
> the third of xxvii ynches
> the iiii of xxiv ynches brode in the mouthes.

The commissioners were able to report in 1553 that the plate and jewels of Herefordshire amounted to £1213 1s 3d and the weight of the bell metal 9 tons 6 cwt. 28 lbs. worth £190 5s 0d.[1]

The bells were to remain for 200 years and played an important part in parish life. They heralded both joy and sadness, probably warned of danger, called the faithful to prayer, and mourned their passing. They represented a substantial run on the parish purse and, although the first book of parish accounts does not commence until 1741, one can be certain that the bells would have featured regularly in previous expenditure. From 1741 to 1756 the following extracts are typical and introduce us to the language of bell maintenance.[2]

William Baugh, smith work for ye whele	3s. 0d.
Timber, hoops and bords to make a nugh whele	5s. 0d.
Sharbows, straps and nails for ye bell whele	3s. 0d.

Richard Baynham for making ye whele/fasning in ye stoks	5s. 6d.
For halling to ye pit strake sils, rowls and scaffel poles	1s. 6d.
Paid John Beavan for mending the clapper of ye bell	1s. 0d.
Due to the parish for a roap 10½lbs. at fower pence a pound	3s. 6d.
Paid for oyle and nailes for ye belles	10d.
Paid Mr. Mic Bramton's bill for ropes 59¾ lbs and nails	1. 7s. 0d.
Paid Mr. Bramton for 35 foot of bords at 1½d ft.	4s. 4½
For a rafter pole to make stays for ye bell wheels	2d.
Paid for one pint of oile to oile the bels and for the pottle	1s. 2d.
Wm. Davies for 8 days work a'mending the bells	10s. 8d.
2 days his son, Wm. 2 days his son, James	5s. 4d.
4 days Wm. Cook a'helping Davis	4s. 0d.

A parish meeting in 1753 decided 'that the bells be cast into five, and sent to Mr. Rudhall in order that they may with all convenient speed be recasted'. The Rudhall family were the foremost bell founders of the day, several generations casting, at their foundry in Gloucester, bells which went all over the world. Even today some of their machinery can be found in the equally well-known Whitechapel Foundry in London. It was further agreed that the bells be taken by the cheapest possible route to Gloucester which was probably down the Wye to Chepstow and back up the Severn. The estimate for the work was £50. The Rev. Richard Vaughan and Mr. John Parry of Arkstone each donated one guinea towards the cost. There were gifts amounting to £10 while Mr. Richard Russell of Dunswater gave a further £10, which probably accounts for his name being engraved on one of the new bells. They were inscribed as follows:

Peace and Good Neighbourhood	1756.
Prosperity to this Parish	1756
Ex Dono Ricardi Russel	
Abel Rudhall cast us all	1756
Jno. Herring. Ch.Warden	1756[3]

The re-hanging of the bells was the subject of a fascinating entry in the parish records which encompasses many facets of bell-ringing. What interest and excitement there would have been when they arrived back, probably harnessed to several horse-drawn farm wagons plodding along the road from Hereford, pretty rough going in those days. No doubt there were plenty of helping hands required and proffered and a few pints of ale downed in the process. Mine host at the Bull Ring would have had a profitable day. Perhaps he was a member of the bell-ringing team him

Taking down the old bells.
L to R: L. Evans, R. Powell, E. Hoad and T. Gundy. *HerefordTimes*

self. The project was completed in 1756 and Mr. Rudhall was paid shortly afterwards.

Court fees of 4s 6d were paid 'for ye bells whilst at Hereford'; presumably they were in storage on the outward and return journeys waiting for the appropriate carriers. Thomas Pritchard was paid for the use of his pulleys, timber was needed for the bell stocks, and Mr. Cooke was paid 'for his worke and for ye gudgens for ye bells'. The latter charge amounted to £14 18s 0d, an extra item which had to be accounted for, while sixpence was sufficient to pay 'for helping up with ye bells'. It was decided to have four new ropes to complete the job properly and a shilling was paid for 'running' them. An entry reads, 'The one key of the coffer in the Church was left at William Burgum's, Clarke of the Parish, to put in the roaps belonging to the parishners the third day of February in the year 1757'.

A note of 1762 states 'It was ordered and agreed that no person in future shall be buried in the body of the church unless a rope or 3/6d in lieu of it be deposited in the hands of the Churchwarden'. The old ropes were sold and in 1772 the going rate for 66 lbs. was sevenpence per lb. New ropes were required every three or four years, while nails, staples and hasps for the 'bell soller door' were often needed. In 1899 more restoration was done and a chiming apparatus installed and in 1903 a sixth treble bell in memory of Mr. Edwin Wathen of the Green Farm was hung at a cost of £43 17s 8d. It was cast by Barwell of Birmingham and was inscribed: Te Deum Laudemus Reginald Hereford Bird, Vicar/James Farr, Churchwarden. 1902. The necessary funds had been raised by Edwin's daughter, Annie Catherine Wathen.

The old bells continued to ring out until the mid 1980s when it was realised that a great deal of money would be required to restore them and to provide a new bell platform. The opportunity arose to acquire, at a very reasonable cost, a ring of eight bells cast by Taylor's of Loughborough early this century. These were housed in the belfry of the Church of All Saints, Llanbradach in South Wales. Sadly, this church had to be closed due to mining subsidence making it unsafe for further use and it has since been demolished.

It was decided to purchase these bells even though it was realised that, in the long run, the cost would probably be almost as much as that of restoring the existing peal. The chance to acquire eight bells perfectly matched, in excellent condition and with relatively little wear and tear was considered too good to turn down. Kingstone has always had a strong bell-ringing tradition and the challenge that was offered was taken up with extraordinary alacrity by the bell-ringing team.

The ancient bells of Kingstone were purchased by the parishioners of the Church of the Cross and Stable, Milton Keynes who were delighted to take on the restoration in the realization that a new peal at today's prices would be far beyond their resources.

The old bells awaiting transport to Milton Keynes.

The fund raising that took place in Kingstone for several years before the installation of the bells in 1987 was amazing. Coffee mornings, jumble sales, sponsored walks, organ recitals, barbecues, charity shop days, whist drives, bingo, discos; the list was never ending. The brass plate on the vestry wall says it all.

> The ring of eight bells in this tower was installed in November 1987 through the inspiration and dedicated service of Reginald and Evelyn Powell, the bells were dedicated by the Rt. Revd. Ian Grigg, Bishop of Ludlow, on 13th February 1988. Thanks be to God.
> Brian Gillett, Rector. Doris Watkins/Colin Brothers, Churchwardens.

Mr. Reg Powell is captain of the bell-ringers and, together with his wife, kept the momentum of events going, a great achievement. Reg became a bell ringer in 1931 when, after several years in the church choir, his voice broke. As was the normal practice in those days, he was asked if he would like to take up bell-ringing. His teacher was Mr. Bert Colcombe who, with his two brothers, Ted and Allan, were regulars in the team. Ted started bell ringing at the age of thirteen and a half and continued for seventy years. In those days many of the bell-ringers worked on local farms. Bert Colcombe worked on Dunswater Farm, like his father before him, and with a normal working week of sixty hours, bell-ringing took a back seat. It was cancelled between April and October since farming commitments were paramount. The team at that time consisted of the three Colcombe brothers, Mr. F.A. Oakley senior and his two sons, Fred and Arthur. Reg was so well taught and such a keen student that within two months he was able to ring in rounds for the 1931 Christmas services at 6a.m. and 7a.m. These days there are ten regulars in the team with three girl and two boy trainees.

The Llanbradach bells ready for the journey to Kingstone in November 1986.

The new bells, which hang in a modern steel frame designed by Taylor's who originally cast them, consist of a treble, 2nd, 3rd, 4th, 5th, 6th, 7th and a tenor, and have a combined weight of nearly two and a half tons. The inscriptions are as follows:

Treble — Let him that is athirst come
2nd — God save His Church
3rd — God save King George V

4th	Thanks be to God
5th	Praise ye the Lord
6th	Edwin Edwards Vicar
7th	Parish of Llanbradach formed 1904
Tenor	Clark Thomas Patron and Benefactress

The removal of the bells from Llanbradach was a sad day for the local folk who showed us photographs of church events there in the past. They were pleased that the bells had not gone too far away. I felt a little upset too that, in due time, the old bells would be leaving Kingstone for very different surroundings, a modern church in a new town.

The tower of Kingstone church has for centuries been a meeting place for much camaraderie by those practicing the art of campanology. The blacksmith, William Baugh, worked there often; Richard Baynham would have left his fields when needed; William Davies and William Cook, with their lads, were there 'a'helping'; while today the local team 'run the ropes' in very much the same way as their counterparts through the centuries. The bells may be different, but the friendship, enthusiasm and skills are little changed.

Bell ringers, 1995. *L to R:* R. Powell, E. Hoad, Rev. B. Gillett, N. Cooper-Tomkins (visitor), T. Gundy, M. Powell, S. Geary, P. Hornsby and S. Hornsby.

REFERENCES

[1] *Church Plate of the County of Hereford.* Hon. Berkeley Scudamore and H.C. Moffatt. Constable & Co., 1903.
[2] Kingstone Parish Records. Hereford Record Office.
[3] *Church Bells of Herefordshire,* Vol.II. Frederick Sharpe, F.S.A.

9 ARKSTONE COURT

The earliest reference to Arkstone occurs in the Herefordshire Domesday[1] where it is identified as being the Cobhall mentioned in the original Domesday Book of 1086. The Herefordshire Domesday of circa 1160-1170 was really an attempt to update the original. There is a marginal note stating 'Archeteleston, the estate of Arketel'. This could be a corruption of an old Scandinavian personal name, Arnketill.[2] Hugh de Lacy was the holder of Cobhall and Arketel would have held the land from him. After the accession of Henry I to the throne in 1154, there was an endowment by Hugh de Lacy to the Abbot of Gloucester and the Monks of St. Guthlac which included two parts of the tithe of the estate.

Other references to Arkstone are as follows:

Archelestune	1173	Hereford Cathedral Charters.
Arclestun	1243	Testa de Neville.
Arcleston	1303	Feudal Aids
Arkeston	1316	Feudal Aids
Arclestone	1334	Episcopal Registers
Arkeston	1484	Inquisitions Post Mortem[3]

Arkstone Court, 1996. Note blocked windows to avoid window tax. The building on the right has old stone foundations and is probably part of the dairy and kitchen wing of the original building.

In 1291 an inquisition was held into the right of one Hugh of Ploufield to succeed to the messuage, land and rent of Arcleteston on the death of his uncle, William de Radnor.[4] It appears that the Radnor family had held Arkstone for some time. An Elias de Radnor had been treasurer of Hereford and also Bishop of Llandaff from 1230 to 1240, while a William de Radnor had been treasurer to Llandaff, and later bishop after receiving royal assent in 1256. He died in 1265. A history of Llandaff states that William de Radnor had gifted to the bishop and chapter of Llandaff one carucate of land (approximately 100 acres) together with a messuage in perpetuity to support two chaplains there to say Mass daily for the souls of William and his brother Simon.[5] There is no record of an Arkstone chapel in Llandaff Cathedral today but there was once a chantry in Hereford Cathedral endowed by a Simon de Radnor circa 1270.[6] Browne Willis quotes the record as 'the Manor of Arcleton in perpetuity'.

William de Radnor, it would appear, had made this agreement with the Bishop of Llandaff. In return he was to receive twenty marks sterling for his life and, at his death, the chaplains at Llandaff would say Mass for him. Five marks would be paid forever for the said tenement, presumably to William's heirs. However, there's many a slip twixt cup and lip, as they say, and the bishop died before this convention (as it was called in the inquisition report) could be observed. William re-possessed his gift but after some three weeks was turned out by the Guardian of the Bishopric of Llandaff who claimed it for themselves. Perhaps it was all too much for William who also died. It fell to his nephew, Hugh of Ploufield (near Preston-on-Wye), to petition the bishopric of Llandaff and the sheriff of Hereford. The hearing or inquisition was heard at Hereford in 1292. The jury found in favour of Hugh but, since the original agreement was confirmed in 1337, presumably Hugh had let it stand. For how long Llandaff retained an interest in Arkstone is difficult to say. It was in the ownership of the de la Hay family until the middle of the fifteenth century when David Morgan arrived on the scene. It remained in the possession of the Morgan family until 1621. David Morgan's will, dated 1524, is the earliest I have located and is very detailed. It is lodged in the Public Record Office in London.[7]

DAVID MORGAN

David Morgan was born at Wernddu, Llandewy Skirrid, close to Abergavenny, about 1445. He married the heiress to Arkstone, one Margaret de la Hay, whose family are believed to have originated from Alt-yr-Ynnis, adjacent to Pandy/Longtown. His will commences with bequests to the church including Llandaff, the Grey Friars and the Black Friars of

Hereford, the Abbey of Dore and its daughter house, Grace Dieu, and to the parish church of Kingstone. With regard to the latter, the money was to buy a set of vestments. The cathedral church of Hereford, the rector of Ludlow, the priory of Aconbury, the church of Brecknock and the church of Llandewy Skirrid were also beneficiaries.

The vestments were listed in 1552 when commissioners appointed by Edward VI came to make an inventory of church goods with a view to taking away anything considered to be in excess of simple worship such as statuary, plate and jewels. Kingstone church had two old green vestments, a cope of 'sike color blewe', and 'a vestment of velvet ....aysed [emblazed?] with braunches of venys gold, the crosse browdered with images and braunches of venys gold'. I think the vestment of velvet was that bought with David Morgan's bequest. It was not considered to be old and the cross on it was embroidered with images which was not to be tolerated. It was taken away but the blue cope and the old green vestments were allowed to remain 'for every day'. The blue cope had an 'orphag' embroidered with images but, as this was the border of the garment, it may have been permissible.[8]

This was nearing the end of the era when it was customary to give land or money to religious orders who would undertake to pray for the soul of the donor and the souls of his ancestors. The setting up of chantries in this way was very common amongst the wealthy. David asked his heir to give 'for the tyme being yearly viii bushells of whete to pray for my soule, myn ancestor's soules and all expired soules for ever'. 'I will that my Executors ordayn in time of my burying xii torches, 30 lb. wax and more if need be at theirdiscretion. To xii pour men that shall bere xii torches, xii blak gownes'. The number of twelve was very often stated as it was the number of the apostles less the traitor, Judas Iscariot. The emphasis on the provision of wax for burning of candles was a very special part of all church ritual.

He also wished his executors to 'fynde an honest preest of good conversation, able in synging and redynge and waged by them ....alway to say daily masse yf he be disposed at the alter of Saint Stephyn in the Chapell of Arxston and there to have his chamber, fynding wax, bred and wyne and to say disige after the ordnance of the Church every Fryday...'.

This seems to indicate that the chapel is at Arkstone but he then goes on to say '...if any person, being myn heirs, will interrupt the said prest to sing and say mass in the said chapel of Saint Stephyn in the form above said, I will.....the said prest to sing and say mass himself...at the alter of the Trinity in the parishe church of Kyngeston'.

He mentions 'Saint Stevens landes lying in Arxston' and also wills three acres of land in the Brookfield at nearby Thruxton together with six kine 'to be sett to hire and with the profits and increase thereof to keep reparons and vestments of the said chapell and to fynd wax'. There appears to have been land already on the estate for the benefit of a chapel to which he is willing yet more. It is the luck of the draw that, although he was astute enough to request that his wishes should be recorded in the Dean of Hereford's register, and he made Canon Hugh Greene an overseer of his will, there is a gap in the records at this time. Although earlier chantries can be traced nothing has yet been found to prove just where the chapel of St. Stephen (or Arxton) was situated.

The north chapel, now St. Luke's Chapel, in Kingstone church was built long before David Morgan's time and, although he mentioned the church as his burial place, he qualified it by saying 'or in some holy place where it shall please my executors'. No memorial stone to him has been found although there are two earlier ones, quite unconnected with him, which were placed in the chapel when the church was restored in 1890. There is no record of a chantry being in existence there at the dissolution of chantries which took place some twenty-five years later. Although not all such dissolution certificates survive, in view of the church being a Dean's Peculiar a reference might have been expected somewhere. Arkstone Court was largely rebuilt in the late eighteenth century replacing the earlier building. It was sometimes the custom when a house was rebuilt, or when a chapel was disused or demolished, to retain a stone for insertion into a wall of a building on the land where it once stood. At Arkstone there is a curious ancient stone set into the wall of a barn facing the present house.

The ancient stone of unknown origin set in the wall of an outbuilding.

There is a mention in the seventeenth century court rolls of the 'Chauntray Leasow adjacent to the Marshe' but this is also the position of 'the Stevens'. The purpose of the field seems to have lived on by the latter name given to it by David Morgan himself although, in practical terms, there is nothing in church records to suggest that the chapel in Kingstone church ever received any finance from it.

Inventories of goods belonging to later occupants of Arkstone list some of the rooms. These included the parlour, kitchen, dayhouse (dairy), kitchen chamber, dayhouse chamber, little chamber, fellow's chamber, the new room, the buttery chamber, the great chamber, the green chamber, the backhouse (sometimes used for brewing), and simply 'at the stairhead'.[9] Some years ago, when alterations were being made, an original Tudor fireplace was uncovered in the then kitchen area. Quite recently, during more building improvements, several more fireplaces, one behind the other, were found. There is also a small portion of linen-fold panelling from the original building.

In David Morgan's will his son, John Delahay, was to have 'the bed in the wardropp with the heling of brodour [embroidered bed covering]'; daughter Anne, 'a wrethed cupp of silver with a cover'; 'William ap Morgan 2 oxen'; 'Roger Vaughan a goblet with a cover'; and, lastly, 'my chayn of gold, my cropp of graynes in Hereford and all movable goods to bury me and to pay debts, legacy and bequests'. His executors, one of whom was Sir John Taillour, pastor of Thruxton, and his two overseers were to have black gowns. His son was to have a 'doblet of silk' in addition to a black gown. His debts included £3 3s 4d to the vicar of Kingstone, Sir John Roberts, and 7s 6d for wages to his servants. There were many other gifts of oxen, heifers, bullocks, kine, geese and wheat to friends and to Canon Hugh Green, who was to act as adviser and overseer of his affairs, he bequeathed the sum of £10, quite a deal of money in those days. Most of his beneficiaries received 6s 8d rising in some cases to £1.

Morgan possessed land around Abergavenny. Rents from land in Llanwenarth were to be set aside for a priest to be paid eight marks a year to say Mass in the church of Llandewy Skyrrid for a year following his death. His grandson was to have 'the best salt of silver, the best flatt pees, 8 spoons of silver with the hole stuffe that resteth at Llanthenoye [Llanthony]'.

David Morgan's son died before him and it was his grandson, Thomas, who succeeded to the Arkstone estate. He and his wife Elizabeth Whitney had a son and eight daughters. One of the daughters, Anne, married Henry Carey whose mother was Mary Boleyn, sister to Anne Boleyn. Henry Carey, Lord Hunsdon, was a cousin to Queen Elizabeth and one of her most trusted advisers. He received his peerage in 1559 soon after her accession to the throne. On his death in 1596, the Queen paid for his funeral which cost just over £1000. His tomb, which towers some thirty-six feet high in Westminster Abbey, is quite remarkable if only for being the loftiest there.[10] Surely he must have visited Arkstone, the home of his wife's family? An article in the Woolhope Transactions in 1928 states that his grand-daughter, Philadelphia, later to become Lady Wharton, resided there but no authority for this statement is given. I have located portraits of both but have not found any other reference to confirm this statement.[11]

Henry Carey, Lord Hundon (1526-1596).

Mr. R.J.H. Berkeley, Berkeley Castle: photo Courtauld Institute

Philadelphia's father, Lord Hunsdon's youngest son, Sir Robert Carey, was English warden on the border marches for the last ten years of Elizabeth's reign. Lord Hunsdon had been warden of the eastern marches and was responsible for keeping order on the Scottish border. Sir Robert was present at the death of Queen Elizabeth and had galloped in sixty hours to Edinburgh with the news for the new monarch, James I. One of Lord Hunsdon's daughter's, Catherine, married Lord Howard of Effingham, later appointed Lord High Admiral by Queen Elizabeth to command the fleet that sailed against the Spanish Armada in 1588. She was David Morgan's great, great grand-daughter.

Lady Philadelphia Wharton (1596-1654).

The trustees of the Grimsthorpe and Drummond Castle Trust: photo Courtauld Institute

The last Morgan to live at Arkstone was Charles Morgan, the great-grandson of David Morgan. Charles was a ward of Sir George Carey by 1593. The wardship deed mentions that the Morgan estate included not only the manor of Arkstone with five messuages, two watermills for corn, five gardens, five orchards, one dove house, lands in Eaton Bishop and Kingstone but also the lordship and manors of Kilpeck and Kivernoll with lands in Treville, Thruxton and St. Devereux. In addition three other messuages were held from Sir Thomas Lucy who was Lord of the Manor of Kingstone. Charles was knighted at the time of the coronation of James I in 1603. By 1614 he was in financial difficulties, Walter Pye of the Mynde Estate in Much Dewchurch paying some of his debts. In 1617 he gave up Kilpeck and Kivernoll with their attendant holdings to Sir Walter Pye for the sum of £2700.[12]

The old Arkstone must have echoed with many different voices and varied dialects, from the humble dairy maid, waggoner, ploughman and cook, to the all powerful, since Lord Chamberlain was one of the offices held by Lord Hunsdon. Since Charles Morgan was a ward of a member of the Carey family it is possible that Lady Philadelphia could have lived at Arkstone, although, from what I have been able to discover, she was born about 1596 and married in 1611 and, since her husband Sir Thomas Wharton was from Easby, Yorkshire, she would more likely have been living there after 1611, by which time Charles Morgan was of age.

THE PARRY FAMILY OF ARKSTONE

Arkstone was sold by Sir Charles Morgan to Serjeant Hoskyns between 1617 and 1621. The latter exchanged it with Stephen Parry in part payment for the manor of Morehampton in the parish of Abbeydore.[13] The Parrys lived there for many generations until the death of the heiress, Mary, who was then the wife of another Charles Morgan of Ruperra and Tredegar House, Newport, Gwent. She willed the property to James Pritchard, a relative, on condition he took the name of Parry.

John Parry is the first of the family who speaks to us through his will. The son of Stephen above, he died in 1689 at the age of seventy-two.[14] He mentions mortgaging 'my lands and Mills Grittuals [Grist Mill] lying and being in the parish of Eaton Bishopp comonly called and known by the name of New Mille' for the sum of £250 with a promise of redemption. He bequeathed to his two daughters the title to the mill and lands but stated that if his son, Milo, would redeem the mortgage and give his daughters £150 each within a year of his decease, he could have the mill for himself and his heirs. He left the sum of £10 for his grandson John to be bound apprentice at the age of fifteen.

His inventory amounted to £542 of which £36 was owed to him in rent for the New Mill and £124 for forty-four trees and timber which had been felled on the estate and would be sold in due course. The trees are listed as being 'in Arkstone Parke'. He was a wealthy man. An interesting item was that of 'arrears of Chief Rents, but not known what it will amount to until a Cort be kept'. This indicates that there were freeholders in possession of land on the manor who owed a rent to John Parry as Lord of the Manor of Arkstone. His gravestone stands adjacent to the new vestry and is somewhat puzzling since it is a thirteenth century coffin lid. The inscription mentions his grandson John who was to be apprenticed and died in 1759. The initials and date J.P.P. 1791 are incised on the stone. This would be James Pritchard Parry who added the name Parry on inheriting the estate.

Manuscript notes on parishes in the Webtree hundred made in the late 1800s list some of the memorial stones in Kingstone church.[15] Prior to the 1890 restoration the coffin lid later used by the Parrys was recorded as lying in St. Luke's Chapel. The restoration included making the chapel into the vestry and the stone was moved to another position, possibly its present one. Other stones listed in the notes were also moved. Could the coffin lid have belonged to a member of the Furches family? Alternatively, could it have been moved from Arkstone itself? If so, it would still date from a long time before the setting up of David Morgan's chantry, wherever it was. The fact that the lid was at one time in St. Luke's chapel, together with other stones of the Parry family, points to the chapel having been used as a burial place for the Parrys of Arkstone from the late 1600s, even though there are also Parry memorial stones in the new vestry or tower. There is no doubt that many stones were relocated in the 1890 restoration but, sadly, no record was made of what was done.

The next Parry on the scene was Milo or Miles, John's son.[16] He died only four years after his father in 1693, leaving a widow and three children. John was the eldest, followed by Thomas and Elizabeth who were aged ten and seven. Thomas was left £300 and Elizabeth £400, plus £50 for their maintenance until they reached the age of twenty-one. Presumably John was heir to the estate with all the livestock, implements and goods that were detailed in the inventory amounting to £330 with no debtors. There is a large flat gravestone in St. Luke's Chapel at Kingstone which bears the name of Miles and his daughter Elizabeth who died a spinster aged thirty-three. Nearby is the grave of Mrs. Jane Ballard, wife to Miles, who re-married and outlived her daughter Elizabeth by ten years.

John Parry (apprentice John) died in 1759. He did not appear to have any heir and the estate passed to Thomas, the youngest of Miles's children. Thomas married Mary, a daughter of Robert Mynors of Treago

Castle in St. Weonards, and lived to the ripe old age of ninety-two. He died in 1774. There is a large memorial tablet on the wall in St. Luke's chapel erected by 'his sorrowing wife and daughter'.

Thomas's daughter, Mary, is more than a mere shadow from the past. She married twice; firstly to Robert Mynors Gouge of Treago, who was her cousin, and after his death in 1765 she married Charles Morgan of Ruperra Castle and Tredegar House in Monmouthshire, who was also M.P. for Brecon. Poor Mary had no children, and died at Brickendonbury, Hertfordshire, one of the Morgan family seats, in 1777 at the early age of forty-two. She lived both at Treago, where her second husband Charles Morgan carried out various alterations to the property, and at Tredegar House, Newport where her name can be seen today on the Morgan family tree on view to the many visitors to the mansion, now owned by Newport County Council. She and her husband Charles, who died in 1787, were buried in the Morgan chapel of St. Michael's church, Machen, near Ruperra Castle, the original family seat.

This ancient church at Machen has fine painted hatchments of the Morgan family mounted on the walls. Mary's can be seen close to the organ and the Morgan chapel. It is a remarkable coincidence that on leaving Kingstone and Herefordshire after thirty-seven years, my husband and I returned to live at Machen, his birthplace, and we regularly worship there. How I wish there was a portrait of her somewhere but to date nothing can be found in the Tredegar House archives or local collections.

In her will she conveyed various parts of her estate to her mother, her husband and, after their deaths, to a relative, James Pritchard, on condition that he obtain a Royal Licence to assume the surname of Parry which he did on 15th September 1787.[17]

It was James Pritchard Parry who built the Arkstone that we see today. To date there is no way of knowing what it looked like before although a deer park has been mentioned together with the names of Great Park Field, Lower Park, and Hopyard field, etc. J.P. Parry's will is lengthy and indicates that he had a considerable estate near the old Wye Bridge in Hereford including a malt house, stables, buildings and lands. He leased a large farm at Abbeydore from the Duke of Norfolk, and owned land called the Great Hill (Grithill), together with lime kilns, adjoining Thruxton parish.

He died in 1791 soon after assuming the name of Parry. His two sons carried on after him. The estate was bought by the Clive family who held it for a short time until James Martin from London and Ledbury (Martins Bank) acquired it some time prior to 1840. It remained with the Martin family until 1940 when James Hamilton Martin was killed in the

Hatchment of Mary Morgan who was born at Arkstone Court in 1735 and buried in 1777 at Lower Machen, Gwent.

North Sea in a naval action. The estate was purchased in 1942 by Guy's Hospital, later by Mr. Charles Clore and, in the 1980s, became the property of the Prudential Assurance Company. Today, as we approach the twenty-first century, the farm is once more owned and farmed by a family who have lived there for several generations. John Watkins and his family, his parents Bill and Rosa, and his grandparents have all in turn taken over caring for and improving the acres which have been cultivated through many centuries of change.

What would the many squires of Arkstone think of it today? The field patterns of the estate have changed a great deal; hedges have gone and large fields have taken their place. Some of the ancient names on the tithe map are becoming less familiar; Stephen's meadow (the Stevens), Ox Pasture, Great Park Field, the Squares and Cherry Orchard, Tumpy Close, the Slingets, Birchy Leasow, and so on. Yet, one feels when wandering through the lane past the entrance and on alongside the common to the Brookfield, that David Morgan, Miles Parry, old Squire Thomas Parry and his daughter Mary, would recognise it, although they would miss some of the old buildings in the vicinity. Indeed, they would surely gaze in wonder at the Arkstone of today.

Seventeenth century Little Arkstone Farm, now demolished.

There still remain large gaps to be explored in the history of Arkstone. It was known to the bishops of Llandaff, to the powerful Bohun family who were Earls of Hereford, to the Carey family who were related to Queen Elizabeth and, perhaps most importantly, to the many yeoman farmers who made their home and living from its lands through good times and bad.

REFERENCES

[1] *Herefordshire Domesday.* Edited by V.H. Galbraith and J. Tait. Pipe Roll Society, London, 1950.

[2] *Domesday Book: Herefordshire.* Edited by F. and C. Thorn. Phillimore, 1983.

[3] *Herefordshire Words and Phrases.* A.T. Bannister. Walsall, 1887.

[4] Inquisitions Post Mortem.
[5] *Description of the Cathedral Church of Llandaff.* Browne Willis. 1718.
[6] *The Cathedral Church of Hereford.* A.T. Bannister.
[7] PRO Wills. Prob.11/21.
[8] *Church Plate of the County of Hereford.* Hon.Berkeley Scudamore and H.C.Moffatt. Constable & Co., 1903.
[9] Deanery Wills. John Parry. Hereford Record Office.
[10] *Death Burial and the Individual in Early Modern England.* C. Gittings. Croom Helm, 1984.
[11] H. Reade. Transactions of the Woolhope Naturalists Field Club, 28.8.1928.
[12] Mynde Collection, no. 221.
[13] *Mansions and Manors of Herefordshire.* C.J. Robinson.
[14] Deanery Wills. Hereford Record Office.
[15] Mss. Webtree Notes. Hereford Reference Library.
[16] Deanery Wills. Hereford Record Office.
[17] J. Bradney. Transactions of the Woolhope Naturalists Field Club, 28.8.1924.

10 THE OLD MILLS

The Kingstone Mill, also known as Arkstone Mill, is mentioned in 1661 as paying a chief rent of ten shillings to the manor of Meer Court indicating that it was a freehold.[1] In 1670 William Rogers, a yeoman of Kingstone, was granted a lease of fifty years, or the term of the lives of the grantor's wife and daughter, at a rent of £8 per annum.[2] The mill was described as a 'messuage, water corn grist mill, Kingston's mill, with garden, orchard and land, with all gardens, orchards, water course, stankes, ponds, dames, wayes, commons, profits and heraditaments'. In much later years it belonged to the Arkstone estate as evidenced by the sale particulars of 1825 where we read of '...power to drive a water corn mill with 2 pairs of stones...'.[3] It was not until 1957 that Guy's Hospital Estate released it for sale as opposed to leasing. It was bought by Mr. and Mrs. W. Parry who had been in occupation for some years. The property then comprised about fourteen acres including the mill and orchard and the mill pond.

Arkstone Mill, also referred to as Kingstone Mill.

The mill is situated on a tributary of the Cage Brook. It is a three-storey building with brick upper part on a stone base, most probably rebuilt or enlarged. The two pairs of millstones were of French burr and there was a wooden pulley for sack-hoisting. The gears were of iron and the great spur wheel was wooden.[4] Although it probably ceased milling by the 1920s, Reg Powell said everything was intact and could have been used when his family lived there about 1928. There was a 300 yard leat bringing the water from Dunswater, although it originated from the Grange higher up. The head of water was too low, well under the level of the brook, and it was necessary to keep three pumps running to get the water up for use in the house. It is a great pity that nothing remains of the original machinery or the wheel although the sluice structure can still be seen. Inside the house there was an oven inserted in the wall by the fireplace and upstairs evidence of cruck beam construction with a huge beam running width-wise through one room.

There are memorials in the churchyard to two families who were millers for most of the 1800s, namely those of Eustance and Mayo. Prior to that the land tax records show Richard Blackway and his wife Ann were milling there in the late 1700s.[5] The last to grind there would probably have been James Farr who was listed in a 1905 trade directory as both farmer and water-miller of Arkstone and Arkstone Mill. The 1891 census shows the mill as unoccupied.

New Mills, although in the parish of Eaton Bishop, is also on the Cage Brook and is mentioned in a deed of wardship dated 1593 when the young Charles Morgan of Arkstone was put in the care of Sir George Carey until he came of age to inherit. The deed lists all the properties owned or leased by his deceased father, Thomas Morgan, and includes 'two water mills for corne'.[6]

David Morgan of Arkstone died in 1524 and gives directions in his will for his various 'landes and tenements, medowes, lesos and pastures with their appurtenances lying in Bishops Eton, *except* the newe mylle, Croft corner ploke and the water course to the same mylle which I will that myn heir shall have, paying the Bishop rent of 6s.8d.' This would indicate that he owned the mill and was paying a chief rent for his freehold to the bishop who was lord of the manor. He mentions one mill only.

The Morgan connection with Arkstone and the mills ended in 1621 when Edward Morgan, the youngest of Thomas Morgan's sons, renounced any claim to the estate and confirmed the title to John Parry, son of Stephen Parry.[7] Previous to this there had been exchanging and mortgaging between John Sergeant Hoskyns and Stephen Parry.

With regard to New Mills, it is interesting to note that when John Parry came to marry Elizabeth Delahay of Allt yr Enys in 1642 he settled all his lands and manors in trust to her brother but states in the marriage settlement 'excepting only water corn mills called New Mills in Eaton Bishop'. This seems to reinforce the inference in the wardship deed of 1592 that there were two mills.[8]

The mill wheel, dismantled in 1940 in response to appeals for scrap metal for the war effort.

In May 1685, needing to raise money, John Parry mortgaged New Mills to Mary Trist, a widow of Hereford. He died in 1689 and it will be remembered that he had mortgaged 'my lands and Mills Grittuals [Grist Mills] lying and being in the parish of Eaton Bishop commonly called and known by the name of New Mills' for £250 with a promise of redemption. He wished his son Miles to redeem the mortgage but Miles died in 1693 shortly after his father. In 1697 New Mills was still mortgaged to the Tryst family when John Tryst assigned the mortgage to a Richard Welsh of Hereford. Richard Welsh, or Walsh, had married Anne, one of John Parry's daughters. The other daughter, Joan Morse, a widow, was the other party. Having at last redeemed the mortgage, they were able to lease the mills to Edward Brewer of Luggbridge Mills, Holmer for ninety-nine years for a payment of £100 and a rent of £12 a year. The lease states 'New Mills. Two water corn mills in Eaton Bishop'.[9]

In 1718 another John Parry, Miles Parry's heir, gave over any rights he had in the New Mills to Richard Walsh, who conveyed them to James, Earl of Caernarvon. The earl leased them back to Walsh for his life and the lives of his daughters, Ann and Helena. The estates of the Earl of Caernarvon were eventually bought by Guy's Hospital in the 1730s but it was not until 1754 that they gained full ownership on the death of Lady Caernarvon, the wife of his eldest son. In 1754 the representatives for Guy's visited New Mills and reported that they had been leased by them for lives at £2 per year for some time and the lease had recently been assigned to Thomas Parry. Once more Arkstone held the lease to the mills but they were owned by Guy's Hospital Estates.[10]

Today there is but one mill, the New Mill. It is weather-boarded with some brick and stone and a half-timbered mill house. All the machinery remains including two pairs of French burr stones and an external overshot wheel of iron measuring 10ft x 4ft 6in.[11] The mill has been sympathetically restored, presenting a pleasing picture of a part of our early industrial history which was an integral part of village life. In common with Arkstone Mill it is noted on the maps of Taylor in 1754 and others of later date, including the tithe maps. It is thought that the Lewis family were milling there from about 1840 until the 1930s. By the 1920s, the milling side of the business proving uneconomic, the family turned to wholesale corn merchandising which continued into the 1950s. The present owners are Mr. J.R. and Mrs. W.L. Knight.

Adjacent to the mill are three cottages which were originally known as Upper, Lower and Middle New Mills. They were attached to the mill lands, probably built for those working at the mill, although this would indicate that it was a sizeable undertaking to employ more than the miller and his own family. The deeds of Upper New Mills owned by Mr. and Mrs. Brian Watkins date back to 1701 when Edward Brewer leased the mill. Domesday Book lists a mill in Bishops Eaton valued at five shillings which could have been the Ruckhall Mill. The Cagebrook Mill, although in Clehonger parish today, was also close by. It seems that New Mills, which is also the name for the area, was a highly valued part of the Arkstone Estate since the Morgans and Parrys were anxious to retain it for as long as possible.

New Mills, Eaton Bishop.

REFERENCES

[1] Mynde Collection. No.5135.

[2] Kingston Mill Lease. 7th March 1670. Hereford Record Office.

[3] Webtree Mss. Hereford Ref.Library.

[4] *Water Mills of the Middle Wye Valley*. S.D. Coates and D.G. Tucker. 1983.

[5] Land Tax Assessments. Hereford Record Office.

[6] Grant of Lordship and Wardship Deed. G.87/25/28. Hereford Record Office.

[7] Whitfield Estate Archives. AW.28/13/3. Hereford Record Office.

[8] Ibid. AW.28/13/2.

[9] Ibid. AW.28/13/7.

[10] Guys Hospital Estates. C.99/111/235. Hereford Record Office.

[11] Coates and Tucker, op.cit.

In the name of God Amen I John Parry of Clyton within the Fifth of Kingston in the County of Hereford gen being weake in Body but of full perfect memory praised be to God Allmighty Doe make and declare this my last Will and Testament in manner and forme following ffirst I commend my Soul into the hands of Allmighty God my maker and Redeemer and my Body to be Buried in Christian Buriall by the direction of my Executors hereafter named Item whereas I have mortgaged my Lands and Mills scituate lying and being in the parish of Eaton Bishopp commonly called and knowen by the name of new mills unto mary [illegible] for the Consideration of Two hundred pounds with a Provisoe of Redemption Item I devise give and bequeath all my Right Title and Redemption in the said mills and Lands with the remainder thereof unto Joan and Anne my two Daughters and to their heires for ever But my whole intent and meaning is that if Miles my Sonn shall pay the mortgage moneys and the sume of one hundred and ffifty pounds to my said two daughters within one year after my decease the said Lands and Mills shall be to my said Sonn and to his heires for ever Item I give and bequeath unto my Grand Child John Sonn of my Sonn John [illegible] pounds when he shall accomplish the Age of ffifteen yeares for the binding him Apprentice and untill that time to be maintained by my Exors Item my Debts paid my ffunerall Expenses discharged all my goods Cattles and Chattells moveable or unmoveable in what kind soever I am owner of I give and bequeath to Joan and Anne my daughters and to their heires for ever And I nominate constitute and appoint Joan and Anne my daughters Executors of this my last Will and Testament and I utterly revoke and disanull all other Wills and Testaments by me ever made or bequeathed In Wittness whereof I have hereunto putt my hand and Seale the ninth Day of Aprill in the ffirst year of the Reign of William and Mary King and Queen of England Scotland ffrance and Ireland defender of the faith etc Anno in the year of our Lord God one thousand six hundred eighty nine.

Sealed and delivered in the presence of
Hester Parry
Tho: Morgan
Morgan Powell

John Parry

7o. die Decembris 1689
Jurat fuerunt Executrices in hoc Testamento nominat [illegible]
Coram me
Ja. [illegible]

Probatum fuit hoc Testamentum apud Hereford Septimo die mensis Decembris Anno Dni 1689 coram [illegible] [illegible] Georgio Benson Sacrae Theologiae Professore [illegible] Hereford [illegible] Joannam Parry et Annam Parry fil [illegible] [illegible] [illegible] [illegible] [illegible] [illegible] [illegible] Johanne [illegible] [illegible] [illegible] [illegible]

John Parry's will mentioning the New Mills.

11 RICHARD KING

Richard King, who died in 1688, lived at Mawfield which was often twinned with Kingstone in early documents. He was vicar of Clehonger and Allensmore and prebendary of Hereford Cathedral. A glebe terrier dated 1672 for Allensmore, listing all the land owned by the church there, ends with an item stating that the tythe wool and lambs payable from Meer Court were to be apportioned between the vicar of Kingstone, then Christopher Whiting, and the vicar of Allensmore, Richard King, when the dean next visited.[1] The parish boundaries run through part of Meer Court so Whiting was entitled to his share of that portion of tithe. Today the villages are united in one parish.

His lengthy will, full of interest with regard to its phrasing, hints at an intriguing link with Arkstone. He was a very wealthy man; the value of his possessions listed in his inventory is the highest of any that I have seen. The content of his will indicates a man of great integrity, tempered with much humility.[2]

Mawfield, Allensmore, home of Richard King.

King's home was well furnished with an abundance of pewter, cooking utensils, bedding, linen, provisions, etc. He had eight oxen, a few cows, two mares, sixteen 'swyne' of all sorts, and seventy-seven sheep and lambs. His land was planted with oats, barley and peas valued at £30, while corn of all sorts in the house and barn, threshed and unthreshed, together with more in the city of Hereford, was valued at £50. The total of such items amounted to £228 but the bulk of his estate was comprised of debts 'due by bond or otherwise' which amounted to £1029. All debts were meticulously listed from one of £380 owing by Herbert Aubrey, squire of Clehonger, down to £5 from Thomas Price of Allensmore.

He wished to be buried privately under 'ye great stone in ye chancell of Allensmoor'. If this wish was carried out, there is no record of it and no memorial to be found there. Victorian restoration work may well have erased any trace. He left £4 each to the poor of Allensmore and Clehonger and five shillings to every servant, but 'Jane' was to have forty shillings.

He was childless but provided liberally for his niece, Hanna, and nephews, Thomas and Richard King. Thomas was particularly fortunate, since he was to have all Richard's wearing apparel, coats and hose. Money was invested for the three until they came of age. Another nephew, John, seems to have well and truly blotted his copy book. Every time the others are mentioned the will states 'except John' and later, '..to John I will leave nothing, he having idly consumed the porcon I gave him'.

Richard King ordered the following items to be sold for the use of his brother's children: 'The cider mill and screw, ye furnaces, one tableboard in ye hall and frame and syde draw there and ye clock, one table board and frame in ye kitchen and frame bench and joynt settle there, all my hogsheads, save two for my wife. The frame and cheesestone in ye dayhouse and cheese ring except my wife hath occasion to use them for her dayry. One great vat with iron rings, one bedstead in ye chamber over the parlor, and bedding and furniture there and great workt chayre there, one bedstead in the little chamber over the cheese ring, one great chest in ye chamber over ye backhouse, one chest in ye chamber over ye great butry and great vat, one long table board in my chamber over ye dayhouse and tressle'. This list gives a good idea of what the interior of Mawfield looked like at that time. A butry was a store room, used mainly for food and drink, and a cheese ring was a wringer or press or could be another name for a cider press, since the apple pulp was sometimes known as 'cheese'. I would like to think that the 'great workt chayre' was bought by a parishioner or donated to Allensmore Church since they have two very old chairs there, one of which could well be Richard King's as regards style and date.

The will refers at great length to a deed covering some land 'which was speedily to be done but not yet executed because of my weakening'. This land had been specified as being of two acres in Gethinfield in Clehonger. In fact it was only one acre and Richard intended giving the

The 'great workt chayre' in Allensmore church.

other party, Thomas Jones, land from another field or money to equal it, or to exchange it for another close to it. He mentions that his lawyer had measured the land and that an account of it was in his study.

The transaction was obviously very much on his mind. He writes '....if this exchange does not go on, I charge all persons concerned if they take more money from ye poore man Thomas Jones than yet one acre in Gethinfield arable now soed with barley by me, it shall never bye on my conscience to do wrong though I did this for ye reason aforesaid, yet not with any intention to defraud at any time, but only for his and my convenience.........but this declaration by me is sufficient to settle it, and those honest gentlemen to whom I have disposed my estate will act squarely according to my Will for I claime no right to those two acres of ground, nor were ever in my possession or ever should, unless ye exchange be effected'.

As the writing becomes barely legible Richard King adds various items that come flooding into his memory; 'the standing of books to my cousin John Parry' (Arkstone), 'I have a bull at Mr.Sydell, lent him', 'I have a 3 year old bullock and 2 yearling calves at Richard Perris at Wynall'. To Simon Tranter and Richard Poole, the trustees of his will, he writes 'I doo give them Thirty shilling a peece to buy them two rings to wear for my sake with this motto, I live in your love R.K. earnestly desiring these are to see my will according to equity and conscience without wasting of words'.

Now to the intriguing part of the will, namely the large parts of it which relate to Richard's wife, Elizabeth Lenthall who came from Hardwick, an estate in the Herefordshire village of Pembridge. She was

> 'to have twenty bushells of wheat and thirty bushells of rye to be delivered by my Executor and Trustees and yt [that] very good, and all the provisions for housekeeping yt is in my house, and all the hempe, flax yet is in my house,or about the outhouses and yards, and thirty bushells of barley, if there be not thirty bushells of malt in my house and what is wanting of thirty bushells of barley malt, ye rest to be to her delivered, and if it be more in my house, she is to have it all as well oates and barley'.
>
> 'I doe assign my wife for her conveniency the Hall Parlor, great Butry, the chamber over ye parlor and ye hall chamber with her conveniences, to use ye backhouse and brewhouse and what other rooms my Executor and Trustees shall think fitt.....till ye sale of my estate'.
>
> 'I allow my wife all the wood about the house to be disposed of as she pleases to burne whilst she is at my house and to be carried away for her by my Executor when she intends to leave, *see it be*

not to Arkston'.

'I doo hereby order yt my cattles and wains carry my wife's goods and what is heere left her to any places within ten miles of my house, and if my cattle be sould before she have yt occasions yt my Executor pay ye charge out of my estate, *see it be not to Arkston*'.

Elizabeth was to have an allowance of £30 yearly for life, paid quarterly from his estate and, if she did not receive it at the correct times, she could claim £1 a week until it was paid. Richard made his mother, also named Elizabeth, his executor and ordered his wife to deliver to her 'my heve deske with all ye deeds and wrighting therein, and in my study, and all the letters and bonds and papers and one coffer in the chamber now over the little butry.....'. He also mentions that some of his wife's belongings may be listed as belonging to him and, if so, she is to be paid to the full if such items are sold.

It seems a strange way to act unless Richard and Elizabeth were estranged. Or was she not sufficiently responsible to deal with the winding up of such a large estate? Perhaps they had not been married for very long. I have been unable to trace their marriage. The references to Arkstone point to some measure of distrust directed at the Parry family. He certainly did not want her to end her days there and yet leaves his books to his cousin, John Parry, who was residing there. Elizabeth, at the time of Richard's death, was about sixty years of age, his mother presumably much older. The relationship between the two women may not have been a happy one.

Richard's injunctions were not in the event to be realised, however, since Elizabeth King did go to Arkstone. Her memorial stone can be seen on the floor of St. Luke's Chapel in Kingstone church. She left a will and inventory, the former, far from indicating a weak mind, is clearly set out and was signed by her. Attempts to trace her exact relationship to the Parry family have failed. She leaves money to her cousins, John and Thomas Parry, and to their sister Elizabeth, her god-daughter. The word cousin was often used in those days to denote a relative or kinsman, nephew, niece or even a very great friend.

INVENTORY OF ELIZABETH KING

It is not known when Elizabeth King moved to Arkstone but she died there in 1699. From the fact that her inventory lists all the rooms in Arkstone with contents which amounted to only £38, she presumably had possessions which were to be found all over the dwelling.[3] I find it intriguing that there was a brass clock in the hall and the furniture there closely resembled what was in the hall at Mawfield. Did they make their way to Arkstone too? Her goods included all the usual items: cooking, dairy and brewing utensils, a malt mill, three pairs of wooden scales, salt barrels, straw skips and baskets (a skip was a small basket often made of willow), a voider which was a large basket or tray, butter tubs, and four smoothing irons. Even a tub of feathers was noted. In her bedroom, apart from the normal items, there was her Bible and a looking glass. She seems to have learned some of her husband's business acumen since she was owed £300 in two bonds of £150 each. There is no mention of farm stock, implements or crops so it is possible she may have taken over the housekeeping of Arkstone. The cousins mentioned in her will were all under age at the time of her death. Their father Miles Parry had died in 1693 and their mother Jane married John Ballard of Monmouthshire as her second husband.

REFERENCES

[1] Glebe Terrier of Allensmore, 1672. Hereford Record Office.
[2] Deanery Wills. Richard King died 1688. Hereford Record Office.
[3] Deanery Wills. Elizabeth King died 1699. Hereford Record Office.

12 KINGSTONE GRANGE

The Kingstone Grange of today dates from the late 1500s or early 1600s. It is built on a sandstone rubble plinth and to an E-shaped plan with wings extending south-eastwards, a projecting staircase wing on the north-west side and a modern addition at the north-east end. The south-east front has exposed timber framing, except the three gables which are tile hung. Lying well back from the road, surrounded by fields, trim hedges and undulating hills and woodland it is a perfect setting giving a glimpse of what the countryside might have looked like in the reign of Elizabeth I. The fields would have had fewer hedges and more strips but the topography has remained constant.

Kingstone Grange, 1927. *RCHME Crown Copyright*

The origins of Kingstone Grange are almost as old as the parish church itself. Grange indicates a small monastic farm. Kingstone Grange was just this, a part of the possessions of the Cistercian monks of the Abbey of Dore. The abbey was founded in 1147 by Robert, son of Harold of Ewyas. Robert was also a benefactor to the monks of Ewias Priory and to the Priory of Craswall but he chose to be buried at Dore where his tomb can still be seen. The ground on which the monks established Kingstone Grange was given to them circa 1170. It is recorded that 'Baldwyn Sitsylt gave certaine lands in the township of Kiggestone unto the Moonkes of Dore, and granted unto the same moonkes freedom of common and pasture and other liberties in his woods'.[1] The Sitsylts were ancestors of the Cecil family whose descendants were great statesmen in Tudor times.

There followed gifts of land from Walter of Kingston, Robert of Clifford, Geoffrey of Kingstone and John Lightfoot from 1250 to 1305. Walter gave his land in return for a promise of burial in the abbey, while Geoffrey's land is recorded as six acres. There are two ancient field names which indicate their monastic connections, Monk's Mears (boundary) and the great and little Horston fields. The first named rector of Kingstone was Henry of Llantony. The name Horston, as used in recent years, is a corruption of Austin as noted at the time of the Enclosure Act. Llantony was a foundation of the Augustinian canons, known as Austin Friars. Prior to 1250 Walter de Haia, a Prior of Llantony, gave a grant of sixpence from land in Kingstone to the church of St. Mary and St. Ethelbert of Hereford (Hereford Cathedral) and canons there.[2]

The Grange lands lie in Abbeydore as well as Kingstone which in 1239 gave rise to a dispute between the rector of Kingstone, one William Rufus, also referred to as Philip Rufus, and the monks of Dore. William appeared to be entitled to one third of tithes from the monks as well as tithes from assarts (clearing of trees) of the forest of Treville. The abbot and monks proved that they had 'an indult on tithes of lands which they cultivate'. In other words, they had permission to depart from the normal church laws so William waived his claim. The Cistercian order had been granted exemption from payment of tithes in 1132. Parish churches in the areas where the Cistercians had farms must have suffered loss of income as a result.

William's entitlement to one third of tithes from 'land before the door of the Grange at Kingston' or the gate of the Grange at Kingston, was set out in a document, now in the Public Record Office in London, in which the bounds are given. The document states:

> 'namely the third sheaf of the tithes from the land before the gate of Kingston Grange, from the folla [?pit, valley] of Kingston as far as the way which leads towards Coeghere [or 'Cotghete'? from Cockyard] and divides the land of the Forest of Trivel from the territory of Kingston, and so by the same way directly as far as the bridge of Hoppeleg and so from the bridge, descending by agreed bound as far as Aylburgewelle, excepting the new meadow within that land next to the way which leads to the grange'.

Hereford Record Office has a perambulation of Abbeydore parish made in 1822 which states 'this neck of land is declared not to be in Kingston Parish' and is thus described in Latin, 'excepto novo prato juxta viam que ducit ad Grangeam', 11th August 1239.[3]

It is difficult to decide just where the exact boundaries were but the reference to Aylburg's well is helpful. The well is to be found across the fields at the back of the Grange towards the valley of Kingstone. The bridge of Hoppeleg is adjacent to the Cockyard to Thruxton road, close to the old hollow way, which was the original road, before one reaches the lodge house at the entrance to Whitfield. Those familiar with the area will know that on the road from Kingstone to Abbeydore, the Cockyard, there is a well defined lane leading off to the the Grange. At one time there was a very prominent marker stone at the top of it. No doubt this was placed there for a good reason, quite possibly to mark the boundary between the Grange and the territory of the demesne farm of Kingstone, Dunswater, and to define the parish boundary. It is possible that the 'pit' could refer to the quarry or marl pit which was adjacent to the lane just mentioned. Another possibility is that the way to the Grange could be the way that William de Furches gave to the monks on his demesne in Kingston, going from the garden of their Grange and leading to 'the king's way' which they were allowed to enclose and ditch. This was a pathway through the fields from the Grange meeting the B.4348 between the Bull Ring and Dunswater, marked as a footpath to this day. Either way the description equates with the land before the Grange which remains in Abbeydore parish. The name Hoppilegh is noted by the Rev. A.T. Bannister as an area in Treville which also contains Fernilegh.[4] Fields known as Hopleys or Hopless and Fern Field appear on the Abbeydore tithe map and in an old map of 1790 showing the Grange lands.

There were other disputes with the monks regarding tithes and forest boundaries at Treville, where they had bought land from Richard I in 1198, and King John in 1215, paying him 600 marks and ten palfreys for all the land between the river Dore and the Treville brook. A year later they paid a further 300 marks in order to clear the woodland. The woodland was obviously valuable to the monks, both as standing timber, which they needed to build and maintain their farms and lands, also as a saleable commodity and later, when cleared, as land for cultivation. A notable historian of the time, Gerald de Barri, better known as Giraldus Cambrensis, Archdeacon of Brecon and Bishop-elect of St. Davids, intensely disliked and distrusted anything to do with Dore Abbey. Consequently, any of his writings in relation to its abbots and their deeds have to be treated with caution. He accuses the abbey of obtaining grants of land and forest by devious means, sometimes by downright trickery. According to him they tricked Richard I into selling part of Treville Wood for 300 marks by describing it as a wild place giving shelter to Welsh rebels and robbers who were terrorising the neighbouring villages. Giraldus also comments that the monks were 'changing an oak wood into a wheat field', since a survey taken of the forest in 1213 showed that the abbey owned more than half of its 2013 acres and that the basis of their farming was arable and wool yields.

It must be born in mind that the area was very close to the ancient Archenfield, a veritable cockpit of the continuous strife in the Marches between English and Welsh. The abbey was regarded as being in Wales while it was attached to the diocese of Hereford. No doubt there was some truth in the assertion that the Treville forest provided hiding for some raiders, in which case it may have been expedient to clear parts of it.

The monks were great sheep farmers. Dore's wool with that of Tintern, another Cistercian foundation, was the highest priced monastic wool in England. By 1291 they had fifty-four cows, 2740 sheep and mowed fifty-one loads of hay on their lands. Wool from sheep grazed on the pastures of Kingstone Grange was sold to merchants in Italy, France and Flanders in the thirteenth and fourteenth centuries.

Most of the seventeen granges belonging to Dore Abbey were situated within a day's journey of the mother house. Each would have had a chapel, a barn, sometimes a mill, and accommodation for the lay brethren as well as buildings for their implements and stock. The land was worked by lay brothers but, as time went on, the granges were leased to tenant farmers. By the early 1500s the abbey farmed very little of its land; indeed half of Kingstone Grange was leased to Thomas Goff at £3 per annum for sixty-one years. In 1517 Thomas ap Gore (probably a descendant) gave up the lease. From 1529 the Baskervilles appear to have been in possession, together with Morehampton Grange, although the latter was sold by the Crown about 1546 to Stephen Parry, grand-father of Stephen Parry of Arkstone, with Thomas Baskerville remaining as tenant. It would appear that the woodland was still greatly prized since leases, including Thomas Baskerville's in 1529, incorporated a clause that the tenant could have sufficient 'housebote and heybote out of the Abbot's wood at Dore, but he was not to cut the grete oke, elm or polle wood'. In 1540 another lease mentioned the fact that the land in question was 'closed with a hedge containing 120 acres, whereof 13 acres be of fifty years growing, and the residue of an hundred years growing and above'. This indicates careful management of the forestry rather than the heavy-handed approach to assarting that Giraldus wrote of much earlier.

Baskerville's lease in 1529 was for sixty-nine years. In addition to the clause regarding use of the woodland, it provided that he was to build 'a dwelling house, a barn, and other cottages meet and convenient' while he was allowed the wood to repair and maintain his hedges and dykes within the precincts of the grange. There are two wills made by women living in the Grange; one dated 1618 by Margaret Williams, a spinster, and the other by Elizabeth Baskerville dated 1652. I have not discovered any relationship between them. Margaret left 'my brasse pann, my brasse pott and my featherbedd' to her nephew, and Elizabeth left 'my featherbed, boulster and coverings and the standing bedstead in the chamber over the parlour at the Grange, and one other featherbed in the custody of Bodenham Gunter of Thruxton, gent, and the feather bed in the chamber at the Grange aforesaid , one coverlett' to her son Steven Baskerville. The rest of her goods, including cattles and chattles, were given to her other son, Tristram Baskerville of Kingstone Grange. It appears that the Baskervilles inhabited the building for several generations. I have seen references to Baskerville's Park in leases which indicates they were well established for the name to carry on in that way.

Thomas Baskerville was the last steward of the abbey. It was dissolved by 1536. By that time there were only nine monks and sixteen servants within its walls. The yearly value was stated to be some £100. Its main lands were granted by the King to John Scudamore of Holme Lacy. The remains of the beautiful building, which it must have been, have become the parish church. John Scudamore bought most of the contents at a sale held at Dore on 1st March 1537, paying £2 for the roof, slates and timber of the Frater, 'the old house by the wayside next to the bridge' and the 'organs in the quire'. Others bought the vestments which included five chasubles, four pairs of tunicles, three copes, together with thirteen palls and four stained frontals. It was John Scudamore's great-great-grandson, the first viscount Scudamore, called 'the Good Lord Scudamore', who undertook the repair of the church in 1632.

The household goods in the kitchen at the time of the dissolution comprised eight platters, six pottingers (soup bowls), three saucers, a broach (spit for roasting meat), a chafern (for heating water), two gridirons, two brass pans, an iron dripping pan, a frying pan and a hogshead. The parlour had a table-board with trestles, a chair and a cupboard. The brew-house contents included a kneading trough, two bran tubs, a moulding board, a mash vat, two brass furnaces and a hogshead.

Implements of husbandry included four corn wains, eleven iron towes (chains), four shares, twelve yokes and two pairs of horse harrows. Twenty-four oxen were sold for £16, twenty kine for £8 6s 8d and four horses for 13s 4d (1 mark).

John Scudamore had been appointed the crown receiver by Henry VIII to supervise the dissolution of the monastery. He lists among his accounts the payment of 6s 8d (half a mark) to John Wellington, a plumber,

The Cistercian Abbey of Dore (1147) now the parish church.

for melting the lead and moneys paid to masons and labourers who assisted in the demolishing of parts of the building. The churchwardens were allowed to buy two of the bells. The gilt chalice was also left because 'of the clamour made about it by the parishioners'. Good for them! Although they had to leave the abbey, the nine monks and some of the lay officials appear to have been allowed pensions or were given work.

We shall never know how far the monks and monasteries which were dissolved by Henry VIII allowed their original ideals to become eroded to such a degree that this action was necessary. Dore itself was never a very wealthy foundation but others were, to the point of accumulating great wealth and lands, sometimes to the point of destroying villages in order to acquire a vast amount of pasturage for their sheep. To me it seems needless desecration to let such priceless gems of architecture moulder away in the name of financial expediency. Dore was often in financial difficulties, and certainly the tenant of Kingstone Grange, Harry Griffith, was no help to them; when he died twenty years after he was given the lease, he together with several others had failed for many years to pay rent amounting to over £160. This was a great deal of money.

Kingstone Grange was considered primarily an arable farm of 329 acres as reported in a survey in 1623. Morehampton was important for its pastures which, in an inventory of 1291, yielded forty loads of hay while Kingstone yielded a paltry three loads. The acreage of the Grange in those far off days was very much more than today or even at the time of the tithe map (156 acres). It would appear that it included the Bigsty farm (95 acres), or part of it, since the woods nearby are mentioned as being insufficient to repair the houses and hedges there.

Thomas Baskerville lived at Pontrilas Court. He died in 1551, is buried at Kentchurch, and had two illegitimate sons, Walter and William. Possibly Elizabeth Baskerville, who died at the Grange in 1652, was a descendant. William Hoskyns, the younger son of Sir Bennet Hoskyns of Harewood Court, made his home at the Grange, endowed the almshouses in Kingstone, and died in 1721. It was later acquired by the Moore Greens of Cagebrook, Eaton Bishop, whose descendants owned it until the Rev. Archer Clive of Whitfield purchased it in 1860. After William Hoskyns died, a James Fisher was named in court rolls through the mid 1700s as being of the Grange. Then a Williams family were tenants for a while in the 1800s. James Deacon was in possession by 1867 and James Hoddell by 1900.

The survey of 1623 describes the farm as having a 'dwelling containing four rooms of old decayed building', 'a good barn of four rooms', 'a sheepcot of three rooms, some twenty acres of meadow and sixty-four of pasture'. The remainder was arable. When the Royal Commission visited in 1927, they dated the barn and sheepcot as seventeenth century, so they may have been the buildings referred to above. Returning in 1952 they referred only to the larger barn and put the date as possibly mid-eighteenth century.

Elizabeth Baskerville, in her will of 1652, referred to the chamber over the parlour and the chamber at the Grange. If we include a kitchen, that would seem to account for the four rooms of old decayed building. Today the parlour is lined with old panelling and has moulded ceiling beams. The 'chamber over the parlour' has beautiful early eighteenth century panelling with cornice and dado rail and incorporating earlier work. The fireplace has an early eighteenth century moulded surround and shelf. Other rooms have original panelling and ancient ceiling beams. The staircase is also early eighteenth century and the hall has original moulded ceiling beams. It seems likely that the Hoskyns family were responsible for improving the house and that some of the original panelling was retained.

Kingstone Grange today is farmed by the third generation of the Winney family. Nigel's father, Kenneth, and grandfather, Hubert, gained a county-wide reputation for their fine heavy draught horses and Friesian dairy cattle. Many supreme championship awards, cups and trophies were won by their animals, some outright after successive wins, for example, in 1949/50/51. It was jokingly said by Mr. H. Winney 'Winney by name,

A prize-winning pair from the Grange with Archie Pitt.

and winner by nature' and so it would seem.

On one of our visits to the Grange, we were taken upstairs to one of the attics to look at a relic that had been there for many years. We discovered it was an old box mangle invented in the mid-eighteenth century. As the photograph shows, it was very large and heavy, about 6ft x 4 ft. The clothes were twined round the wooden cylinders made of beech wood and placed on the lower part of the frame. The oblong wooden box, which can be seen inside the frame, was filled with heavy stones and mounted on runners at each side of the frame which propelled it over the rollers by straps fitted at each end of it. They passed over the upper roller in the middle, which was carried round by a winch. It must have been a very exhausting process to propel it back and forth. The handle can just be seen. Sometimes a male worker was called upon to assist the laundry maids on large farms and estates. Seemingly, the clothes needed little or no ironing afterwards and smaller items were wrapped in a strong sheet first, possibly of flannel, to protect shirt buttons. The tenants of the Grange in this era were James Fisher and William Williams, buried at Abbeydore and Madley respectively. No doubt the mangle was considered to be quite a status symbol in its day!

The box mangle. The handle version was patented in 1779.

REFERENCES

[1] *Abbeydore.* Edwin Sledmere. Jakeman & Carver, 1914.
[2] Calendar of Cathedral Muniments. Book 3, no.1269.
[3] Perambulation of the Parish of Doore. R.70/1. Hereford Record Office.
[4] *Place-names of Herefordshire.* A.T. Bannister. 1916.

Also much useful general information from *White Monks in Gwent and the Border* and *Welsh Cistercians: aspects of their economic history* both by D.H. Williams.

13 ENCLOSURE

The first information we have of how land was distributed in Kingstone comes in the Domesday Book of 1086 which details that there were four hides, probably about 500 acres in 1066, and that the sheriff added more land in Earl William's time (William FitzOsbern who died in 1071). It will be remembered that this included one virgate (about thirty acres) which belonged to the Abbey of Cormeilles in Normandy. This would not have included scrub-land, or land not considered taxable, so the acreage was probably a great deal more.

Land was given by various local donors to Kingstone Grange between 1250 and 1305 and, during the reigns of Henry III and Edward I (1216 to 1307), surveys of land holdings were made giving the names of some of the folk who held small acreages together with the rents they paid. We learn that Thomas Ameysey and his mother Rose had eighteen acres which was worth 7s 6d yearly, while Walter Wytside held four acres and one messuage (dwelling), the four acres being worth 20d and the house 12d. The Abbot of Dore had four acres and one acre of meadow for which he paid 3s. One also learns that Henry the Frenchman had twenty-eight acres, and part of his service was to 'carry letters of the lord King whenever they come into the county of Hereford at Clifford'.[1]

In 1587 cathedral archives list the glebe lands of the Dean of Hereford, held by him as rector. The list is to be found in the court rolls of Kingstone with Allensmore. Kingstone was sometimes referred to as Kingstone in Mawfield while Meer Court was at one time a manor belonging to the Bishop of Hereford, both dwellings being in Allensmore. Allensmore church was appropriated by the dean. So, way back, there was a link which has now come full circle, since Allensmore is part of the present parish together with Clehonger, Eaton Bishop, Thruxton and Kingstone. The Kingstone glebe lands were spread over the common fields, namely Low Field, West Field, Brookfield, Thornfield, Christfield, Kipperley Field and Mill Field. These were mainly in small strips of half to one acre but there were also two sizeable fields 'adjoyning to the King's Way leading towards the Cockyatt commonly called the Flax Mears'.[2] Flax Mears had become known as Flaxmoor by the time of the tithe map in 1842. In later years the glebe was attached to Green Court Farm, the tenant leasing it from the dean. The acreage in 1587 was about seventy-five acres.

In addition to the glebe, there were the lands belonging to the College of the Custos and Vicars of the Cathedral, known as the vicars choral, which were interspersed over the parish. These holdings were known as the Kingstone Farm so far as cathedral records were concerned, but land tax accounts refer to them as the 'College lands or the College Farm'. They were not attached to any one farm, which is very misleading since the Whitehouse Farm of today was known in the mid 1800s as the Kingstone Farm.

A lease of 1556 by the dean and chapter to Richard Lane, husbandman, states that their property consisted of 'all that their lands lying at Kyngston withyn the countie of Hereford called Grene lands belonging to a Vycarage funded in the quere [choir] of the seyd Cathedral Church called Philypps Ruffs vycarage, and also..... all that their lands lying in Kyngston......called Whytteneys lands belonging to another vicarage funded in the quere called Kyngstones Vycarage'.[3]

The former refers to Philip or William Rufus who was rector of Kingstone, circa 1239, and was involved in the Kingstone Grange tithe dispute. This was before the church was appropriated by the dean. When perusing the deeds of Church House it appears that the area of ground on which the two adjacent bungalows were built was known as Green's Acre, while the orchard was referred to as Lord's Land. Likewise, the deeds of Brook Cottage also mention a Green's Acre.

The other mention of 'Whitneys landes' in the same lease must, I think, refer to David Morgan's bequest discussed in Chapter 9, in which he mentions St. Stephen's lands and willed more land for maintaining the chapel of Arkstone. David's heir was his grandson, Thomas, who married Elizabeth Whitney, daughter of James Whitney, who held the important post of receiver of the many estates in Monmouthshire and the Marches belonging to the Duke of Buckingham. Buckingham, who was executed for treason in 1521, had been Lord of the Five Hundreds, of which Kingstone was one. Thomas Morgan was his father-in-law's deputy and it seems likely that the lands mentioned in David Morgan's will became known as 'Whytneys lands'. I have come across a reference to them in cathedral records dated 1529 as 'Whytneys londes at Kingston', and also mention of a chapel in 1517. 'Sept.17. Inspect a letter of appointment to Kingston's vicarage chapel, now in ruins and neglected. Duties given, stipend 20/-'.[4] The vicarage chapel, wherever it was, obviously had money bequeathed for its upkeep. There is also a reference to an account of the custos of the cathedral which included a payment of £6 13s 4d (10 marks) to 'Richardo de Arclestone, capellano [chaplain]'.

Amongst the many deeds of exchange, leases and eventual sale documents at the Hereford Record Office are some referring to Greensland and Whitneys lands as 'void vicarages'. These documents date from mid 1700s to early 1800s and show that the lands were still being leased by the dean and chapter who administered the lands of the College of Vicars Choral.

All these church lands were listed at infrequent intervals on a document called a terrier which in 1775 listed the glebe under field names and showed two different types of measurement. The ancient measurement was more generous than the statute measurement. By 1775 the old glebe, which had risen to eighty-four acres, ended up as sixty-one acres.[5] The college lands were listed on a separate terrier in 1743, and were eighty-two acres, old measurement.[6]

Strips were listed, with compass points, and varying descriptions, for example:

> Kipperley Field. One half acre lying underneath west hedge. A piece near the last, only one between them.
> Thornfield. One acre on the south side of the field, Russell north and south.
> Lower Field. One acre under the Hop Yard hedge. One acre by Mattocks close [Maddox]. Two acres lying by Hereford roadside.

Sometimes the name of the tenant can be very helpful and, just occasionally, an old name like Threepenny Plock is even better. In those times, as today, when one talks to people who have lived in an area all their lives, it was unnecessary to go into detail, everyone knew everyone else so 'over by Russell's' was probably deemed quite sufficient identification.

The glebe terrier makes it clear that the Kingstone common fields, of which there were more than the three main areas that remained in the early 1800s, were cropped for two years and lay fallow for the third. It was common for the fallow to be ploughed several times in order to keep down the weeds. This also applied to the areas that had been enclosed quietly through the centuries as one gathers from some of the entries in the court rolls. So the land surveyor who listed the land in 1775, and assessed the value of the tithe, detailed it thus:

Wheat 126 acres Two thirds of which are	84 acres	at	5/-
86 acres Every years land	84 acres	at	6/-
126 Lent grain Two thirds are	84 acres	at	2/6
90 acres Two thirds are	60 acres	at	3/6
50 acres Meadow		at	1/6

Lent grain was oats and barley, grown on less fertile land than wheat, so the nature of the crop presumably dictated the price put on the assessment. What is perplexing in Kingstone is the fact that Arkstone, Meer Court (the part which was in Kingstone), and the Grange had not only certain acreages which paid to the tenth, the normal tithe, but others to the fifteenth, and to the thirtieth. So far as Meer Court and Bridge Court were concerned, a yearly rent in grain was sent to the canon's bakehouse which was presumed by James Clarke, who rented the tithe from the custos and vicars of the cathedral in 1750, to be equivalent to one third of the value of the tithe due from them.[7] The other half of the tithe was let by the dean, as rector, to the tenant of Green Court Farm. James Clarke was accounting for the tithes which he and his father Francis before him had rented for many years. He says: 'As for Arkstone and the Grange, I cannot find they pay anything [possibly referring to grain] and yet they pay tithe as follows:-' and goes on to quote the different acreages paying to the different assessments of tenths, fifteenths and thirtieths. He suggests it ought to be regularized so that all the farms pay to the tenth and the value increased two thirds in Kingstone and other areas. Naturally, he had a vested interest. He goes on to say: 'Mrs. Parry [Arkstone] has lately enclosed some land, and plowed up the moors, and as there are different tithes paid from this land, I fear one day it will not be known how the tithe is paid'. Newly ploughed land was assessed differently. I cannot help feeling that if James Clarke could not get to the bottom of it, my chances nearly 250 years on are slim.

There are many factors which must have entered into the equation. The starting point with the Priory of Newent and the Abbey of Cormeilles which originally had all the tithe, was followed by the granting away of part of Arkstone's tithe to St. Guthlac's. Then came the old dispute of 1239 with the Grange and the fact that one half of the tithe was leased on behalf of the custos and vicars by the dean and chapter, while the remaining half was leased by the dean as rector to the tenant of Green Court, who also farmed his glebe. This presumably came about after the church was appropriated in 1281.

A survey of the parish made for the rector in 1792 mentions various estates and farms, owners and occupiers, and the acreages due to pay the great tithe of corn and grain.[8] Different assessments are denoted by symbols as being of the twentieth or half, two thirds or the fifteenth, and five sixths or the twelfth. The twentieth or half is explained by the shared lease. The rest seems linked to ancient custom which endured through the centuries. The fact that the farms involved were Kingstone Grange, Arkstone, Meer Court and Bridge Court points to ancient demesne and land belonging to religious houses. Bridge Court is the exception, although it sent grain to the canon's bakehouse, which indicates some involvement with the church.

There appears to have been a certain slackness in the way the custos and vicars administered their affairs. Francis Clarke mentions:

'1/4 of an acre joyning ye said way and shooting towards, Grithill, Mr. Clarke on E, and the said way on W, mentioned in the old Terrier 1693 to be two half acres but ye best piece of ye two (a reputed acre) is lost by ye negligence of ye Custos and Vicars not bringing an action for it before ye evidence dyed.'

This is the type of thing that happens when someone has been accustomed to using a piece of ground that appears to belong to no one; over the years it ends up as belonging to the user and no one can dispute it. Life changes but little in many things. How many ancient footpaths have disappeared in the same way?

Francis Clarke also draws attention to:

'1 acre lying in lands called the Barrow ground belonging to Hanley Court's farm, enclosed with 1 acre of Hanley Court land, adjoining to Kipperley Common Field, mentioned in the Terrar in the College of 1693 to be lying in a common field called West field, but had been enclosed with ye Barrow Farm out of West field, time out of mind before the terrar of 1693 was put into ye College.'

The 1693 terrier cannot be traced in the cathedral archives but, once again,

Hanley Court as it was in the 1920s. The lean-to building on the left has now disappeared.

there is mention of early enclosing of land, of a farm called the Barrow Farm and of West Field being a common field. The phrase 'time out of mind' serves to remind us how lovely was the language of yesteryear. What an interesting character Francis Clarke must have been. He believed in getting the facts straight even if it did offend the powers that be.

Bridge Court early this century.

Land tax was paid at a rate of 4s in the £ on land valued over £20. The assessment lists for Kingstone run from 1777 through to the 1830s. Owners and tenants are mentioned with the amounts due, with some of the farms being listed, but there are many cases where the only identification is, for example, 'late Chadnor's or late Hull's'. These names often go back many years, sometimes as much as a century and longer, so unless there is a continuity of maps and leases, it is well nigh impossible to trace exact locations. Often the tenant of a large farm would be paying for small acreages elsewhere which are listed as 'for Green's land', 'for Lord's land', 'for the Grithill', 'for Pipe Lane', and so on. Greensland and Lords Land referred to the void vicarages but, bearing in mind there was also a proprietor named Moore Green, and there were dwellings clustered round the village green, one has to consider all possibilities.

The Enclosure Act for Kingstone was passed in 1812 covering the un-enclosed land in the common fields which amounted to 200 acres. By that time there were only three fields that were considered to be common fields. The distribution was thus:

	Acres	Roods	Perches
In the Brookfield	115	3	0
In Chrisefield	63	3	13
In Kipperley	20	3	8

To enable enclosure to take place, a petition was made to parliament for permission. Such a petition only required one signature. The Bill was then considered and, if approved, became law. A commissioner was then appointed to visit the parish, the land would be surveyed, and the commissioner would hear all claims made by the parishioners who had open land or common rights. He would then allot land to each claimant in proportion to the rights he or she had enjoyed in the past.

Permission to enclose was most often granted provided a sufficient proportion of landowners were in favour. Since most of the land was usually owned by a few wealthy proprietors, the wishes of the small farmer did not hold much weight, should he be against the proposal.

With regard to Kingstone, it was not all plain sailing. Sir George Cornewall petitioned for enclosure in 1801 without success. There was another attempt made in 1811. However, William Croome was possibly a smoother operator since it was eventually finalised in 1812. It was said that 'difficulties had arisen as to the terms of the enclosure, the consents of several parties could not be obtained until a few days before the last day for present Private Bills.' All expenses were met by William Croome, so perhaps that was the factor that won the day. He was the principal landowner at that time.[9]

There has been much emotive argument regarding the effects of enclosure. The cottager, who had been allowed to graze his few animals on the commons, was often denied that right, while the small farmer or cottager, who was allotted land, often found he could not afford to enclose it or, in many cases, that it was not large enough to provide a living. The result was that many who had been reasonably self-sufficient were driven from the land. Since large enclosed fields often led to increased sheep farming, particularly in Tudor times, there was not so much arable farming for those who worked in the fields. On the other hand, there was the need to diversify and increase the crops to feed the ever growing population in the cities and towns, expanding to accommodate the demands of the industrial revolution and attracting many people away from the land.

This was the time of the Napoleonic Wars and of great fluctuation in the price of corn. The years between 1793 and 1814 produced poor harvests. Starvation among the poor was common. The coming of the threshing machine meant that the farm labourer had less winter work and the loss of grazing rights in the common fields and on the commons undoubtedly caused great hardship. The writer of the following verse, Joseph Arch, who founded the National Farmworkers Union in 1872, voiced the feelings of many at that time, but the words would have been just as apt at the beginning of the 1800s.

> They hang the man, and flog the woman,
> Who steals the goose from off the common,
> But let the greater criminal loose,
> Who steals the common from the goose.

Kingstone poor law books show record doles being paid. Large quantities of corn were bought and stacked in a parish store which had to be padlocked. The growing of potatoes, clover, root crops and hops, in addition to grains, meant that cattle could be fed all the year round and did not have to be killed before winter as had been the custom in the past. The crops also cleaned the soil and, by proper rotation, it was not necessary to have land lying fallow. Drainage schemes were essential to bring about good yields and this could not be carried out where holdings were small and scattered.

Prior to the Act there had been a great deal of exchanging and leasing of land in the different fields between the dean, the college of custos and vicars, Sir George Cornewall who had bought Hanley Court and different pieces of land in the early 1790s, John Moore Green who owned the Grange, and William Croome who later bought Hanley Court and Dunswater, thus becoming lord of the manor. Kingstone was a village encompassed by several large farms whose owners owned most of the land, some of which was leased to tenants who occupied the dwellings within the village centre.

Many years ago I located in Hereford Record Office a map which had been drawn for Sir George Cornewall in 1791. It shows 'estates lately purchased' with numbers given to all the strips and closes but very few names. All I could do was to endeavour to fit the descriptions on the college terrier to the map. Recently material from the Moccas estate has been deposited at the record office. It includes valuations of the land and, much to my delight, the names of tenants which match the numbers on the map. What do they say? Everything comes to he who waits. This piece of good fortune enabled me to trace the void vicarage lands, which formed the estate of the custos and vicars, something I had thought impossible.[10]

By 1791 Greensland and Whitneys lands were part of the estate of

John Merrick of Turners House, who took over the lease from James Clarke, son of Francis Clarke. John Merrick was allowed by the custos and vicars to transfer his lease to Sir George who, having bought Hanley Court, set about integrating the many strips into larger units. Within a few years these were ready for enclosure and were parcelled out to the owners and tenants of the big farms, and those who had smaller claims. John Merrick was farming about sixty-seven acres of college land, together with 108 acres of his own freehold land, which was also purchased by Sir George. In addition, he had some fifty acres adjacent to Turners House which he retained.

It appears that Sir George's purchase of land in the parish led to a very much better ordering of the way in which the various acreages were worked. By 1807 John Merrick's estate, comprising some of his freehold and the college leasehold amounting in all to 175 acres, had been added to Hanley Court (twenty acres), Dunswater (fifty-four acres) and the Grange (eleven acres). John Merrick and his son, Arnold, rented back about sixty acres and William Baugh, the village blacksmith, held the remaining thirty acres. Sir George ensured that the sixty acres rented by the Merricks were all adjacent in the area just above Barrow Common, which now forms part of Dunswater. Likewise, the other strips were added to the farms in which they had been lying.

The college lands were leased on a seven year tenancy. John Merrick had to pay a fine of £60 to the custos and vicars on renewal, plus rent of 42s per annum, and sixteen bushels of wheat. The strips were in Horston or Austin Fields, the Brookfield, Barrow Field, Great and Little Lowfields, Portway Croft, the Marsh Plocks, Canon Meadow, Tumpy Close and all over Hanley Court lands. When one sees the clearly defined boundaries as they are today, it is hard to believe what a patchwork picture it must have presented. Imagine the time it must have taken a farmer to get to and from his various strips with his plough, before he actually set to work, particularly when using oxen.

By the time the Kingstone Enclosure Act was finalised, William Croome had bought Hanley Court and Dunswater. The details of the allotments show him receiving and exchanging land from the dean and from the College of Vicars although, in reality, the re-arranging had been put in place by Sir George Cornewall a few years earlier.

As previously mentioned, William Baugh, the blacksmith, was leasing thirty acres of land. He also owned some strips, together with several cottages. His widow, Mrs. Ann Baugh, was allotted one and a half acres in Kipperley which were later acquired by John Seall, the village carpenter. The tithe map of 1842 lists eighteen people who had a few acres of land close to their homes and eighty-two people who had cottages with sizeable gardens.

The vicar was allotted seven acres in Brookfield as glebe, and an additional acre in Christfield for the use of the poor. The latter was exchanged with William Croome for land in Little Hales which is occupied today by a pair of semi-detached houses. By 1842 the other seven acres had been taken over by Queen Anne's Bounty, a fund set up in 1704 for the maintenance of poor clergy, augmenting livings which were below £50 p.a. The vicarage of Kingstone, in the Liber Regis of 1787, was recorded as having a clear value of £18 19s 6d.

The custos and vicars were compensated for their sixty-seven acres by allotments and exchanges in the Brookfield where they ended up with sixty-one acres leased as part of Dunswater. The lease was in force until 1957 when the Ecclesiastical Commissioners finally relinquished it, selling to the Whitfield Estate.[11]

The old college lands included just one building, namely Payn's barn, which in 1791 consisted of two bays and a tiled threshing floor. It stood on about half an acre of ground surrounded by a small hopyard. It is the site of Dean Pool Cottages which were built about 1829. At that time there were only two cottages. By 1842 the tithe map shows the three cottages that exist today.

The glebe lands remained reasonably compact, varying little from the first mention in 1587. They were all sold in 1859 by the Ecclesiastical Commissioners to the sons of William Croome who inherited Green Court from their father.[12] The larger pieces were added to Hanley Court and the Grange, while one piece of Green Court land had earlier provided the site for the school. The ground on which the tithe barn stood, with a small hopyard, became the site for the old school house. Many small strips were absorbed into the Whitehouse Farm fields and Mill field which today is farmed as part of Arkstone.

The earliest maps I have been able to peruse date from 1790. They cover the estates of Kingstone Grange, Hanley Court, Dunswater and Green Court. In addition there is the map drawn for Sir George Cornewall in 1791, and copied in 1809, which has already been mentioned. These maps have proved invaluable as a 'before and after' picture of the way the farms in the parish have evolved.

KINGSTONE GRANGE

Kingstone Grange was owned, towards the end of the 1700s, by the Moore Green family, heirs of John Smith, a barrister of Cagebrook, Eaton Bishop. They were sheriffs of Herefordshire in 1748 and 1796 and owned Smallbrook, Whitehouse Farm, parts of Hanley Court and the Marsh Farm by the early 1800s. The Grange lands, when surveyed in 1623, included the Bigsty farm and amounted to 329 acres, which by 1790 had shrunk to 192 acres, sixty acres of which were on the opposite side of the road running towards the mansion of Whitfield. The Bigsty farm had been added to Hanley Court Estate. There was another thirty-eight acres adjacent to Cockyard farm, of very ill assorted shapes, including Upper Monks Mears and Great Horston (Austin) field. No doubt much of the original land had been bought by local landowners and added to their holdings. Some of the land was over the parish boundaries in Abbeydore.

In 1808 John Moore Green exchanged land, including Monks Mears, with Sir George Cornewall who had plots of land, including part of Austins Field. Enclosure did not have an immediate impact on the Grange. John Moore Green was allotted some eight acres adjacent to the Grange which enabled his heir, J.S. Gowland, in 1820 to exchange the sixty acres near Whitfield, mentioned above, with sixty acres Mr. E.B. Clive already owned. By the time of the tithe map in 1842, the farm was much easier to cultivate. After the deaths of J.S. Gowland and his wife, their two daughters inherited and their respective children retained the estate until, in the 1860s, the Grange lands finally passed to the Rev. Archer Clive. Today the pattern is much the same as it was then, apart from some fields being merged, and totals 203 acres. It is farmed as part arable and part stock.

HANLEY COURT

The first mention of Hanley Court that I have found is of a mortgage and sale deed granted in 1737 indicating that it was part of a very large estate which included lands and messuages in eight Herefordshire villages, in addition to property in Brecon, Somerset and Gloucester. Originally owned by a widow, Elizabeth Hands, it passed to a Thomas Cholmley, an Berkshire innkeeper, whose father was Thomas Cholmley, a clerk in holy orders and a member of the vicars choral of Hereford. The vicars choral do seem to appear where one least expects. Thomas Cholmley's mother, Ann, was related to the Clarke and Gunter families which came from Brecon, the Clarkes eventually acquiring the Willocks Bridge estate and settling in St. Devereux.

It was obviously a family inheritance since the mortgage was taken over by Thomas Chamberlayne of Bristol, whose wife was an aunt to Thomas Cholmley the innkeeper. I was particularly pleased to find this out since one piece of the vicars choral lands is described thus: '1 acre, a piece of wood and bushes land near by Biggstye lying lengthways between ye 2 Mitchells woods and other lands formerly Mr. Gunter's now the lands of Mr. Thomas Chamberlayne called the Biggstye and Hanley Court lands'. Until coming across this lease I had no idea how these folk fitted in, apart from a reference in the Rev. Charles Robinson's wonderful *Mansions and Manors of Herefordshire*.

By 1777 Thomas Chamberlayne and his heir, Richard Combe, had died. Land tax records from 1782 to 1791 show Mrs. A. Combe, Richard's widow, as proprietor. I think the initials A.C. 174? (illegible) on the gable plaque of the stables could be those of either Ann Cholmley or Ann Clarke, as mentioned above. Various members of the Wathen family were tenants from around the 1740s until the early 1800s. In later years Charles Adams, Jonathan Dale, William Hobbs, John Wall and Albert Meats were tenants before the Bevan family who have lived there since 1932. I have not come across any wills or inventories which mention the farm by name. When the various tenants had land in so many different places it becomes increasingly difficult to establish which farms they lived in.

In 1737 the estate consisted also of the Bigsty farm, a Barrow Farm and a Bayes or Boyes farm. It is possible that the cottage known as the Thatch, long since disappeared, might have been the Barrow Farm since it is listed on the 1812 map of Dunswater and Hanley Court estates as 'Barrow house and garden'. Several of the closes nearby had the prefix of Barrow. Barrow Croft, Barrow Meadow, Barrow Field and Barrow Plock. With regard to Bayes or Boyes Farm, the court rolls of 1594 mentioned a John Boye several times. He appears to have been non-conformist, since he was presented along with several others for not wearing cloth caps on Sundays and fined twopence. He was presented with another likely lad, Roger Crosse, for illicit games and fined sixpence. If that was not enough, he was also presented with Roger for peddling and fined yet another sixpence. If he made any money out of the hard pressed villagers from his trading, and perhaps gambling with dice, he soon lost it. To make things even worse, he was told to make a good hedge between his close and the 'gret ditch meadow' (Mitch Meadow?) within ten days, otherwise he would be fined 7s. Possibly his farm was near the Barrow Common too but since holdings were so piecemeal one cannot tell. It does show, once again, that 100 or 150 years was nothing once a name stuck. The Bigsty farm has long since fallen into decay, but one reminder of it survives in the will of William Popkin who lived there in 1607. The Ross family who lived there in the 1920/30s are mentioned elsewhere.

In 1791, Sir George Cornewall of Moccas had bought Hanley Court, and, by 1809, William Croome, the Cirencester banker, had acquired it together with Dunswater. On his death, two of his sons, the Rev. Thomas Boys Croome and James Capel Croome, took over and finally sold in 1874 to the Rev. Archer Clive of Whitfield.

When Sir George considered selling the Kingstone estate, his agent prepared a very detailed land valuation, whether it was arable, meadow, pasture or woodland, and the amount rented to various tenants, including the leasehold lands of the custos and vicars. The description of Hanley Court is as follows:

> '.....a substantial farmhouse built with brick containing a hall, kitchen, 2 parlours, brewhouse, dairy and scullery, 5 lodging rooms and 4 atticks, grainery or room for men servants over the brewhouse and scullery. Cellar under the parlour, shed for cyder mill, cyder house for 40 hogsheads, stables for 12 horses, loft over grainery, 3 threshing floors and 5 bays, sheepscott, ties for 5 oxen and 10 cows. Hackney stable and hopkiln with grainery over. Calf cott, pigsties, sheds, wainhouse etc'.

The agent valued the timber on the estate in 1808 at £2592, a considerable sum, also noting the number and species of the trees in each meadow or grove.

	Oak	Elm	Ash	Value
Meadow behind buildings		51		100 0 0
Lower Nitchel Grove	220		50	750 0 0
Rick Yard		12		40 0 0
New Pasture, Barrow & Daniels	50	2	4	84 0 0

The 1812 map of Hanley Court, compared with the one drawn in 1791 for Sir George Cornewall, shows that many awkward-shaped closes and fields had been tidied up. Although the map is somewhat worn, when one looks very closely at it, the very faint lines that were drawn by the estate manager, or perhaps William Croome himself, become apparent, as they endeavoured to make a more coherent pattern of the whole estate. I felt I was looking over their shoulders as they worked, and found myself wondering where, and in what surroundings they would have been meeting to discuss the plans.

From the eighteenth century the acquisition of farms and land as a reliable means of investment seems to have been common-place amongst the nobility, merchants, bankers and traders. Likewise, it was these people who provided mortgages to farming families wishing to purchase their holdings. In William Croome's case, his investment in Kingstone coincided with his marriage to Jane Girdler at St. James, Piccadilly. His ancestors were from Cirencester where William was a Justice of the Peace, and deputy lieutenant of Gloucestershire. His descendants lived at North Cerney for many generations. One of his ancestors was a Rev. Thomas Boys who hailed from Buckinghamshire, the name being handed down the family.

The acreage of Hanley Court in 1874 was 384, of which some 112 acres were in Abbeydore parish. Today it is 363 acres, some twenty acres being taken off to improve the woodland as part of the set-aside policy. It is both an arable and stock farm, specialising in cattle. A tenancy agreement for the farm was made in 1792 between Sir George Cornewall and Mrs. Elizabeth Wathan at a rental of £170 per annum. It was stipulated that Sir George would build a kiln, allowing Mrs. Wathan to sell lime provided 'no injury is done to the wood, or the land by the road being cut.' The location was adjacent to the Bigsty woods and the old farmhouse and is noted as Lime Kiln Field on the Abbeydore tithe map. Care for the woodland was considered important two centuries ago. It is good to know that the need to conserve it is equally understood today.

DUNSWATER, also known as KINGSTONE FORGES MANOR

The origin of the name of Kingstone Forges has already been explained, as also the fact that the various people who were involved in mortgaging and leasing it from 1703 until William Croome purchased it in 1812, were, for the most part, direct descendants of Sir Thomas Coningsby who had acquired it in the late 1500s. Where an heir had three daughters, it meant each of them had an interest. Although William Croome was a party to a release in 1809, it was not until 1812 that he became full owner. Counsel's opinion was sought in order to clarify the title and this covered the years from 1703 to 1809.

The manor was advertised for sale in the Hereford Journal of 30th December 1773 and was bought by a Dansey Dansey of Ludlow, from whom it was bought by William Croome. The particulars of the sale, which was on the 18th November 1808, give much food for thought. Originally Dunswater had been leased to Richard Russell in 1703 for himself and two other lives at a rent of £5 per annum. By 1773 the advertisement states it is for Richard and one life, and that the rent will be worth upwards of £200 when the lease expires. By 1808, the farm is tenanted by John Goode who is paying a rental of £520 per annum. Dunswater is a beautiful and well maintained building with a wealth of beams and traces of its original timber framing dating from early seventeenth century, including original carpenter's assembly marks. The sale details rather scathingly comment 'the house may, at a small expence, be improved and made suitable for the Residence of a genteel Family'. The particulars continue 'there is a considerable stream of water which runs through the Lands, Fold Yard, etc. and irrigates a large Part of the Estate', and also mention fish ponds.

This 'excellent farm of rich and fertile land' was to be sold by auction at mid-day on the 18th November 1808 at Garraway's Coffee House in Exchange Alley, Cornhill. London coffee houses were very popular places where the well-to-do rubbed shoulders with the local worthies.

Alcohol was not available, but coffee had become a normal and popular drink due to increased trading abroad. They were meeting places where news was sought and business transacted. Many folk had their favourite coffee houses and regarded them as a type of club. The famous insurers Lloyds of London began life in the coffee house of Edward Lloyd. Property sales would have been quite a normal part of the day's activities.

When the tithe map was drawn in 1842, the odd strips of land in Cristfield common field, situated opposite Hanley Court and Kipperley, had been allotted to William Croome and incorporated into the main fields. In addition, there were the sixty-one acres leased from the vicars choral in the Brookfield eventually sold to the Whitfield Estate this century. The farm also included some 117 acres of the Marsh Farm in Kingston parish, and land behind the church running up to Kingston Mill. This brought its total to some 430 acres. The Marsh Farm does not feature in any records I have researched but there was a Marsh family in the parish for several generations, at one time tenanting Dunswater. It formed part of the estate of John Moore Green and, in 1837, consisted of 143 acres when it was sold by his descendants. Presumably William Croome acquired it then, having leased it before. By 1874, when his sons sold up the Kingstone estate, it had been dispersed. Dunswater today has 318 acres and is given over to arable and stock farming.

TURNERS HOUSE

Turners House has provided another mystery in the Kingstone story. In a later chapter I have mentioned the possible source of its name. As it is remembered by older folk, and seen by us today, it is a medium size, double-fronted dwelling built early this century. Documents in the record office show that, nearly 300 years ago, it was a sizeable farm. It formed part of the marriage settlement of Francis Clarke, then living at Gillow, when he and Elizabeth Addis of Sollershope were wed in 1709. Its land was widespread; in the Dean Pool area, the Mill Field, Great and Little Lowfield surrounding Whitehouse farm, near Coldwell, in Kipperley, and in Brookfield, and was referred to as 'Turners Old Lands'.

By 1739 Francis Clarke was living in Kingstone, at Turners House, and was prominent in local affairs. He appears regularly in the old poor law books and church accounts. He is noted in the terriers of church lands as owning freehold lands next to strips and, of course, rented the lands belonging to the vicars choral, in addition to Turners House lands, some of which he leased to under-tenants. James Clarke succeeded his father and, after him, the property devolved on the Merrick family who were related through marriage. There is a memorial plaque in the church, partially obscured by the organ, which records that John and Susannah

Merrick of Turners House died in 1825 and 1824 respectively. They had also lived at Haywood. The farm, with its remaining fifty acres, was contracted for sale to Thomas Wathan, who occupied nearby Bridge Court, and remained attached to that farm for many years. The house was in ruins by the end of the 1800s. Mrs. Ruby Meats remembers her mother saying it was a black and white building and that she thought it must have been quite an important dwelling at one time.

John Merrick transferred the lease of the college land, with the approval of the custos and vicars, to Sir George Cornewall in 1792, also selling part of his freehold lands. Since he had six children, three of whom were not of age, this involved setting up a trust for the younger ones, the elder ones being paid their share. It was necessary to do this so that Sir George had a clear title to the freehold lands. Another comment in the correspondence regarding this is interesting since it mentions an ancient custom of 'odd marking', which entitled the outgoing tenant to sow and take away one third of the arable on the farm when he quits. This also occurs in the will of William Popkin in 1605. It would appear that Merrick, or his under-tenant, had sown more than the usual oddmark, intending to take away 'more straw and produce than custom allows him as a going-off tenant.' Sir George's agent commented that if the tenant refused to quit when he should, it would be possible to take an action against him and distrain on the growing crop.

Sir George's tenants were expected to fallow and manure the land every third crop with dung or lime, some of the land being laid down with grass seed.

BRIDGE COURT

There is very little information on Bridge Court farm. At the time of the tithe map in 1842 it was a farm of 119 acres, to which could be added fifty acres from Turners House, both farmed by John Wathan, son of Thomas. It was tenanted by Arnold Rogers until his death in 1727, then the Barrell family by the 1760s until the Wathans took over soon after 1800, remaining there until the late 1930s. From 1939 to the present day, it has been owned first by Mr. C. Watkins and then by Mr. W. Watkins. Joseph Barrell's will of 1787 passes on his 99 years lease from R. Gorges of Eye Manor, Herefordshire to his wife, but that is the only mention I have found of an earlier owner. The National Monuments Record date it as early 1800s but it was mentioned in land tax records well before that. Architecturally it bears a marked similarity to Arkstone, partly re-built about 1790, so Bridge Court may also have replaced an earlier building. Joseph Barrell made some of the charity jackets and clothes. When visiting the cellars some years ago, my husband and I found stones the size of a tennis ball with a hole in the middle which could have been loom weights. Today, Bridge Court's 174 acres are farmed with Arkstone Court.

Whitehouse Farm before conversion.

The triangle on which stood the village pound. Green Court in the background, Yew Tree Cottage on the left.

GREEN COURT

In 1726 Green Court was known as the Church Stile Farm and later on, in land tax records, as the Pound Farm. The area around the church is regarded as the most likely site of the medieval village. The small triangular piece of land nearby could have been the site of the pound or market place. In 1762 a Walter Gunter was living in Yew Tree House (originally called Green Villa) and was presented to the court for enclosing part of Kingstone's Green. We can safely assume that this was the hub of village life and the place where a pound was most likely to be erected, together with the stocks and whipping post. Indeed, on one small map denoting church lands in the area around the church, a small square has been drawn in, which probably indicates the pound. This is very close to the road, opposite the Bull Ring, at the bottom of the entrance to the church. By 1874, when the farm was sold with Hanley Court and a small part of Dunswater, it had become known as Green Court Estate.

It was this farm to which the glebe lands were attached, including the tithe barn. It was owned for many years by a family named Hill who are commemorated by a wall memorial in the chancel of the church. The first member of the Hill family I have found, James Hill, was leasing the tithe and glebe in 1632,[13] and the last member, Mary Hill, died in 1786, leaving her property to William Wathan, who took over. The lease of the great tithe was shared at one time between the tenant of the college lands, and the tenant of Green Farm, who farmed the dean's glebe lands.

A lease for twenty-one years, dated 1799, states that Nathan Wetherell, Dean of the Cathedral (father to the Rev. Henry Wetherell) and proprietor of the parsonage at Kingstone, lets the lands, tithes and premises (tithe barn) of the parsonage at a rent of £5 10s 0d payable half yearly to the cathedral, while he was to pay the vicar of Kingstone £1 6s 8d and eight bushels of wheat per annum.[14] Many of the clergy who served at Kingstone lived at Green Court since there was no vicarage house. I can only think this was a condition laid down in the lease of the glebe and tithe. When William Wathan died, he bequeathed the lease of the tithe and glebe lands to his wife Martha. The constitution of the Ecclesiastical Commissioners, in 1836, led to all church lands being brought under their jurisdiction. In 1859 they sold the glebe land to the Croome brothers, who put Green Court up for sale in 1874. At that time the farm had 94 acres. I think Green Court Estate got its title about 1844 when William Croome bought it. At that time its acreage was 109. Robert Berrow, who was living opposite at Whitehouse Farm, signed a declaration confirming this just before the sale. It continued to be the Pound Farm well into the 1830s in land tax records.

Edwin Wathen, resident there until his death in 1879, made a declaration at the time of the sale in 1874. He stated that he 'knew and was well acquainted from my childhood with William Croome'. He rented Green Court for many years from him and, after his death in 1855, he had continued to rent the farm from his sons. He goes on to mention a cottage and garden near Green Farmhouse which he knew since he was a boy. About 1871, James Capel Croome told him to pull it down. Edwin had occupied the garden and site of the cottage ever since. This is shown on the tithe map in 1842 as two cottages, but is occupied today by the property named Caradoc. I was very pleased to know that William Croome did have contact with the village, and would like to think, from Edwin's statement, that he knew it well. Perhaps he would visit yearly on rent day to meet his tenants, travelling in his coach or venturing on the new railway from Gloucester to Hereford.

Green Court is owned now by Mr. George Williams whose father bought it in 1917. Previous occupants were the Wathan family, Benjamin Watkins and Dr. J. Frost. It has fifty acres and is a small stock farm.

WHITEHOUSE FARM

The origins of Whitehouse farm are very obscure. The house was built in the early to mid-seventeenth century, typical of a well-to-do yeoman's home. By 1782 it belonged to John Moore Green and, from then until 1874, was occupied by a family named Berrow. John Berrow, then his children, William, Robert and Amelia, are all named on land tax records, maps, conveyances, and on the abstract of title to Kingstone Grange Estate. Robert Berrow, in yet another sworn declaration, says 'my parents leased a farm in Kingstone (unnamed) from John Moore Green and his heir John Gowland, and I was born there'. This was in 1862 when he 'was upwards of 70 years'.

He appears to have bought the property, then known as Kingstone Farm (trade directory of 1867), on mortgage. Later tenants were John Apperley and Edward Aaron Hancorn. In 1912 it was sold by the then owner, a Mrs. Jane Price and others who were descendants of John Moore Green, and the conveyance states: 'All that messuage, farm lands, buildings...and premises now better known as White House'. It was in 1862 that the Grange Estate was sold up by the trustees of the heirs and heiresses. Many of the lots had to be bought back, so possibly the trustees financed the original mortgage.

At the time of the tithe map Whitehouse Farm covered 96 acres, which had shrunk to fifty acres when it was put up for sale in 1912, being bought by Arthur Watkins of the Grange in Abbeydore. The land which was dispersed is now split in many different ways. Some of it is part of the Grange. Some is part of Bridge Court including Mill Orchard and

Mill Field. A strip next to the vicarage has now been built on, while the high school playing fields, Highland View and Coldstone Cross estates have also taken up a fair proportion.

Today the farmhouse has been sympathetically restored in two dwellings, while the land is farmed by Mr. Martin Phillips, whose parents and grandparents lived and farmed there for many years previous to its sale in 1979. He uses the thirty-three remaining acres as pasture for sheep and cattle.

Cagebrook, Eaton Bishop today. Once the home of John Moore Green.

Bowcott's barn in Smallbrook common field, 1996.

The diagrams that follow show two other small areas where strips were still being cultivated before the Enclosure Act of 1812. The area above the surgery where the vicarage was built has changed somewhat. Another interesting change was in the area opposite Smallbrook Farm, which was called Smallbrook Common Field in the mid 1700s when Charles Morgan, husband of Mary Morgan (Parry), who owned Arkstone, exchanged land with Sir Richard Symons of the Mynde, Much Dewchurch, who owned Meer Court. The two larger areas relate to the strips on either side of the Cockyard, in part of Kipperley field and Hanley Court lands and in Chrisefield (Christfield), which today is part Dunswater and part Kingstone Grange lands.

I hope that this attempt to relate the changes which have taken place over the last two centuries on the land, will give those who farm and nurture it today some idea of how it once was before the coming of mechanisation, quotas, and the Common Market. Believe me, it has been a somewhat difficult, but nevertheless intriguing, trail to follow.

REFERENCES

[1] Testa de Nevill, p.62-73, Temp.Henry III and Edw I. Hereford Record Office.
[2] Kingstone/Allensmore Court Rolls. Hereford Cathedral Library.
[3] Lease, ref. 3354. Hereford Cathedral Library.
[4] Dean and Chapter Act Book, 1512-1566. No.334. Hereford Cathedral Library.
[5] Glebe Terrier. 1775. Hereford Record Office.
[6] College of Hereford Terrier, 1743. Ref. 3966. Hereford Cathedral Library.
[7] Acct. of Tithes. No. 3967. IX. Hereford Cathedral Library.
[8] Kingstone Great Tithes. No.3967. VIII. Hereford Cathedral Library.
[9] Transactions of the Woolhope Naturalists' Field Club. W.K. Parker. 1982. pp.79/90.
[10] Moccas Papers. J.56/111/105. Hereford Record Office.
[11] Whitfield Estate Archives. BB.2/141. Hereford Record Office.
[12] Sale of Glebe Lands. D.360. Hereford Cathedral Library.
[13] Parliamentary Survey 1649. 7006/1. Hereford Cathedral Library.
[14] Abstract of Title. A.43/1. Hereford Record Office.

Details of Conveyance, Leases, Exchanges, etc. from schedule of Whitfield Estate Archives. Nos.BB.2/76 to 2/141. Hereford Record Office.

PART OF COOKS LANE, KINGSTONE

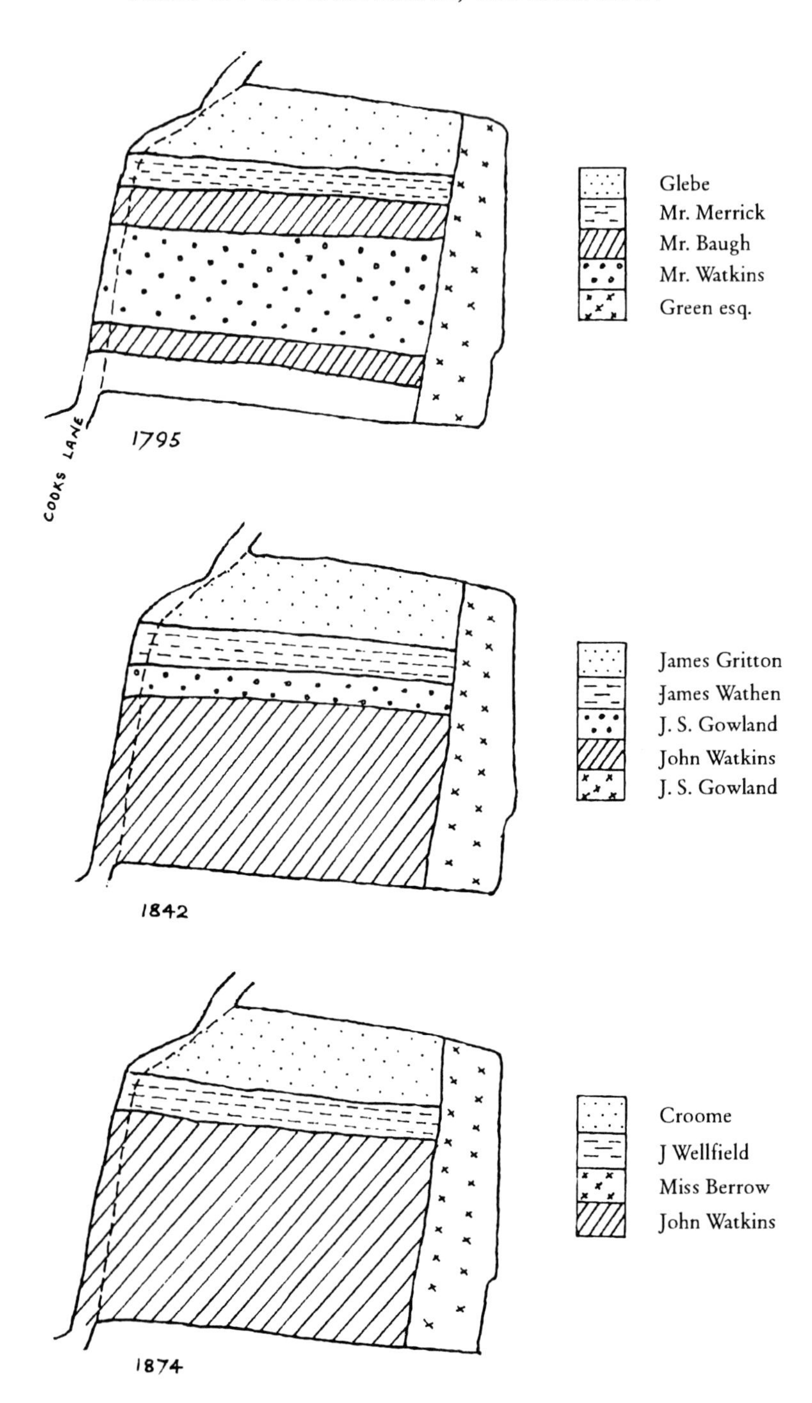

In 1842 the strips were recorded as being in Coldwell Field, Lower Field and part of 11 Acres.

SMALLBROOK COMMON FIELD

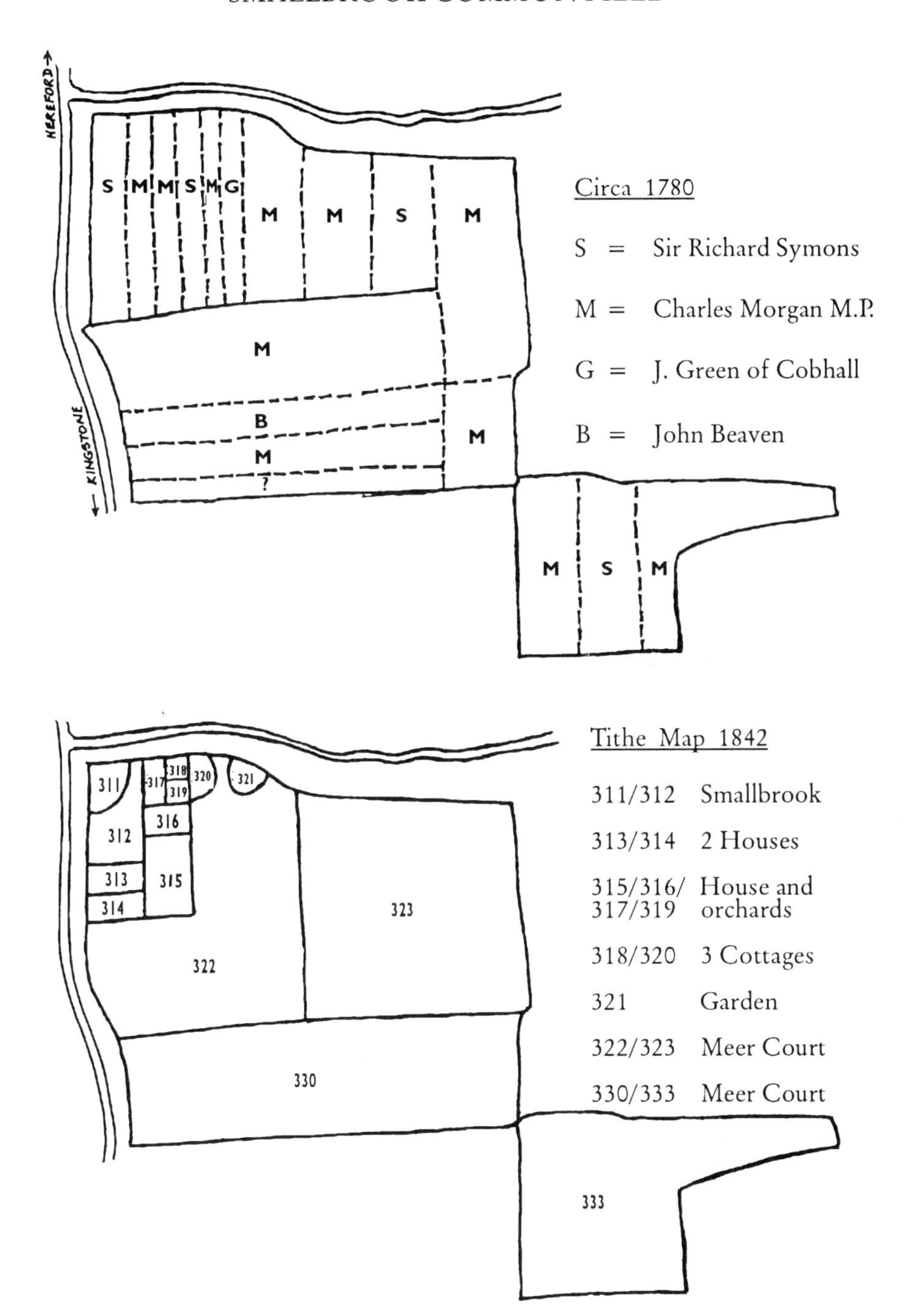

312 was known as Bowcotts Meadow. Thomas Bowcott was tenant in 1777

KIPPERLEY COMMON FIELD

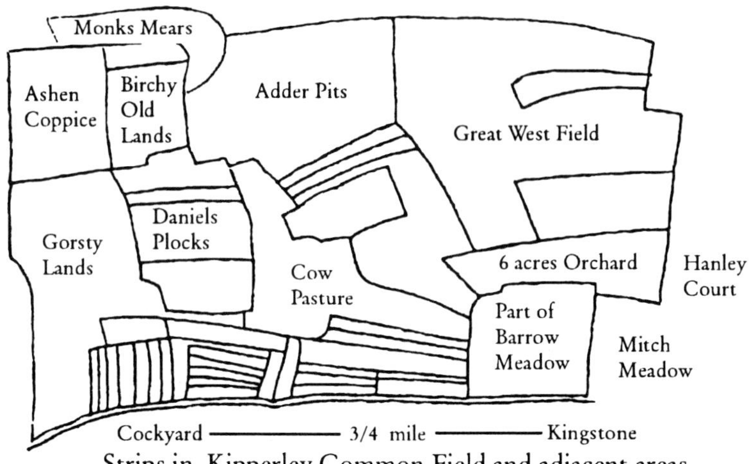

Strips in Kipperley Common Field and adjacent areas

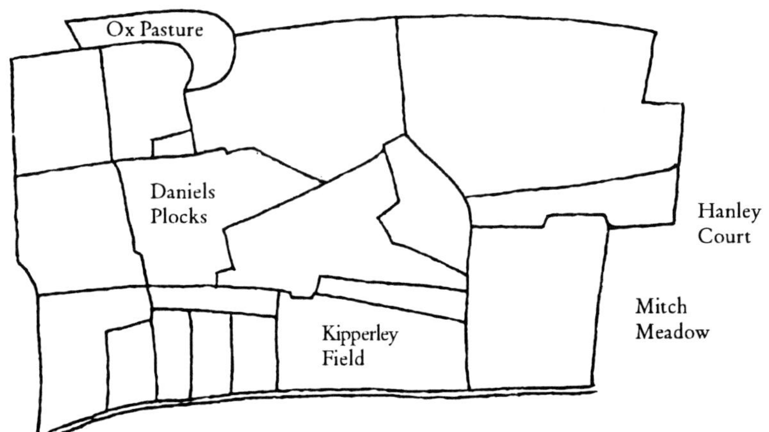

Changes made by William Croome. 1812. Monks Mears now known as 'part of Ox Pasture'. Daniel (Plocks) Williams was Overseer of the Poor and teacher. Died 1764

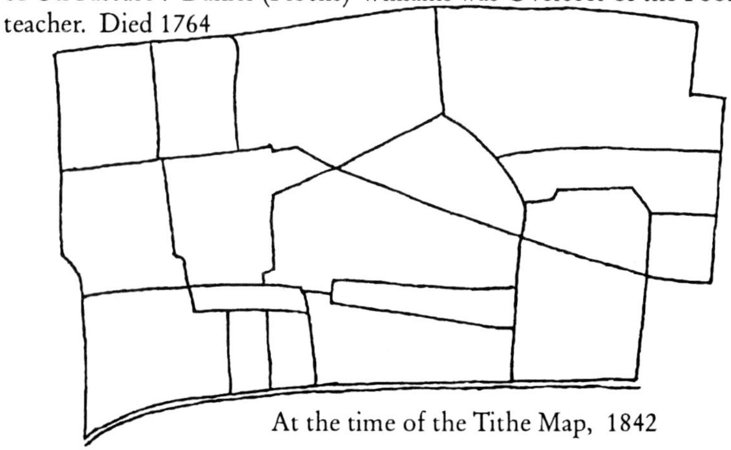

At the time of the Tithe Map, 1842

CHRISTFIELD COMMON FIELD

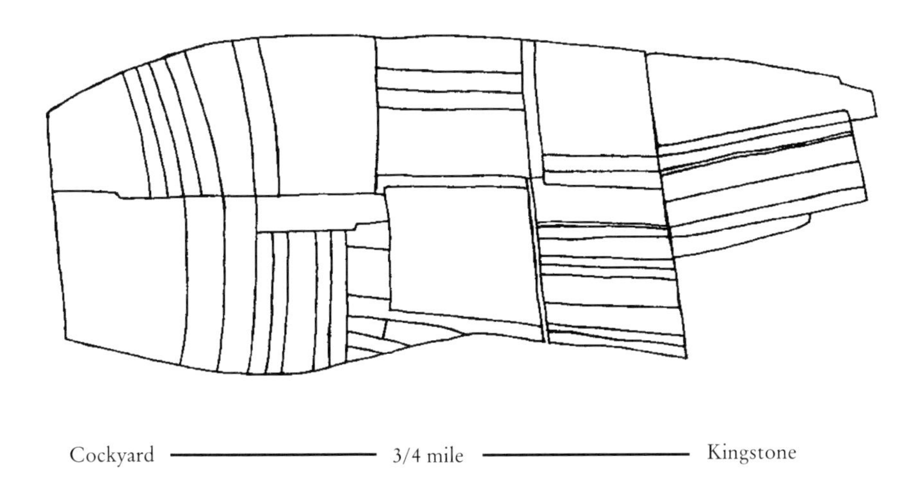

The field in 1791. At this time farmed by tenants and under-tenants of Dunswater, Hanley Court and Kingstone Grange also by William Baugh, John Merrick and William Parry. It included ten strips of glebe farmed with Green Court and the many leasehold strips owned by the college of Hereford.

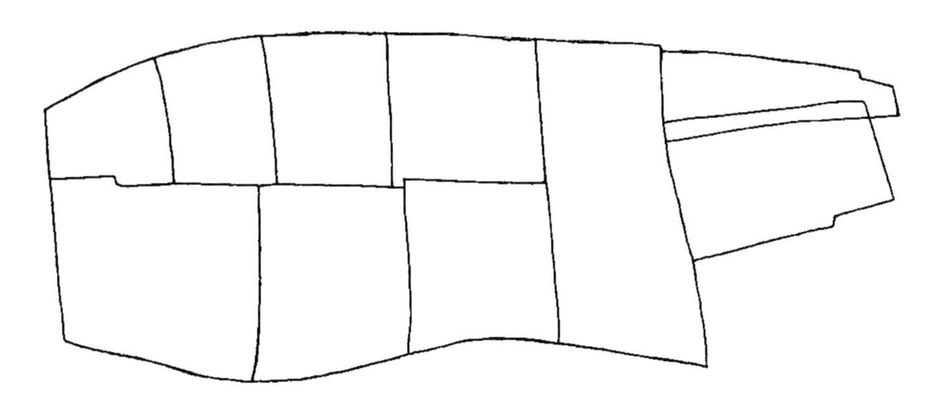

At the time of the tithe map 1842

By 1842 the land was farmed solely by tenants of Green Court, Hanley Court and Kingstone Grange.

14 WILLS AND INVENTORIES

It is possible to get tantalising glimpses of life over 300 years ago from the content of wills and inventories. Country life as depicted in many paintings and prints can give the impression that people lived in cosy thatched cottages, were tidily dressed, cheerful and healthy. In reality there was great hardship and poverty for many. More often that not, it was the better off who had the foresight to make a will in the first place; they had the wherewithal to make it expedient. There are a few instances of others, less fortunate, who had possessions to bequeath or wishes to express that help us to travel, like Alice, through the looking glass to a time when things that are taken so much for granted today were greatly prized and treasured.

The fortunes, good or otherwise, of the majority of those living in such a rural community stemmed from the soil. That Kingstone operated a three field system of farming right up to the nineteenth century is shown in three different ways. Firstly, by the Enclosure Act of 1812, then by an earlier map drawn up for Sir George Cornewall when he purchased land shortly before that date and, thirdly, by a glebe terrier dated 1775.[1] There are other documents which lead to this conclusion. The tithe map gives valuable clues with regard to field names.

A three field system was a method of farming by rotation, two years arable and one year fallow, the open fields being farmed in strips by the villagers and the lord of the manor. The soil in Kingstone is a deep loam, with a subsoil of loam and gravel, well suited to arable farming.

The traditional picture of medieval farming which depicts villagers working side by side with their shares of strips in different parts of the fields, everyone being treated equally in having, good, bad and indifferent holdings, has been much questioned by scholars of late. One thing, however, is certain; it was not good husbandry. If you had strips near John the slacker, who did not keep his ground in good heart and free from weeds, you were obviously a great deal worse off than if your neighbour was Robert the diligent, who knew how to get the most from what little he possessed.

The rules laid down by the manor court were intended to be followed for the benefit of all. A jury composed of locals was there to see fair play but, as time went on and services in kind were commuted to money rents, the need to put strips into more compact holdings, and often to make small 'closes' or larger and more manageable enclosures, became commonplace. This was going on quietly alongside the ancient methods of strip farming so that, when Kingstone had its one and only Enclosure Act in 1812, there was not a great amount of land in the common fields left to parcel out.

Although farming methods as such are likely to remain obscured, the inventories made of a deceased person's goods often referred to farming implements and crops which are useful pointers to some understanding of these methods. It became law in 1529 that if a person died with possessions valued at more that £5, it was necessary for a valuation to be made. These were always entitled 'a true and perfect inventory' but, were they one wonders? The goods were listed by two local worthies grandly referred to as appraisers. It must have been a difficult task to undertake in cases of known hardship or where debts were outstanding; did some items get overlooked or, perhaps, get conveniently smuggled away? In the case of the wealthy, with a wide variety of farm stock to assess, just how disinterested were the men who had to set a price? Certainly, these prices varied considerably from person to person. On the whole, it seems more sensible to concentrate on the goods rather than their value, particularly in view of the difficulty in equating prices with the modern day. Mr. J.W. Tonkin who has spent many years researching and cataloguing Herefordshire inventories states '...it would be fair to multiply them by about 300, perhaps rather more for the early ones'. He also concludes that there was a tendency to down-grade values and that the appraisers varied in their abilities.[2]

References are found to items relating to ploughing teams such as gears, bridles and saddles, plows and drags, together with miscellaneous wagons, oxen wains (sometimes called dissell wagons) and dung carts. No doubt the oft used term 'implements of husbandry of all sorts' concealed a great deal, especially if the appraisers had more than a passing interest in the goods to be sold.

It was a very different matter when it came to farm stock. No doubt the appraisers differed but little from their astute counterparts of today; one look would probably be sufficient for them to fix a price. Pride of place was given to the oxen, which were widely used in the parish up to the early 1700s. Prosperous farmers would have as many as twelve oxen, priced at around £4 a beast, and horses, mares and 'coults' were always noted. Cattle were categorised, i.e. 'six cowes, seven three year ould bests or bullocks, six too yeare oulds, five yearlings and calves'. Sheep were sometimes referred to in pairs, 'twenty three coupuls of sheepe', and also as 'dry sheep', as presumably they were barren. Sometimes wool was entered, weighed by the stone (14 lbs). William Else, who died in 1675, had '23 stone of wooll valued at £13.16.0.', a worthwhile addition, although his sheep were referred to as 'seaven score and 16 oulde sheepe'. Pigs were commonly kept and referred to as 'sowes, store pigs, weaninge pigs, or swine of all sorts'. Poultry was very rarely mentioned. Possibly it was the one item that the women were allowed to call their own. By tradition, poultry keeping was a necessary part of housewifery which helped to provision the larder.

Crops were referred to as those growing and those harvested, thrashed and unthrashed, on the ground or in the house or barn. On 31st December there would be 'hard corn groweing on the land' (rye and wheat) and 'corne, wheat and lent graine in the barn, together with hay, straw and fodder'. In May corn, oats, rye and lent grain were growing on the ground. Hops, barley and peas were also grown, with clover being mentioned for the first and only time in the inventory of John Parry of Arkstone, dated 1689, which was relatively early compared with some parts of the country. His inventory also detailed '38 days mash of hay' while that of his son Miles, who died in 1693, mentions 'corn and malt, wheat, rye, hemp, wool and flax in the house'. It can be safely assumed that flax was a common crop. One of the manorial dictates was that flax was not to be retted in the stream dividing the lordships of Kingstone and Arkstone for fear of pollution. Flax was usually sown in the early spring and harvested for its fibre some three months later, when about half the seeds were ripe. The stalks would be bound into bundles, dried and, afterwards, threshed to remove the seeds. The bundles would then be retted (immersed in flowing water) to separate the fibres. This would take about three weeks and produced a very unpleasant smell. The bundles would be dried again, and scutched, a process similar to carding wool, the fibre being combed with a type of wire brush. Finally, it would be spun into fine linen or, if it was of a coarser type, would be made into rope or rough materials.

William Popkin, a yeoman farmer, leased the Bigsty, a farm bordering on the parish of Abbeydore. The bequests made in his will of 1607 indicate a reasonable standard of living and a concern for the welfare of those around him. His son, William, was to have

> 'one yocke [yoke] of the best oxen now in my teame and one half of all the implements....yockes, tewes [harness], waynes [carts]'.

> 'I give my part of the acres of oattes and pease lying in the parish of Kingstone, in a fyeld called the Ader pitt unto my brother John Popkin, and to my brother-in-law John Spenser at harvest to be equally divided'.

> 'I give and bequeath unto Custan Spenser, my servant maide six lambes to be delivered to goe after shearing time next coming'.

The immediate family was to have the benefit of the fleeces.

William, his godson, was to have 'one cowe and a lambe' and his daughter Mary 'one heifer of 3 years old, when she come of age'. Money was left to his children to be invested until they came of age. At the end of the will the phrase 'it came to my rememberance as to another item' refers to the fact that his brother should have one chamber in the new dwelling at the Bigsty with a bedstead, feather bed, etc. and that he 'shall have his diet provided for himself and his gelding sufficient at all times when he shall please to come or resort to my said house'. There were also bequests of money, furniture and pewter to his family.

There were few who did not brew their own cider and the utensils and storage containers for same merited special mention. Hogsheads, kinderkins, barrels, vessels, wooden wares, brewing vessels, trinds or trends, vatts, all were part and parcel of the mysterious language of cider processing, together with the cidermill itself which was valued at £1 in the 1687 inventory of Henry Marsh of Dunswater.

Richard King of Mawfield, vicar of Allensmore, in his will of 1688 directed 'all the trams on one side under the hogsheads of one side in the great butry.......at my wife's election to her' and 'in case there be no cyder in my house when I dye, I order my wife to take one hogshead of cyder from ye trees for yt year I dye in'. She was also to have two additional hogsheads from his goods. A hogshead held fifty-four gallons, a sizeable barrel.

Thomas Madox, who died in 1762, directed his son William 'to pay his mother £8 per annum for rest of her life as long as she remains a widow, also half the dwelling house, half the garden and 1 hogshead of cyder for every 10 he shall make on the estate, and the running of 1 pigg in the field'.

When the appraisers had had enough they neatly closed the account with the words 'lumberment and forgotten goods', 'all other utensils and things omitted', 'forgotten and unprized', or 'things forgotten or of small value'. Forgotten by whom, one wonders? To the majority of common folk, whose lives were humdrum toil from morning to dusk, dictated to at every turn, and who eked out an existence, everything was of value. On the other hand, the lower the figure of the deceased's assets, the less probate fees there were to pay.

These documents, particularly the inventories, were written in a variety of handwriting, extremely difficult to read at first. As the years went by so the style altered. The local dialect can almost be heard as the words are deciphered; the use of 'ou', and 'ar' and 'ay' in words like ould, carves (not the Sunday joint) and chayers, was very common at the end of the 1600s. The deciphering of these documents has caused me many

In the name of God Amen. I Arnold Rogers of Bridgecourt in the Parish of Kingstone and county of Hereford, being weak in body but in perfect soundness of mind and memory, thankes be given to Almighty God, Do make and ordain this my present last will and testament in manner and form following: First and principally I give my soul to Almighty God and my body to be decently buried by the discretion of my Executrix hereinafter named And as touching the temporal disposition of all such worldly Estate as it hath pleased Almighty God to bestow upon me, I give and dispose the same as followeth: First I will that all my debts shall be paid and discharged and particularly I desire Mr James Davies of Webton to see and take care that Eighty pounds be raised out of my worldly substance to pay my Brother William. Item I give my dearly beloved wife All my Goods cattle and Chattels whatsoever with all advantages and profits arising from the same with all leases bills bonds or writings whatsoever provided she continues a widdow and unmarried all her life after my decease, but if she contracteth marriage to any person then my will is and I do by these presents give and order all my Goods cattle Chattells and substance to be equally divided upon my wifes marriage to a second Husband between my said wife Sarah and my four children: The little House and land in Kingston (when all my concernes are divided) shall be allowed unto my Eldest Son: And I further desire my foresaid friend Mr James Davies of Webton, whom I make Trustee of this my will: that he will see that all things be done and performed according to the true intent and purpose of this my will: And lastly I make my beloved wife Sarah sole and whole executrix of this my will and testament. In witness whereof I Arnold Rogers, to this my last will and testament do set my Hand and Seal this tenth day of August in the first year of the Reign of our Sovereign Lord George the Second King of Great Britain Annoque Dom: 1727

Signed sealed and declared in the presence of us who attest this will in the testators presence

Arnold Rogers

James Davies

Elinor (sign) + Williams

La: Whiting

1o Junij 1728

Jurat fuit Extrix in hmoi testo nominat de [illegible] [illegible] at de veritate Julij [illegible]

Coram me

Richd Waring Sur

Will of Arnold Rogers, Bridge Court, 1727.

hours of frustration, enjoyment and, when something unusual jumped out of the script to solve a particular problem, excitement. It is remarkable that there were people able to perform this task with such efficiency. Some inventories were written so beautifully that they are works of art.

Most of the wills commence with the words 'I...being sick in body, but of good and perfect understanding' or 'I......being in good health and of sound mind and memory, thanks be given to God' and proceed to give instructions as to burial and the listing of bequests. The wording of these has a simplicity, and yet perfect use of English, which is often almost poetic.

> '.....my body to be buried....for as I have lived obscurely, always clouded, and endeavouring to pay every man, and God knows what I have paid, so I desire no pompous funeral'. (1689) Richard King.

> '.....and my will is that neither of my children shall be at the charge of mourning clothes because I believe such mourning is more formality than any way good or useful'. (1747) Francis Clarke.

I find Francis Clarke a most intriguing character. He was a wealthy man, yet obviously of a saving character, whether careful or just downright mean. His will, apart from detailing all his bequests, also gives very explicit instructions regarding his burial.

> 'My body to be buried in the churchyard of Kingstone where I now dwell, at the end of ye Chancell on ye south side of my wife's grave, such a toomb to be erected over my grave as is over my wife's grave with this inscription (viz) here lyeth ye body of Francis Clarke of this parish, Gent, with the day and year of my death and age. My will and desire is that my Executors shall not be at the vain charge of a pall, and to have four or six to carry my body on the bier to ye church and those to be chose out of my servants, workmen or tenants, each to have a good pair of usefull gloves, only to invite half a dozen relations or friends.......each to have a good pair of usefull gloves and a silk hatband........the minister ye same and ye like to as many of my children as can come to my burial, and to send the like or the value in money to those children as cannot come, and to have no wine, cakes or biskett, to have a plain shroud and coffin without hinges, to use the Church cloth to cover my coffin and bier'.

There is no trace of these graves. He had three sons and two daughters, and all were left sizeable sums of money, and items of furniture.

The most valued item in homes was a bed, and all kinds of these were listed. The main item was the feather bed with 'boulster, pillow biers [pillow cases, only the wealthy had the latter], blanketts, sheetes, coverlets'. Most often they were described as 'beds with everything belonging thereto'. Then came four-poster beds with tester (hangings), truckle beds with casters on, and standing bedsteads. William Popkin, before mentioned, bequeathed to his two daughters,

> 'Unto Joan, my daughter, the second feather bed now in my house with appurtenances thereto belonging viz; one bedsteed, one double canvas, one pair of flaxen sheets and 2 pair of hurden sheets'.

> 'Unto Mary, one feather bed, one coverlet, one double canvas and pair of flaxen and one pair of hurden sheets'.

It is to be hoped his wife had the first feather bed. Why Mary had one pair less of sheets than Joan we shall never know. Perhaps that was the sum total of linen available and she was, after all, the younger. Hurden sheets were of a much coarser weave than the flaxen ones.

Whereas the less well off had, at most, one or two beds with accompanying sheets, often scornfully labelled as 'ould' by the appraisers, the yeoman farmers had surprisingly extensive stocks of linen. Henry Marsh of Dunswater had twenty-three pairs of sheets, nine tablecloths, and three dozen of napkins. He also had two other items not generally met with, a pair of birding guns and a looking glass. The inventory of John Parry of Arkstone lists his linen as 'napery ware' and goes on to specify 'flaxen sheets and corse sheets', 'three dozen of flaxen napkins, three dozen of the second sorte', 'foure flaxen tabell cloathes and fouer of ye second sorte', a nice change of wording. Napkins were often found in the wealthier households being used in place of forks which, although introduced into England in 1611 from Italy, were not much used until the next century.

Henry Marsh died in 1687 and his inventory gives us a good idea of Dunswater at that time. Items are listed as being 'in the parlor', 'little chamber by ye parlor', 'ye best chamber', 'ye red chamber', 'ye hall chamber', 'ye kitchen chamber', 'ye porch chamber', 'in the cocklofte', 'ye hall', and 'ye servants end chamber'. His guns were to be found in the parlour, while the looking glass was to be found with the linen in the red chamber and, even if it was the best chamber, it was still the place where he kept three stone (42 lbs) of hemp and flax. Incidentally, this is the only reference I have come across to a cockloft, a small upper room or attic often reached by a ladder. It could be a space over an attic and, as the name would imply, could house fighting cocks. It was more often used as a sleeping area for servants and, in the case of Dunswater, it did contain a bed and bedstead and a truckle bed. His inventory also lists a quiver. Was this a family heirloom perhaps, or was archery still practised?

Furniture was often willed to relatives. Here again, the well off had sufficient to warrant very good description, while the lesser mortals tended to have their treasured pieces lumped into items like 'trumpery over the kitchen' or 'ould sheets, ould cupboard', etc. Richard Williams, a yeoman, in his will of 1775 gave 'my desk and two beds to my daughter Penelope and Ten Pounds', 'to my daughter Theodotia, my chest of drawers and two beds and Ten Pounds' while to his son he gave 'all my wearing apparell, my watch and Bible, and my mare with saddle and bridle' and, of course, 'four hogsheads'.

Returning to Francis Clarke, that man of substance who places himself firmly in the history of Kingstone by his regular appearances as landowner, tenant, church warden and overseer, he bequeathed to his eldest son James 'my picture of my Great Grandfather and my Grandfather which is in one frame in the parlor, for a family piece'. His daughters received linen, and shared silver spoons that had belonged to his wife. Two other children had 'bed, bolster, two pillows, bedstead, blankets, rugs or quilts and other appurtenances'.

Storage in most homes was confined to cupboards or more often wooden chests or coffers as they were called. There are numerous references to these in kitchens, parlours and chambers, also to stools and chairs, sometimes reference to 'joynt chayers' and tables. In larger houses, there were often table boards, with trestles or frame, and settles. Elizabeth King who died at Arkstone, owned 'eight leather cased chairs' and 'six chairs cased with cloth'. John Merrick, who died in 1825, had been living in Turners House and his land was under contract of sale to Thomas Wathan at nearby Bridge Court. He left the 'bookcase and pictures in the parlour, and the great table in the hall and ornamental pictures over the fire place' to his daughter.

At one time all my attempts to trace where Francis Clarke lived in Kingstone came to nothing. It is only now, thanks to documents recently deposited in Hereford Record Office, it emerges that his residence was Turners House. I had noticed earlier that Francis bequeathed family pictures to his son and that John Merrick left pictures 'in the parlor' to his daughter but this was not much to go on. Marriage settlements and leases now make it clear that not only Francis Clarke, but also his son James, lived at Turners House, and that John Merrick married James Clarke's niece. So the Clarke family portraits stayed in the home for many years.

The Turners House that stands today was not built until 1915, replacing the building inhabited by the Clarkes and Merricks. I find the name puzzling. Turner was not a local name but, when Francis Clarke married in 1710, Turners House was part of the marriage settlement so the name was already established. Clarke's grandfather, who died in 1656, was Sir Clement Clarke whose tombstone is part of the floor under the altar in Kingstone church. The Clarkes, I find, were an important family related through marriage to the Crofts and Garnons. They dominated the office of town clerk of Hereford for much of the sixteenth and seventeenth centuries.[3] In those days the town clerk was a member of the council and, in addition to a salary, he was in receipt of fees from the mayor's court where he acted both as clerk and attorney. Francis Clarke's great-grandmother was Mabella Garnons. One close in his freehold lands was named Mabel's close. When he married in 1710 he was living at Gillow but in a later lease he was resident in Kingstone, as he states in his will.

If the Clarke family owned Turners House and had lived there before Francis, as recorders or judges of Hereford, could the name be a corruption of the Attorney's House? There are no documents extant about Turners House before 1710 but, since Sir Clement Clarke was buried in Kingstone, he was most likely residing there at the time of his death in 1656.

Other items which were obviously very important to everyone were cooking utensils, which naturally included equipment required for the fireplace. Dishes of pewter, porringers, plates, cooking kettles, brass pans, brass and iron pots, frying pans, spits and coberts or cobirons, dripping pans, cullenders, earthenware, tongs and fire shovels, skillets, flesh forks, andirons (to support the spit), bellows, chafing dishes, all were part of inventories. Women's wills often referred to 'my little brass posnett' or 'my big brass pan', while in the dairy or dayhouse, as it was sometimes called, were salting stones, cheese rings, cheese stones, butter tubs and all types of wooden wares. A 'furness' and 'wetting vatt' are mentioned at Arkstone. A 'furness' was a large boiler or pan, often made of copper, and a 'wetting vatt' appears to have been a cider-making term which can be either the vessel that actually presses out the liquid, or the bed of the cider press.

In 1652 Elizabeth Baskerville willed 'my still and limbeck' to her friend Katherine Siddall. Housewives distilled their own recipes for medicinal and culinary purposes. A limbecke (from the Latin *alembic*) was a still used for making liquor such as aqua vitae, the ancient name for brandy or whisky. Since grapes were unlikely to be available, Elizabeth probably used for her distilling grain or potatoes flavoured with aromatic seeds and spices, which would have been in more general use. A still consisted

A true and perfect Inventory of all ye goods Cattle and Chattells wch Myles Parry of Arkstone in the County of Heref: gent lately deceased was seized & possessed of, taken & valued & prized by the persons whose names are hereunto subscribed, the 8th Day of August Anno Regni Regis et [illegible] Willmi et Mariae [illegible] nunc Angliae Quinto &c Anno Domi 1693

		£	s	d
Imprimis	his weareing Apparell	10	00	00
Itm	Sixe yoke of oxen and one Bullock	60	00	00
Itm	Thirteen Cowes & a bull	40	00	00
Itm	Sixteen young Cattle	24	00	0
Itm	Seven Calves	3	10	00
Itm	Two Mares and a horse	12	00	00
Itm	Sheep of all sorts	06	00	00
Itm	Piggs of all sorts	08	00	00
Itm	All sorts of poultry	01	00	00
Itm	Waynes and all implements of husbandry	12	00	00
Itm	All plowboote & other tymber belonging to husbandry	01	00	00
Itm	One trunk wth 19 pairs of flaxen and holland sheets, and other diaper & damask napkins & towells	15	00	00
Itm	One trunk wth seventeen pair of course sheets wth course napkins & table clothes	05	00	00
Itm	one feather bedd wth all other furniture in ye Hall Chamber	08	00	00
Itm	one ffeather bedd wth ye furniture in ye dairhouse Chamber	06	00	00
Itm	Two ffeather bedds for servts in other lower roomes	03	00	00
Itm	All ye furniture in ye parlour	10	00	00
Itm	In the Cellar seven hogsheads of syder	07	00	00
Itm	All empty hogsheads & kinderkins	04	00	0
Itm	one cheese-press and all other rudiments belonging unto the dairy	01	00	00
Itm	[illegible] one table one brass pott			

Inventory of Miles Parry of Arkstone, 1693.

of a vessel to heat the mixture, a condenser to turn the vapour back to liquid and a receiver to hold the distilled spirit. This is the first and only reference I have found to such a possession in the documents I have looked through and indicates a person of some wealth, which she no doubt was, since she lived at Kingstone Grange.

The following examples show that even the most conscientious appraisers had problems in spelling. They wrote as they spoke, or as they heard words spoken. Yet words like trough and plough were always correct. Perhaps it was a question of common usage.

Cubbert - cupboard. Hockcetts - hogsheads. Cosshins - cushions. Cortons - curtains. Coverlids - coverlets. Too speetes - two spits. Drpin pan - dripping pan, and so on.

Clothes were in most cases referred to as 'wearing apparell' and were nearly always the first item on the inventory. In most cases the figure was £1 or £2, the highest being £15 which related to the wardrobe of William Else of Dunswater whose goods and stock amounted to £738. The attire of Hugh Russell, a churchwarden of Kingstone, was valued at £10 in 1723 with the rather unusual wording 'according to the quality of the person'. Margaret Wathan, in 1785, left to her sister Ann 'my desk, gown and one pettycoat' and to her other sister Sarah 'my blew and white gown and one pettycoat and a tea spoon'. All her remaining apparel went to her sister-in-law Elizabeth Wathan, then at Hanley Court, and her daughter to be equally divided. Mary Hill of Green Court left 'my best wearing apparell' to a relative in 1786, and 'my third best bed, together with any of my wearing apparell not chosen, to my servant, Mary Crump'. Oh, to be an unseen onlooker to see what was left unchosen. She left her large Bible and common prayer book to her god-daughter.

Both Mary Hill and William Else left money for the poor to be given at the church door. William left sixpence apiece 'to such poor as the Minister, Churchwardens and Overseers of the Poor shall thincke fitt' while Mary left £3 to be given out in bread for the poor. This was to be phased over the year on three occasions. Possibly she wanted to be sure that she was still remembered, and also that it might benefit more folk than if given all at once.

If both will and inventory for the same person are available to study, it is a lucky find. More often than not it is a question of having one or the other, but the fact that they are available for all at county record offices after so many centuries is truly remarkable.

William Crump, a tailor, lived at Coldwell in a cottage which, had it survived, would have impeded the building of the new infant block at the primary school. His inventory dated 1737, which amounted to £14, had the following which indicates a comfortable home.

'Two beds with their appurtenances.
One trunk, one old cupboard, three coffers and three boxes.
One spinning wheel, two tables, one bench, one dresser and three chairs.
Three small brass kettles, one small brass pot and a chaffing dish.
A warming pan, two brass spoones, seven pewter dishes.
Eight pewter plates, four porringers and two pewter tankards.
One tin cullinder and one tin pudding pan.
One spitt a pair of andirons, one pair of tongs and a fire shovell.
One brass candelstick one pewter candelstick two pails
and one frying pan.
Three old hogsheads two small barrells two tubs and one trind.
One looking glass. [Very necessary for his customers to
approve their new outfits!]
300 gallons of cyder.
One pair of bellows one flesh fork with some lumber'.

John Bigglestone, who died twelve years later in 1749, had a variety of interesting possessions including a warming pan, a linen wheel and a woollen wheel, six old beehives, a good variety of furniture and utensils including eleven pewter dishes and six plates, wheat, hops and a pike, plus ale in the cellar. All this was valued at £10.

One of the saddest inventories was that of John Jones, a carpenter who died in 1700.

One cowe, and calfe, and one other cow and one littell horse
Two small pigges
Fower hogsheads three barrells one kinderkin
One tub two trindes one payell
One coubourd two cofers
One tabell round one benche
One pott and one small kettell
One pewter dish and one pewter candelsticke
Two ould beades and beadsteeds with coufering and sheetes beelonging to itt
Noue Two acres of couon [corn] growing on the land
Two axes two sawes, six orgers [augers], one payer of cheesells

This amounted to £12 4s 0d of which £7 was for his animals. At the bottom of the page is written 'The parsone deceassed is indebtted to severall parsons the summe of £12 0s 10d'. So, very little was left for his family after his affairs were settled. Perhaps a visit to the overseers of the poor to see what relief could be given was their only course. Could he have been the same John Jones who moved the pulpit in 1666? In which case, the family would have been there long enough to have a settlement.

William Baugh, the village blacksmith, whose father, also William, bought the forge opposite the Bull Ring public house in 1747 for £60 was, apparently, an extremely thrifty man. There were no inventories of goods for either man but their wills speak for them. William senior died in 1766 and left his son 'all my shop tooles in general and large pipe vessell and large table'. A pipe vessell held 105 gallons of cider or ale. It was stored on its side rather than upright as a hogshead would have been. William junior died in 1805 and by that time had acquired the house next to the smithy, known as the Corner House, now demolished, three holdings of four acres and six small cottages, three of which were situated on the site of today's Mona Villa at Dews Corner and were referred to as being 'situate at the Crossway in Kingstone'. Both men held parish offices and were always in demand for church repairs in addition to their normal busy round. There is a fine double gravestone to William senior close to the south door of the Church, the inscription on which reads:

A husband good, a father dear
A faithful friend lies buried here
A neighbour just in all his ways,
He do deserve this word of praise.

An occasional comment makes us realise the strong family undercurrents that were sometimes present in those days. In 1762 Thomas Madox made it clear in no uncertain terms what he felt about his son's future. 'I give and bequeath to my son William Madox the estate that I now lives in with all appurtenances, etc. on condition that he shall not nor will not marry Elizabeth Smyth nor have any converse with her'. He did not give any alternative. Presumably, since he had four other children, two of them boys, young William took the hint and toed the line. Several members of the Madox family appear regularly in the records with no hint of where they lived. My hunch is Whitehouse Farm, but it is only a hunch.

In 1699 Elizabeth King left various monetary legacies to relatives, including thirty shillings for her brother to buy himself a ring. She stipulated 'if either of ye said legatees happen to be dissatisfied or disaprove or shall question or sue for ye same, then such legatee shall loose his or her legacy'. That was telling them!

George Powell, a stone mason, left goods amounting to about £16, in 1721, and his will showed a heart of gold. He wished a twopenny dole to be given to the poor and left thirty shillings to six poor children, 'the most naked children to buy them flanning [flannel] or other clothing to cover them'. To the wife and six children of a deceased relative he gave another thirty-five shillings and to numerous friends and acquaintances, gloves, thirty pairs in all. His godson was to have ten shillings, 'for his particular use, and not for his mother to have it'. Sounds as if he had summed that lady up alright. He also left an educational charity which is mentioned later.

George Powell's inventory below makes one feel that material goods mattered little to him. He had sufficient for his needs, a skilled craft, family and friends. Since no mention is made of his wife, perhaps he was a widower or a bachelor. Although he had saved some money, he was generous enough to help others by loans, which the wording 'Sperate and Desperate' indicates some were unlikely to be repaid.

His wearing apparell	10. 0.
One bed bolster, 2 pair of old sheets, one rug and old bedsteed.	1. 5. 0.
One old hogshead one kinderkin one old tub	7. 0.
Four old coffers one stoole one bench	8. 0.
His tools for his trade	4. 6.
The trumpery over the kitchin	2. 6.
2 Iron potts one little kettle	5. 0.
One pothook one flesh fork	6.
Three old rasors one pike one bill	1. 6.
Two pewter dishes one old brass candlestock	4. 0.
One table one ladder one cupboard one sink 3 hooks	5. 6.
Two hens one cock	1. 0.
The crop in the garden one old grinstone	15. 0.
Money in the house	15. 19. 0.
Money Sperate and Desperate	6. 0. 0.
Total	26. 8. 6.

His possessions were probably well used but 'old' seems to have been applied to almost everything by the two appraisers who were farming sizeable farms. However, this hard-working but soft-hearted man left a more worthy memorial through his charity, which was to educate many children in the village for years to come, than some who considered themselves to be far more important in the community.

It is a pity there are not more records of those who worked the land in the village but the wealth of information that can be obtained from what has survived covers a considerable variety of occupations: gentleman farmer, yeoman farmer, smallholder, blacksmith, carpenter, cleric, tailor, farming widows (there were quite a number) and stone masons. They left their memorials, if not in stone, on paper which in some cases has lasted longer.

REFERENCES

[1] All three documents are in Hereford Record Office.
[2] 'The Goods and Chattels of our Forefathers, 1660-1760' by J.W. Tonkin. In Transactions of the Woolhope Naturalists Field Club, 1985, part 1.
[3] 'The Government of Hereford in the 16th Century', by I.M. Slocombe. In Transactions of the Woolhope Naturalists Field Club, 1972, part III.

All the wills quoted can be found in Hereford Deanery Wills Indexes, these are dated, and indexed by name and parish.

15 THE WORKING OF THE POOR LAW

'We see monuments in many parishes, but they tell only of the Lords of the soil, the deeds of ancestry, the virtues of the wealthy....Not a single monument remains of the poor....their costumes, their habits or their lives. They pass away. Their graves are made in the dust'.

R. Cobbold, 1860[1]

In the early Middle Ages, the care of the poor had been the responsibility of the lord of the manor; then with the birth of the parish, the churches and collection of tithes for clergy, it shifted from the manor to the church. Religious orders, abbeys and guilds all did their share to relieve the poor. In 1391 it was officially decreed that, where a benefice (a living) had been appropriated, a portion of the tithe must be used for this purpose. As the centuries passed it became apparent that ecclesiastical funds were insufficient to deal with the problem. Wars and plagues led to decay and desertion of villages, while the start of enclosure, which turned large tracts of arable land into grazing pastures for sheep, led to less agricultural work. Later still, an increasing birth rate resulted in beggars roaming the country causing havoc to public order. Efforts were made to distinguish those who had to beg, as opposed to those who could work, but it was not until 1601 that the great Poor Law Act of Elizabeth I came into being. This was to be the mainstay of relief for the poor for the next 200 years and it is in this era that the poor law records relating to the parish of Kingstone commence.

The Law of Settlement and Removal which existed within the poor law regulations was also very important. This ordered that any stranger settling in a parish could be removed straight away if he became destitute, so that the parish did not have to provide for him out of its poor rate. It was necessary for people to have a settlement certificate. This was granted if they had been resident for forty days, had been apprenticed in the parish, had served as a parish official, paid a parish rate or had been in service for a year. This slip of paper must have been precious to its holder; it was insurance against bad times.

The task of caring for the poor was carried out by the parish overseers who were also called Guardians of the Poor. Although it was laid down that this was an additional parish office from that of churchwarden, it was common for the churchwardens to fill both offices. This was certainly the case with regard to Kingstone.

The first Kingstone poor law book commences in 1737. The writing is, for the most part, legible and the accounts of different overseers make fascinating reading. They are presented in a variety of ways. Some are meticulously inscribed in beautiful copper plate hand whilst others are most laboriously written, pushed into odd parts of the page, with much crossing out and additions and in accordance with the writer's dialect, e.g. 'payd a ooman for caching a oont'. For the uniniatated this translates as 'paid a woman for catching a mole'.

ADMINISTRATION

The parish officers were elected at the annual Vestry Meeting held in church. However, a short scrappy note dated 1741 states:

> 'It was also agreed that ye Churchwardens and Overseers of the Poore shall pay the expenses not exceeding 2/- at any parish meeting lawfully called that should be held for ye future at any publick house in the parish for ale and syder then drank. We do allow of the above amount'.

This declaration was witnessed and signed by Zacharias Whiting, vicar at that time, and other local worthies. It was also quite usual for the entries to commence with the words 'at a meeting lawfully held in Kingstone Church ajourned to ye Bull Ring'. Since it is not unknown for the church to be somewhat chilly, even with the provision of modern heating, one can understand the desire for the warmth of the Bull Ring if for no other, more obvious, reason.

Parish officers had plenty to do as there were no lines of demarcation in those days. One officer in 1744 agreed 'to serve as Overseer of the Poor, Collector for Land Tax, and Lights or Window Tax and Surveyor of Highways'. It was financially expedient to combine several offices and to appoint those who had a settlement and were reasonably well off. Although in law a settlement could be gained by serving a parish office, research has shown that in practice this rarely happened. Since there were not a great many people with the requisite qualifications in small parishes, it was necessary to combine several offices. In the case of Kingstone, at one time, the bigger farms were listed and the occupiers were appointed in rotation.

The window tax, introduced in 1695, was very unpopular and, although it did not affect poorer homes with few windows, it certainly affected the more affluent yeoman farmers, rising gentry and the clergy who lived in large rectories. Many of these objected strongly and sacrificed sun and fresh air by having their windows bricked up. Arkstone has several blank casements. The tax continued until it was repealed in 1851.

The surveyor of highways had to survey the roads three times a year, report to the justices regularly, attend highway meetings elsewhere, sort out the days on which work was to be done, supervise it, and report defaulters. He also had to check the numbers of animals used with vehicles to ensure that there was no excess likely to cause too much wear and tear on paths and bridleways that served as main roads and trackways. All materials and haulage were paid for out of the parish rate, but the labour was unpaid and compulsory. Every able bodied man had to give six days a year, while anyone providing teams for hauling was excused rates. No wonder that when the parish nominated someone for the job, he had to be sworn in by warrant. There was no getting out of it although, having once served, it would be a while before having a re-run and would give a settlement in the parish.

Few highways accounts survive apart from the brief mention in the general poor law accounts.

Pd.Quarter Pay and Bridges Money	11. 11½
Stone for the bridge	5. 3
Survayors Warrant	2. 6
John Price, repairing the road	7. 0
Tools for the highway	9. 6

The office of parish constable is thought to be the oldest of the parish positions. Here again the duties were linked with all the others and individual details are hard to find. He was in earlier days responsible for keeping the peace and maintaining the parish archery butts which were often sited in the churchyard.

The constable was responsible for the stocks and whipping post. John Bevan was paid 1s 6d in 1741 for swearing his oath when appointed and for mending the 'stoks', while Thomas Jones received 6s 4d for 'making a new whipping post and repairing the stocks', and a further 7s for 'new irons which he put on the whipping post, and for three new locks for the same post'. Often beggars intruding into a parish were whipped and sent on their way. The stocks were used for those giving short weight and measure amongst other crimes. It was usual for these to be set up in the vicinity of the church or on the village green.

By 1764 the constable was paid a salary of five shillings which appears to have been a type of retainer since James Powell, then constable, was paid £1 10s 0d for apprehending a miscreant. A constable was required to accompany those who had to be taken back to their place of legal settlement and to apprehend runaway fathers of illegitimate children. Judging by entries which follow later, these journeys were most likely a pleasant interlude from the dull routine of parish affairs. An old constable's account for nearby Eaton Bishop shows that in addition to purchasing swords, bills, and a pike, new bandoleros were also needed. These were leather belts worn over the shoulder to carry cartridges. No doubt most parish constables were similarly equipped.

The overseers were responsible for a great variety of duties for which they could claim a small salary at the end of each year, often with the simple words 'For my trouble and serving the office...5/-'. Occasionally, there will be a sly touch of humour in the wording, perhaps intentionally: 'Paid Mr. Clarke on ye parish account for long letters and his short journeys £1 10. 0.'.

Even in those days, there were plenty of forms and general paper work to be dealt with.

Pd.for signing the indentors for Thos. Morgan	2. 6.
Postage of a letter from London [Payment on delivery]	9.
The ringers on November 5th. [Day of rejoicing, foiling of Gunpowder Plot]	5. 0.
Wrighting paper for the use of the parish	1. 6.
Sneed the Cryer [Kingstone must have had a town crier, very few mentions]	1. 0.
Mr.Williams', Clark, showing the Statue [Statute] Book touching settlements. [Checking a point?]	1. 0.
Filling 3 sertificates	3. 0.

APPRENTICESHIP

Children were regularly apprenticed within the parish. This could be a voluntary contract between those concerned but, so far as parish records go, it was the pauper children who were allocated by the overseers to various masters and mistresses. Records vary greatly from village and town; there are no actual apprenticeship indentures remaining although they were drawn up, signed and sealed as evidenced by many entries in the poor law books. The indentures were usually in two parts, one for each signatory, and are referred to as a 'paior' of indentures, 'Paid for two paiors of Indentures 7/-'.

At best apprenticeship gave a child the precious right of settlement in the village (which he or she probably had already) and, hopefully, a roof and reasonable sustenance but, if it turned out to be the opposite, there was little or no choice for the children concerned since their parents were in receipt of poor relief, and the overseers had little compunction in dealing with any resistance.

'1746. Stopped 6d. out of 2/- a week from Ann Davis until she brings her son George back to the parish that he may be bound an apprentice to the parish.'

There is no record of George returning to the parish. His mother was a widow and there are several references to her receiving wood in addition to her dole.

The apprenticed children were allocated to their new lives at the parish meeting.

'1764. It was agreed that Elizabeth Griffiths should be placed as apprentice with Isaac Roberts at the next Justices' meeting or sooner if possible'.

Isaac Roberts was landlord of the Bull Ring so little Elizabeth would have had plenty of fetching, carrying and scrubbing to do. Most children were sent to farms, the girls to work in the house or dairy, the boys on all types of labouring. These were referred to as housewifery or husbandry. There is no evidence of how they were treated. Occasionally, the blacksmith, cordwainer (shoemaker), wheelwright or clockmaker would take an apprentice giving the opportunity to acquire some worthwhile trade skills.

The master or mistress was paid £1 and the child was given a new set of clothes which was listed in the parish book: '1 hat, 3 shirts, 3 pairs of stokins, 1 pair shoes, 1 frock [smock]. James Very is gone as servant to Mr.Armitage with the above allowance for 1 year'. Mr. Armitage farmed at Webton Court. In 1793 and 1794 a total of ten children were apprenticed to the larger holdings in the village including Dunswater, Bridge Court, The Grange, Arkstone and the Forge.

The following entry gives food for thought: 'for a girl brought to bed at Bridge Court'. This covered maintenance for the time prior to the birth, 'the lying in period', as it was called, and nursing of the child for months afterwards. This indicates the poor girl was an apprentice since the parish was taking responsibility for her.

THE MILITIA

This was really the forerunner of Dad's Army, while also being the continuation of King Alfred the Great's 'fyrd' which was formed to combat the Danish invasion in the ninth century. The constant warring with the French and threat of invasion made it necessary to have an army mustered in readiness. By 1757 the parish itself was responsible for providing a list of men eligible to serve. These were chosen by lot and compelled to serve for three years or, failing this, £10 had to be contributed towards a substitute. This was another of the parish constable's concerns. By 1802 another Act was necessary which directed that families of the militia men or their substitutes had to be given parish relief. This would have been a common occurence for, with the head of the family away, life must have been hard for those he supported. In 1764 Kingstone rates paid £5 for a militia man, and £2 2s 0d to support his family. In 1798 £3 3s 0d was paid towards a substitute, while the following year two men agreed to go and were paid £5 each. One item in 1802 states: 'Paid the Solder's boys, 52 weeks, £12 10s 0d. This was a dole payment to the young sons of militia men. There was much difficulty in procuring anyone to serve by 1804 and the parish was fined the heavy sum of £20 for not complying. The overseer notes:

'Journey to Hereford concerning the Twenty pounds fine	2. 6.
Paid the fine for the Army of Reserve	20.0. 0'

However, the parish shortly afterwards decided to spend £2 2s 0d on counsel's opinion as to the legality of the Act so they had problems of interpretation but, the law is the law, and so it went on.

The last few years of the eighteenth and the early years of the nineteenth centuries, the era of the Napoleonic Wars, yield many references to the cost of finding volunteers. In 1805 the parish paid £10 to buy a man out of the militia. Why he was considered so valuable is not apparent. There seems to have been a need for more men in 1813, the prelude to the Battle of Waterloo, when the large sum of £14 14s 0d was paid out as 'bounty money for 7 local militia men'.

During this era of hostilities there are many instances of the payment of money to soldiers and sailors passing through Kingstone. In 1789/90, the total of 11s 6d was paid to sixteen men on passes at different times. In 1807 thirteen sailors were helped and in 1812 fourteen sailors were paid, entries usually stating 'Pd. a sailor on a pass'. Having done the duty required of them they were making their way home. The showing of a pass guaranteed relief by way of a cash payment from the poor rate at different stages of their journey. It was a well thought out system on the part of government. What is amazing is that these local officials were well versed as regards their obligations.

THE RELIEF OF THE POOR

The foregoing has dealt with the general aspects of items that came within the orbit of poor law and parish administration. The relief of the poor, an immense responsibility, was taken out of the hands of the parish officers when the Poor Law Act of 1834 decreed that all relief was to be given in Union Workhouses. These were dreadful places, made purposely so to discourage 'scroungers'. There must have been frightful hardship for the genuinely poor who had to choose between trying to eke out a pitiful existence in their homes, if they were allowed to, or going to the workhouse where husband and wife, mothers and children would be segregated and were often never able to be together again.

Up to 1834 the parish had full responsibility for its own poor. There is no doubt that inhuman treatment was sometimes meted out by the Overseers and Guardians of the Poor to the unfortunates who were under their jurisdiction. However, there are instances where the wording of the old records makes it clear that there was real concern for the people who needed help. We have to try to understand the problems of the parish officers in those days having to deal with beggars and vagrants roaming the country, ready to steal and make trouble and seeking dole money, which was sometimes difficult to raise from the ratepayers. Just as today, not everyone paid their dues. There were times when the officers applied for a warrant for those that 'refuse to pay ye yers lewn' (old English for levy or rate). In addition, the parish was responsible for maintaining the church, a vital part of their lives, and for maintaining the highways. When researching the ancient records it is noticeable that, although there is great variation in the amount of manuscript records surviving in parishes, the methods of administration, even to the wording of disbursements, differed very little indeed. When comparing this present age of technology with the seventeenth and eighteenth centuries, the age of ploughing with oxen, horse and cart, of mail coach, stocks and whipping post, it is a sobering thought to find that an Act of Parliament could be enforced in a parish within a few days of it becoming law. Also worthy of note is the fact that those holding parish offices knew their duties and were not inhibited in dealing with the local justices and attorneys, or taking their grievances to the Courts of Quarter Sessions. If they wanted clarification or felt they were being put upon, they were quite prepared to battle it out. There are many stories of strangers who came to Kingstone and found this out, often to their cost.

A brief background has already been given to the working of the Law of Settlement. Kingstone by the 1700s was a well-settled and reasonably compact village. The medieval area was situated adjacent to the church, with the village green and waste surrounding it on the land known today as Green Lane, with hamlets at Coldwell and Coldstone. The villagers were quick to check up on strangers and newcomers were required to show the vital piece of paper showing their lawful place of settlement. In 1754 a parish meeting decided 'to apply for a warrant to bring all persons that have intruded into the parish to be examined, and to indict James Jones for harbouring them'. James Jones may have been doing a kindly act by helping the strangers out, or perhaps he was hoping to make a bit of extra cash by providing board and lodging. He might even have been a local innkeeper. Sheltering vagabonds was an offence liable to fines ranging from 10s to 40s.

In 1744 an entry reads:

> 'It is agreed that the Churchwardens and Overseers shall take the opinion of any able attorney or counsel about Wm. James' case relating to his legall settlement, he being sent home by an order from ye Parish of St. John the Baptist in the City of Hereford where he has lived near 48 years'.

This appears to be a sad and flagrant case of injustice and, if so, Kingstone were within their rights to take it further. Presumably poor William was too old to fend for himself any longer and, after forty-eight years, was sent away from his home in Hereford to his place of birth, Kingstone. On the other hand, is it possible that he wanted to end his days in his birthplace and hoped that he might be allowed to do so? In a few cases, a parish would send money to another parish to cover a person legally settled in its midst. Unfortunately, attempts to trace what happened in such cases are fraught with difficulty.

In 1741 another entry reads:

> 'It was agreed that James Wathan.....shall apply to obtain a warrant against William Rogers who has left 3 children in our parish with Thomas Madox who threatens to put them upon ye charge of the parish to maintain, and to apprehend him and bring him before 2 justices to sware his last legal settlement, and to remove him and his children to his last legal settlement, and also to take out an order to remove Thomas Gray to Malmesbury the place he has sworn his settlement'.

The cost of the warrant was 6d. What was the cost in terms of human misery?

At the same time fifteen people were listed as being 'idle persons who have no visible way of getting a livelihood' and a warrant was being sought to bring them before a magistrate. On the other hand, occasional relief was given to persons passing through the area on their way home, as distinct from the soldiers and sailors mentioned earlier.

> 'Taking a poor woman and a boy that was lame that was brought by a pass too ye Bullring and for their yetables [eatables] and drink and for taking them on their way to the next parish 1s 4d'.

They were given food and firmly passed on to the next place thereby eliminating any chance of settling in the parish without being noticed. Another entry states: 'Paid a poor woman that was big with child to help her on her way'.

The last thing the overseers wanted was to have a confinement to cope with. This was a costly enough business when it was a Kingstone inhabitant, let alone an unknown pregnant woman.

The account for 1752 gives an illuminating record of the removal of Evan Davies who had entered the parish and was able to prove his lawful settlement was at Penbrai, near Swansea.

Evan Davies 4 weeks pay [dole]	2/-
Going to the Justice with him	1/-
A going for the Order to remove him	1/-
For the order	2/-
For one pair of shoos for Evan Davis	1/-
For eating and drink and horses hay and oates at the Hay the first night we set out with Evan Davis	4/2
Do. at Brecknock the first night	7/10
Do. also Dinner at Trecastle and drink and horses	4/2
Do. night and morning at New Inn	7/10
Do. dinner at Carmarthen and horses	4/6
Do. night and morning at Kydwiley [Kidwelly]	8/-
Do. dinner at Penbray and horses	4/6
For a guide to bring us to officer	1/-
At Carmarthen the night wee came back	7/-
Do. dinner at Langadock and horses	3/9
Do.at Brecknock night and morning	7/-
Do. at the Hay at dinner and the horses	3/6
Spent going and coming back	2/6
3 horses six days at 2/- per day	1. 16. 0

One has a sneaking feeling that the Overseers had a six day holiday, paid for out of the poor rate. Possibly they were rather saddle sore at the end of it, but there was no way that Evan was not going back home. It is quite a fascinating exercise to follow their journey on a map. Whether Evan was an elderly man or ill, or likely to be a difficult customer to deal with is impossible to say but two men went with him, possibly the overseer and the parish constable. Anyway, he had a new pair of shoes, was well fed for six days, and it cost the parish £5 8s 9d out of the annual expenditure of £14 7s 7d.

Another case which merits attention, if only for the spelling, is that of Percy Poole.

Persey Poolls settlement	
Going two Mr.Aubry on Persey Poolls acct.	1/-
For keeping Persey with diet 3 weeks 3 days at 1/9 per week	5/6
For two peny worth of salt for Persey	2
For going to Mr.Delahay to bring him over to take Persey Poolls depsition	2/6
The charges for taking Persey Poolls away to Tuksbree	1. 19.0.

It was usual for the overseer to take the person concerned to the magistrate, who would examine by way of questions as to his or her past employment, writing down the details and then, if satisfied, the order of removal would be issued after hearing the pauper swear to the authenticity of the statement. Some parishes have copies of these orders of removal. Unfortunately Kingstone has none. Since Percy was given lodging and food for a few weeks, and it was also necessary to fetch a justice to take his statement, he was probably not fit to travel. In such cases the order would be held over until the person involved was judged to be reasonably fit and then the removal was carried out.

With regard to maintenance of illegitimate children, the overseers were fair to the unfortunate women if they were from the parish. One case was dealt with by Elizabeth Wathan, overseer and churchwarden in 1788. Celia Powell was taken to Pontrilas to swear as to her condition and then to Hereford which, with the hire of two horses for each journey, cost 10s. When the father's identity was disclosed, the village constable was dispatched to find him, which he did. Thomas Jones and David Watkins were paid 6s for 'looking after him' and Thomas Preece, landlord of the Bullring, put in a bill 'for keeping the man in care for six days 16/-'.

Later on, a villager was paid one guinea for Celia's lying in month plus 2s 6d for the midwife, and a further 2s was expended on a warrant to apprehend the father. Often the father was put in gaol, then fined. Sometimes a wedding was arranged or the father had to sign a bastardy bond agreeing to support the child. Celia's child was then '..to be put out to nurse at the chepist price it can be and all expenses aloud by the parishioners'. What became of Celia and the reputed father the records do not say but for many years Celia's child, a boy, received money and clothes.

Celia Powell's child nursed for 52 weeks at 1/6d by Dorothy Walters.

A yard and half of flannon for Celia Powell's child	2/-

Mrs. Steward for close for Celia's child	13/2½
Miss Jones for a hat for Celia's child	1/6
Breches and stokings for Seala's child	
For a shirt for the child at Waters	1/2
A frock (smock) for Sealley's boy	3/2

This was in the early 1790s and it is interesting to note that the name Celia seems to have become Seally within a few years, Sele by 1813 (John Sele, carpenter) and, by the mid 1850s, the Seall family were well established in the village as tradesmen, tailors, carpenters, etc. They were generous in their support for the church. Perhaps this was the beginning of the name. A former vicar obviously thought so as he irresponsibly underlined some entries in blue crayon in the old poor law accounts.

Seventeenth century Rose Cottage, now demolished, originally thatched and with a heavy iron-hinged, nail-studded door reputedly taken from the church, possibly the door once in the north aisle. It was the home of John Seall, village carpenter, shopkeeper and publican in the mid-1800s.

A great deal of the overseers' time was spent visiting the justices with a view to obtaining warrants, taking people to be examined and obtaining orders of removal. In the absence of relevant documents it is not possible, unfortunately, to follow cases through. The poor law books are valuable as primary sources but so much more would be available if more records had survived.

HOUSING

The poor law overseers were responsible for providing accommodation for those in need. This would take the form of paying their rent, whether for a house they occupied or a room in someone else's house, or providing parish houses. The rents varied from 5s to £2 per year, while yearly rental of a room was 4s. Typical examples in the accounts are:

'Year's rent for Umphrey Carwardine £1
[He went later to the almshouses]
Paid Tho. Joan's grandshar's rent for year £1
Paid William Bergem 12/- for ye Smith's shop at Coldwell and a pane of garden for ye use of Elinor Carwardine or any other person the parish shall think proper.
Paid 10/- to a householder for a room in a house occupied by his tenant for Jane Williams.
Thos. Cooke's wife and children shall be removed to the parish house.
Mary Jones and Elizabeth Hunt removed to the house at the Green owned by James Wathan, to have part of the garden. £1 rent per annum'.

The parish had its own parish houses in addition to the Almshouses or Hospital, as it was then called. By sheer good fortune it has been possible to trace three of them on land which later formed part of the parking area for the one time Orles Nursery at Smallbrook. Through the kindness of the owners who proffered their deeds for perusal this came to light, together with the fact that the houses were jointly owned with the overseers of Allensmore. This was in the early 1700s and, although the tithe map of 1842 shows houses on this land, by then they appear to have passed out of parish ownership. The accounts mention:

Timber to make Frank James a chimley	4/-
Richard Baynham for making Frank James' chimley	4/6
Halling the chimley to Smallbrook	1/6
3 bushels of lime	1/3
Plaistering ye chimley	2/-

A chance perusal of the tithe map for Abbeydore showed that at one time there were three parish houses on the very plot where I used to live, namely The Cockyard. It was a common occurrence for me to find old pieces of brown and yellow glazed pottery in the earth pushed up by moles in the garden. In both cases the jointly owned houses were situated on the boundaries of the parishes concerned. Possibly that made it simpler when it was a shared responsibility or, might it have been a case of 'out of sight, out of mind'?

In 1750 it was agreed 'that two new dwellings should be built upon the Barrow Common for the use of the poor of Kingston'. There is a detailed account of the cost of materials and labour for this project. It seems likely that the houses were built on the plot known as Anne Chelmick's garden, after the benefactress who gave money for the poor. This bequest amounted to £20, and that was the sum expended. Her will was dated 1727. The money had previously been put out for interest amongst local farmers and was then distributed in doles and clothing.

The account of materials listed below indicates a double dwelling but by 1860 it was referred to as 'Barrow Common charity cottage and garden'. A marker stone purchased at the time for five shillings, lettered KCL (Kingstone Charity Land), was sited close by.

Twelve thraves of boulting straw at 3/- a thrave
39 ft. Square timber at 7½d a foot
7 loads of wallstone at 1/6d a load
18 hundred of brick at 1/6d the hundred
Thos. Jones for halling 3 carts load of brick from Donswater 3/-
44 foot of Oak boards for ye outer doors 1½d per foot
1500 hundred of lathe for house walls at 6d the hundred
Broad lathe for the thatcher 4/-
A stepper to go up to the one lodging room
37 perches of brick work in ye chimley 1/2d ye perch
68 pannes of plastering 1½d each panne
Making two new ovens in the 2 houses 8/-
Building the two new dwellings £2.10.0.
1 days work nailing lath on ye house 1/4d.
Sawing 150 foot of boards and squaring the same 4/2d.
2 mantlepeeces for the herths

Finally, the first two occupants were to be moved in and there was an effort made to help them settle in with some semblance of comfort. They were James Lloyd and Ann Davis who, you may remember, was stopped dole until her son returned to be apprenticed. She remained on relief for many years.

100 faggots for Jas. Loyde and Ann Davis at ye new house	8/-
Thos. Jones for halling their goods	2/6
Wm. Davis for putting up their beedsteeds	8

For helping to move them	1/-
Wm. Baugh for a hook and links for Jas. Loyde's chimle	8

The last entry refers to fittings for hanging a kettle, or some vessel for cooking, made by the village blacksmith.

The cottage and garden were tenanted until 1867 but the dwelling was in such a ruinous state that the ten shillings rent was allowed 'for taking down the cottage'. Thereafter the charity records state the rent was in respect of the garden only. The land was sold in 1937. Today the site is occupied by a pair of semi-detached dormer bungalows. The marker stone has long since disappeared.

CLOTHING

There are numerous references in the accounts to the need to see the poor reasonably clothed. It is particularly in this context that the overseer seems to be speaking to us rather than writing; that he was really doing the best he could with the resources available.

10 yds.cloth for sheets and blancett for William James	10/-
For ye making of his sheets and blancett	6d.

Very often a poor recipient appears with unfailing regularity. Such a one was Jack Cut. These entries appeared in 1741 and 1743.

9 yards cloth for 3 shurts, a frock and draws for Jack Cut. 9d a yard and 1d for thread	6/10d
Blanketing to line the frock and for buttons and thread	1/7d
Paid John Wathan for making Jack Cut's frock and draws	1/6d
Paid John Wathan for making Jack Cut's 3 shurts	1/-
Nugh shoos for Jack Cut	3/6d
For a hat and a pair of stoking for Jack Cut	1/3d
Breeches and 2 shurts for Jack Cut	6/6d

Another person on whom the overseers relied was Dorothy Walters. For a period of over twenty years from 1790 to 1812 she was paid to nurse babies, children and adults and to make clothes and provide lodgings.

Paid Dolly to make 2 shirts	2/-
4 pair of hose for boys at Dolly's and 2 hats	
Dolly to making 2 frocks	1/6
Joseph Davies a bill for making and repairing shoes	

for the boys at Dolly's	12/6d
11 yds of cloth for Dolly	11/8d
Paid Dolly for making shirts	3/-
Dolly Waters for the lying in month of Ann Doctor	£1.0.0
Dorothy for pair of stockings for Long Will	10d
Dolly for making a shirt 1/6 and washing 3/-	
Dolly paid for the use of bed	£1.2.0

Dorothy Walters' husband, James, died in 1803. In 1804 she was in receipt of dole of 2s 6d per week. She was buried at Kingstone in 1825. There is an oral tradition of a Kingstone clockmaker named James Walters but no documentary evidence has revealed itself yet, although the 1841 census lists a clockmaker, Thomas Walter, living near the almshouses.

William Bergem (Burgum) and his wife Cibell (Sybil) also provided board and lodging for poor children. In 1756 he was paid £3 per annum 'to keep and maintain Elizabeth Rowbry also Mary, daughter of Joseph Lloyd, 2 shifts to each child, 1 pair shoes each, and stockings and a capp. He agrees to keep ammend all the wearing apparel of the two children as long as they are with them'. They were still there five years later but in 1762 and 1763 respectively Mary and Elizabeth were apprenticed, indentures were signed and £1 was allowed for new clothing.

There are many references to 'the boys at Plowfield'. On one occasion a journey to Ploughfield was charged at one shilling, so this was obviously not in the village. Shoes and stockings were paid for, together with six yards of shirt cloth, gowns and petticoats. One item of £1 2s 0d was for one year's schooling for six boys. The only Ploughfield in the area is at Preston-on-Wye and I visited it with a rather vague hope of finding some link with Kingstone. There is a hamlet half a mile south of the village known as Ploughfield Green. Possibly some pauper children were placed there, either in lodgings or for farm work, but it is impossible to say. It is even possible that they were parish apprentices sent out of the parish in order to gain a settlement elsewhere. This was common practice. My visit to Preston-on-Wye proved inconclusive.

There were several tailors in the village. William Crump who lived at Coldwell, and William Hope who lived in a cottage on Mill Common, were but two. Thomas Williams who lived at Lyndale Cottage was a cordwainer, as was Joseph Davies. John Bartram had a clothing shop at Church House from whence he supplied a pulpit cloth in 1793 and '2 staise [corsets] for 10/-'. The poor law seemed to cater for all eventualities judging by the latter item.

The cordwainers, besides making shoes, were called upon to 'soale' them, to provide heel taps and general repairs. The entries very often give the names of the recipients. Joseph Davies was paid for 'a pair of shoes for Long Will, 9/6d and for soling a pair of shoes for young Long Will 1/9d'. What was the point of surnames when you knew everyone and they knew you? Friendlier by far to think of neighbours in that way. Other entries in the accounts refer to 'two new shifts and cloath for little Jane', 'flannel for John Preece's boys and skins for briches' and 'an apehon, handkerchief and blankett for Hester Sanders'. Thin woollen cloth called camblet, or camlet, was bought for making gowns; also flannel, or flannen as it was often written. The several mentions of leather for breeches, together with the cost of Long Will's shoes, indicate that the overseers did not stint when there was a case of real need. It is interesting to note price rises and inflation apparent in shoe prices between the 1740s and the early 1800s; see Jack Cut and Long Will above.

ILLNESS AND NECESSITIES

The following entries in the overseers' accounts give some idea of the types of relief given in cases of illness.

William Crump [Coldwell] given 3½ bushels wheat in his illness at different times.	
Dr.Exton bill for attendance on Wm.Crump and Elizabeth Meredith in their illness and ingredients	£2. 5.6
Mutton for mother and family in illness for 4 weeks	2.3
Paid Mr.Hutchins on Jack Cut's account when sick of ye smallpox.	
Brandy to bath Ann Davies wound when burnt	3
Beeswax and butter for salve for the wound	1.3
Ale and small beear for Jane Jones when ill	8
Thomas Cook's wife when she lay in.	6.0
Wood for Thos.Cook's wife	3.0
Mault for do	1.3
Drink for do	2.0
A woman to look after her	5.0
Benjamin Crump for bleeding Sarah Golley	6d
Dr.Exton's bill for attending the poor	£1. 1.0
Paid William Brown towards the cure 1 boy and his own finger, in corn and money	16.0
Elizabeth Smith for looking after Wilmot 3 weeks	9.0
Mary Jones for cuting his blister and waching up	2.6
Going to the Dockter for Wilmot	2.6
Mrs.Chapman for Wilmot shop goods at one time	4.7
Neck of mutton for Wilmot 3½lbs. at 6½d.	1.10½

Mr. Wathan for John Wilmot's wooding legg	12. 6
Wooding legg and strap; and altering him	14. 0

Poor John Wilmot had a rough time. It is to be hoped his need for a wooden leg was not due to Mary Jones's ministrations.

Bushels of corn, pecks of flour, beans, butter and cheese were given to the poor in addition to money doles. Wood was often hauled for them and in some quantity, since the entries were for four guineas. This could have been when the charity bequests were presented, namely those of Mary Morgan, late of Arkstone, and John Smith of Eaton Bishop, both of whom willed that wood be given to the poor. At other times, sixpence was paid for cleaving wood and faggots were hauled for those who were ill.

When researching these mellowed and sometimes untidy pages, particularly arresting entries imprint themselves on the mind. The following pathetic story shows how the village cared for the less fortunate 250 years ago.

SUSAN FLOYD OR LLOYD

Susan Floyd, sometimes Flide, and usually Shusan, was a poor teenager and handicapped. In 1746 the sum of 4s 2d was expended to buy 'two shifts for the lame girl'. Soon afterwards Anne Jones was paid sixpence weekly for keeping her and, in July 1747,

> 'At a Parish Meeting legally summoned and held in the Parish Church of Kingstone, it was agreed by us who names are under written that Wm. Meek, the present Overseer, shall take Susan Lloyd to Hereford the better to take Mr. Cam's assistance for 3 weeks or month, and shall pay four shillings each week whilst she continues there for her board and lodgings'.

A month previously Daniel Williams had been paid 1s 6d to take her to see two doctors in Hereford, Mr. Cam and Mr. Lawrence, and 'linnen' had been bought for her, costing another 1s 6d. Daniel had gone to Hereford yet again to 'talk with Mr. Cam about Shusan'. He then went for a third time to find quarters for her. Susan stayed in Hereford for eight weeks, returning home to Kingstone in September. Possibly this was the only time she had ever been outside the confines of the village, into the bustle of a city. How I hope she was kindly looked after for that short time away from those she had grown up with.

In November Mr.Cam was paid £1 1s 0d for dressing her hand. In the following year '½ a 100 of faggots and halling them to Shusan Floyd' is noted in the accounts. The poor child died in May 1748, aged about 17. The accounts reveal that a 'shrend [shroud] and coffin' cost 9s 9d, and a further 2s 6d was paid to the clerk for digging the grave, for drink at the funeral, for going to Hereford to buy the shroud and to Thruxton to look for the Rev. Vaughan to bury her.

There are many entries for the purchase of shrouds, the making of coffins, the digging of graves and the tolling of the bell by the clerk. It was common for six quarts of ale to be purchased on such occasions at the cost of 1s 6d. A family named Built were very poor, often receiving food and doles. In 1812 the overseer tells of 'crape for two coffins for Richard Built's children'. In the late 1800s another Built was listed as being entitled to a new coat and coal from the Kingstone charities.

In the years 1795 to 1815, the era of the French Revolution and the Napoleonic Wars, the amount of poor rate disbursement more than doubled. It was a time of few imports from abroad while disastrous harvests at home led to huge increases in the price of corn. From 1795 the overseers were buying in extra corn and delivering it to the poor. A bushel of corn in the 1740s cost approximately 3s 4d; by 1795 it was 15s. The impact of this on the poor and on the parish purse can be well imagined. The year 1799/1800 was a year of crisis. The accounts show:

'Paid for Corn	694. 7. 5.
Received for it	356. 10. 9.
To be paid by Parish	337. 16. 8.'

This was the figure for the corn alone and did not include the normal expenses of house rents, doles, clothing and so on. It would appear that those who could afford to pay for their corn, did so. The shortage was acute for everyone.

Paid Mr.Eustance for grinding flower for ye poor	17. 8.
Pd. Mr.Crump for the store room	10. 0.
Wm.Baugh for links and staple	6.
Double lock for ye door	2. 0.
Book for corn	6.
For a padlock for ye store house	1. 2.
Delivering out corn, 47 weeks	5. 17. 6.

That it was necessary to go to such lengths to protect the storeroom shows that acts of desperation were anticipated and the overseers were acting prudently to protect themselves and Mr. Crump.

The years from 1795 to 1813 saw a doubling of the number in need

The Disberstments of James Davies the Overseer of the Poor of the Parish of Kingstone for part of the year 1748 and Part of the year 1749

	£	s	d
July 12 Payd then to Mr Robert Simmionds	2	06	06
For my Expence and the Evidence	0	10	06
Payd Ann Davis for her trouble	0	02	06
Payd Thomas Parsonds for his Jurney to give Evidence	0	02	00
Payd John James	0	01	00
Payd Sneed the Cryer	0	01	00
Payd Mr Watman for his Jurneys and Trouble in Bringing Thos Parsonds to apear at Sessoonds	0	14	00
For Me and My Horse for four Days	0	06	00
Brought Anne Davies one Load of Wood	0	08	00
Brought William James one Load of Wood	0	08	00
Spent at the first Parish Meting	0	02	00
Payd Quarter pay and Bridges Money	0	11	01½
Payd at the Second parish Meting	0	02	00
at the Same tim gave Samuell Griffits	.	2	00
Payd Mr Collings for asertificate	0	01	00
Payd for awarrent for Thos Williams	0	00	06
Payd Mr Wathan for Straw to put on Joseph Floyds Hous	0	02	00
Payd John Gynkins for puting it on	0	01	00
Payd Thos Pritchard for making adoor and Winding Walls	0	01	00
For Boards and nails to make the Door	0	00	09
Payd Samuell Griffits at another time	0	01	00
Payd him at another time	0	01	00
February the 15th Spent at aparish meting	0	02	00
Payd for awarrent for the Surveyors of the highways	0	01	00
May the 23d Spent at aparish Meting	0	02	00
Payd Thos Jones late petty Constable for Making the new Whippingpost and Repairing the Stocks	0	06	04
Alowed him for the new Irons that Was put on the Whipping post	0	03	06
Alowed him for three new Locks for the Whipping post and Stocks	0	01	06
Payd Thos Jones for to Warrants	0	01	00
Payd Dunnell Williams the money that he Was out of pocket	0	10	03
Payd Wm James from may ye 29 in 1747 to march ye 26 in 1749: 43 Weeks	2	03	00
Payd Anne Davies from may ye 29 1748 to may ye 29 in 1749: 52 Weeks	2	12	00
Payd Elizabeath Murreaith for 52 Weeks	2	12	00
Payd Mary Jones for 52 Weeks	2	12	00
Payd Sithel Jans for 52 Weeks at 9d p Week	1	19	00
Payd Thomas Williams for awarrant	0	00	06
Payd Mr Thomas Russell for the house Rent of Ann Davies	1	06	00
Payd Mr Thomas Russell for the house Rent of Joseph Floyd	0	10	00
	21	06	11½
Alowed John Floyd for Surving his office 1s	00	01	0
for my trouble in Surving the Affice of overseer 5s	00	05	0
Total	21	12	11½

Payments made by the Overseer, James Davies, in 1748/9. He lived in Yew Tree Cottage, and made the Charity Board in Church. Note payments to Sneed the Cryer, and for stocks and whipping post.

of doles from seventeen to thirty-eight, while the total disbursements rose from £127 to £563.

SETTING THE POOR TO WORK

The overseers, on behalf of the parish, had a duty under the Poor Law Act to help the poor to help themselves. Efforts were made to provide some degree of employment.

Paid for leather for William James	2. 3.
Began to give Joseph Loyd's wife the flax, one pound each week at 6d. a lb.	
2 stone of flax for Jos Loyd's wife	12. 0.
Paid her for spinning	12. 0.
Samuel Meek for whitning and weaving	8.10.
Samuel Meek, weaving, people winding, 4st.2lbs. of yearn.	12. 2.
Samuel Meek for weaving 25 yeards of cloth and 61 yeards Hurden cloth	11. 0.
Pd. William Hampton picking stones	10. 8.
Pd. James Roberts to bye a saw and other tools	2. 2. 0.
Laid out in materials to employ the poor	1. 8. 0.

James Roberts was also set up with a 'bedd, one coverlid, pair of sheets and a tin kettle'.

The foregoing examples are but a few of those recorded in the old poor law books. On balance the poor were looked after reasonably well in accordance with the rules laid down. Those outsiders who fell upon hard times when resident in the parish were not so fortunate as evidenced by many visits to the magistrates for removal orders. Some parishes have removal orders, apprentice indentures, bastardy bonds and so on, but Kingstone's have not survived. Possibly the state of the church prior to the Victorian restoration rendered them illegible due to damp. However, there can be little doubt that once a family was 'on the parish' they had little opportunity to improve their lot. The names were inscribed thereafter for many years. One entry shows that the personal goods of the deceased poor were regarded as belonging to the parish. These were sold, the money going to the poor rate, thus defraying some of the expenditure previously given to the deceased. This was so in the case of a man who had been in the almshouses.

'...take a warrant against Elizabeth Hunt to oblige her to deliver up ye goods and chattles of Thomas Jones lately deceased which she has taken into her possession which belongs to ye parish who imployud her and paid her for looking after Thomas Jones till he dyed'

The woman in question was already in one of the parish houses so this was no doubt causing some annoyance to the officers. The following entry suggests aggravation between overseers and a villager: 'Paid Wm.Powell to stop his complaining to ye Justices 1.0 Paid Wm.Powell's wife for ye same reason 1.0.'

One expense which thankfully was never renewed was that of two shillings for 'six brass bages'. These were bought for the purpose of badging the poor, a requirement which was first ordered in 1697 and not repealed until 1810, but there is no evidence that badges were regularly used in Kingstone. They were to be worn upon the shoulder of the right sleeve. It was common in most parishes for the badges to be made of red or blue cloth bearing the initial P, together with the first letter of the name of the parish. It was a terrible way to treat those who were already subjected to much hardship and had little dignity in their everyday lives.

We will never hear the voices of the poor, they were never loud enough to be heard. We are not able to read their story because they could not write. We can only imagine how dreary life must have been having no trade by which a living could be earned. The agricultural labourer was dependent on a fair employer, fine weather for growth and harvests because he was seldom employed all the year round and, above all, good health. The well-to-do often had poor health in spite of better food and housing so the life expectancy of those who survived on a poor diet and lived in damp hovels was correspondingly worse.

Although the poor remain unheard, they are not unknown because they are recorded in these ancient records. They walked the same roads, lanes and footpaths as the inhabitants of Kingstone today. They worshipped in the same church and stood by the same entrance porch to receive gifts of bread, or a few pence, on the great saints' days when special sacrament collections were made for them in addition to the doles given to them from the wills of their wealthier neighbours.

Many of those who undertook parish offices were craftsmen, indicating that participation was not the province of those who had the larger farms and estates. The parish officers were out and about and able to assess the priorities of the needy. It is to be hoped they had good judgement.

REFERENCES

[1] *Biography of a Victorian Village*. Richard Cobbold's account of Wortham, Suffolk. 1860. Batsford, 1977.

Kingstone Parish Records. Hereford Record Office.

16 CHARITY FOR ALL TIME

Every year at Christmas the older residents of the village become part of the ancient tradition of the giving and receiving of charity in the form of fuel or money. Some ask how this came about, others have the vague feeling it is an old custom. The majority, while being very pleased, have no idea at all of its origin.

While it is not unknown for many towns and villages to have lost their charities through neglect or mis-management, Kingstone is fortunate in having excellent records which tell when the donors gave money or land for those in need, sometimes who they were, where they lived, and how they had gained the wherewithal to give it away.

The Kingstone Consolidated Charities are so-called because they consist of more than one bequest. Since the sums concerned varied greatly in value from £700 to £1, it was decided in 1909 to combine them together under this heading and so they remain to this day. In 1907 there had been correspondence in the Hereford Times suggesting that the Kingstone monies had been poorly administered and that large charities in land or money had been lost. This led to a public meeting, duly reported, which set out the facts clearly, showing that the only money lost was £31 whereas the investment of the other charities had accrued a gain of £350 over their original total, a goodly sum at that time.[1]

The oldest charity on record was endowed in 1667 in the reign of Charles II, known as 'The Merry Monarch', who had returned from exile in France to take over the throne after eleven years of the Commonwealth following the execution of his father, Charles I. Thomas Matthews of Dore, in his will dated 14th August 1667, left the sum of fifty shillings to be shared among the parishes of Kingstone, Thruxton and Allensmore.

20 shillings to 20 of the most needy poor of Allensmore.
20 shillings to the Parish of Kingstone for 10 of the poorest persons.
10 shillings to the Parish of Thruxton for 8 of the most indigent poor.

The money was to be paid out of the rental of Exchequer Court, Thruxton and from rentals received from several arable, meadow and pasture lands on a farm which encompassed lands in the three parishes. A finely penned copy of his will is to be found in the first Kingstone parish register. He was most likely a yeoman farmer though his dwelling place is not named.

The Pye charity was also of long standing. William Pye, son of Sir Walter Pye of the Mynde, Much Dewchurch and Lord of the Manor of Thruxton, owned and farmed much land in the surrounding villages. In his will, dated 24th August 1689, he left an annuity of £20 to be divided amongst twenty-seven villages, of which £1 was for the poor of Kingstone. This was paid by way of a charge on the Thruxton Court estate. The Pye family were great landowners in Herefordshire and the Welsh Marches. They were loyal to the Royalist cause in the Civil War, which affected their fortunes adversely during the Commonwealth.

The £8 left by George Powell, the stonemason who died in 1721, has already been mentioned. He wished the interest 'to be paid yearly for instructing one poor child in the English tongue'. This is one of the smaller charities that unfortunately was lost over the years.

Another charity originated from the wife of the vicar of Vowchurch, Mrs. Anne Chelmick. She gave the sum of £20 to be invested, the interest to be paid forever to the poorest widows of the parish of Kingstone on every Easter Monday. A further £10 was to clothe one of the poorest persons of the parish. Her will was dated 1727. The records show that the money was put to interest amongst farmers in the parish until, towards the end of the century, it was used to buy a plot of land and to build a dwelling for the use of the poor on the Barrow Common. The land, known as Chelmick's Garden, was sold in 1937. It is difficult to trace the connection between Anne Chelmick and Kingstone apart from the fact that she left the money to be administered by her attorney, William Else, whose wealthy father lived at Dunswater Farm in Kingstone. William Else Sr. died in 1675 owning property in Worcester in addition to his farm and stock in Kingstone. William, his attorney son, has an impressive burial stone at Vowchurch where the Chelmick arms are to be found on the chancel screen. She may have been the grand-daughter, Anne, mentioned in the will of William Else Sr.

Mrs. Elizabeth Hoskyns of Kingstone left £5 to be invested and the interest given in bread to the poor on midsummer day. The wife of William Hoskyns of Kingstone Grange, who endowed the hospital known today as the almshouses of Kingstone, she died childless in 1721. The old records show that fivepence was paid out for bread periodically from 1744 to 1792.

John Smith was a barrister who lived at Cagebrook House, Eaton Bishop. In his will dated 19th December 1722, he bequeathed £400 to be invested to provide wood, fuel and coals every winter, and gowns and jackets every alternate winter to poor old men and women of the parishes of Eaton Bishop and Kingstone. His property bordered on Kingstone parish. The money was invested in the purchase of land situated on the Wye at Hampton Bishop together with three small pieces of land on Hampton Common bordering the River Lugg. The land on Hampton Common was farmed in strips. By the 1980s the Kingstone and Eaton Bishop land had become one long strip of about an acre delineated by a large stone at each end bearing the letters E.K.P. (Eaton and Kingstone Poor) with the date 1832. This was perhaps the date when the first Survey of the Charity Commissioners was made, their reports being printed about 1837. The common yields its crop to owner/tenant for six months of the year only, the rest of the year the common is 'stinted', meaning it is thrown open for grazing to those in the parish who have a right to take their animals there.

All this charity land has now been sold, the land in Hampton Bishop being purchased by the farmer whose family had rented it for many years. The strip on Hampton Common is now owned by the Herefordshire Nature Trust who own the whole meadow. The old marker stones have been preserved together with a new stone commemorating the change of ownership. The ancient rights of the commoners are still respected. In the very early days, before the land was purchased, there are entries in the poor law books of wood and money being received from Eaton Bishop every year for the annual distribution.

One of the marker stones on Hampton Bishop common bearing the inscription E K P [Eaton and Kingstone Poor] 1832. There is an identical stone at the end of the strip of land which belonged to the John Smith charity.

John Smith died in 1729. His estate eventually devolved on a descendant, John Moore Green, who owned Kingstone Grange, Smallbrook Farm and what is now known as Whitehouse Farm.

The next two charities originate from the Parry family of Arkstone Court. Thomas Parry, known as the squire of Arkstone, died in 1774 aged 92. He left £100 for the poor which was invested in the Monmouth Turnpike Trust.

His daughter, Mary Parry, married twice and was very generous in her will, leaving £700 to the parish of Kingstone where she was born, and a further £700 to the parish of St. Weonards where she had lived with her first husband. This was a great deal of money at the time.

Mary's legacy was similar to John Smith's; fuel one year, clothing the next. The clothes were made in the village, at one time by Joseph Barrell who lived at Bridge Court in the late 1780s. By 1845 the jackets had been made regularly for many years by William Griffiths, who lived in a cottage on the site now occupied by Kingstone High School car park. He was paid 3s 6d each to make the charity jackets. After his death in 1845, the clothing was made by James Parker who lived in High House, near the Bull Ring. The 1841 census shows that, amazingly enough, there were ten people residing there: James and his wife, two sons who were also tailors, another son and three daughters plus two teenage, apprentice tailors. There is a book amongst the charity records which records in neat, copperplate writing the parishioners who were to receive the charity coats, which were reckoned to last three years. Material for coats and complete gowns was purchased from Barrett and Greenland in the late 1890s.[2]

The price of coal in the 1880s was 17s a ton. It was possible for anything from 45 to 60 tons a year to be allocated. In 1995, sixty-four beneficiaries received cash or electricity vouchers to the value of £18 which is more popular.

The charities board records two pieces of land as having been given to Kingstone charities. Only one can be traced, that known variously as Winney's plock or close, Dean Pool plock and Threepenny plock. The tithe map shows a long strip of land divided in two, both plots being named Threepenny plock. One piece belonged to adjacent Whitehouse Farm, the other was part of the glebe attached to Green Court. The charity plot was this latter one and it was sold in the 1970s. A bungalow was built there after permission had been granted by the charity commissioners to re-route a public footpath which ran through it.

The Canon's Dole, referred to earlier, was an ecclesiastical charity of great antiquity, providing for the distribution of loaves from the canon's bakehouse financed from a fund originally set up to feed and house the residential canons of the cathedral. By 1909 a cash payment of 13s 4d (the value of the old mark) in lieu of bread was being received on a voluntary basis, depending on money available, but this has now ceased.

The Benefactions Board, which notes all the foregoing bequests and charities, hangs in the church and is a fine piece of work in excellent condition. Unlike many in ancient churches, it is made of wood rather than stone, and is referred to several times in parish records. It was made by James Davies, a carpenter who lived in Yew Tree Cottage, now Yew Tree House, near the church gates. His work, for two days, earned him the sum of 3s 4d with another 4s for the borders around the board. The expensive part was the signwriting, described as 'lettering the Donation Table £4.5.0'.[3] An error was made in the Morgan bequest which reads £800, instead of the £700 which was eventually received some years after Mary Morgan's death. This was due to the fact that the Tredegar and Ruperra Estates were locked in chancery proceedings to determine legal ownership, many rents were unpaid and the finances of the estates were in great disarray.

The charities (benefactions) board adjacent to the west door inside the church.

The holy communion service was held four times a year prior to the nineteenth century: at Easter, Whitsuntide, Michaelmas and Christmas. The communion or sacrament money was given to the poor at the church door. This was distinct from the money due from the charities and from the doles, which were allocated from the poor rate that parishioners paid together with a church rate.

When the Charity Commissioners made their first definitive report they mentioned that the church had two pieces of charity land administered by the church council with rents of £1 and £1 5s 0d respectively, carried to the credit of the church rates. They were Church Plock, situated on the Kingstone to Thruxton road, numbered 469 on the tithe map of 1842, and Little Hales, on the corner of the lane leading to Webton Court, adjacent to the Coldstone Cross estate. Church Plock featured in the old account books as far back as 1744 when it was rented for 6s a year. It was also known as Bell Rope piece, probably because the rental was used for this purpose. It was sold when the re-ordering of the vestry took place in 1984 and now forms part of Exchequer Court Farm in Thruxton. The proceeds were used towards the re-siting of the tower clock mechanism, enabling the bells to be rung in safety.

The land known as Little Hales has a rather complicated origin. At the time of the Enclosure Act of 1812 the vicar and churchwardens were allotted land in Christfield, some of which was still in strips. This was part of the Dunswater estate bordering the Kingstone to Abbeydore road. The vicar and churchwardens then exchanged it with the lord of the manor, William Croome, owner of Dunswater, for land which he had been allotted at the Hales. This was common procedure when landowners wished to make their holdings more compact. The allotment and exchange were for the benefit of the poor of Kingstone and, in 1837, the land was rented to William Preece, one of the few villagers to receive an allotment in the Enclosure Act. The Charity Commissioners confirmed in 1895 that this land was under the management of parochial church officers rather than parochial charity trustees. It was eventually sold and a pair of semi-detached houses erected earlier this century.

The parish councillors who look after these bequests today, do so in the knowledge that they are carrying on a tradition which originated in the days when there was no health service, benefit system or pensions; the age of the survival of the fittest, nearly 250 years ago. As a trustee myself for many years, I found it one of the most pleasurable duties of the parish round. It was heartwarming that the other trustees, who were all born in the area, knew everyone that was listed. Long may that happy state of affairs continue.

REFERENCES

[1] The Hereford Times, 9th March 1907.
[2] Kingstone Consolidated Charity Records.
[3] Kingstone Parish Records. Hereford Record Office.

Details of all the charities can be found in the Charity Commissioners Inquiry Report. Hereford Record Office.

17 THE ALMSHOUSES

A more visible charity is that of the almshouses which stand alongside the main road opposite the Bull Ring Inn, which was there at the time they were built in 1712, and rubbing shoulders with Rose Cottage, which dates from 200 years before.

The William Hoskyns Hospital (almshouses) in the 1970s showing the two adjacent cottages that were removed to make way for modern housing.

The almshouses were endowed by William Hoskyns, member of the well-known Herefordshire family seated at Harewood End for many generations. He lived at Kingstone Grange and was buried in Dore Abbey where there is a chapel endowed by the Hoskyns family. Most of Kingstone Grange is in Abbeydore parish and the land belonging to the grange is in both parishes. This is the most likely reason for William's stipulation that there were to be two dwellings for poor men from Kingstone and two for poor men from Abbeydore.

In the beautifully inscribed original lease, now deposited in Hereford Record Office, the buildings are referred to as 'four mansions' and no doubt they seemed so to many at that time. The upkeep of the hospital, as the almshouses were then called, was to be paid for out of seventeen acres of land (Byefields) which bordered the River Wye in the manor of Wilton, near Homme Green at Ross-on-Wye.

The four inhabitants were to be paid £3 a year out of the rental. The parish overseers decided it was too difficult for the poor people to budget for a whole year so they were paid in instalments from the poor rate, and the overseers re-couped the money when the rent from the land at Ross was received. In fact, payment was often tardy, and complaints were recorded that it had been necessary for the overseer to ride over to obtain it, necessitating the entry: 'For a stamp on the auspital money, 2d.'.

When a dwelling became vacant, the new occupant was elected by the overseers of the parish. There are frequent references to relief given by way of food, fuel, and nursing when circumstances required it.

An entry dated 'May ye 28th 1740' states: 'We elect Humphrey Carwardine an Antient poore man to succeed James Williams deceased into the Almshouse in Kingstone and to receive the profits belonging thereunto left by Mr.Williams Hoskyns of Kingstone Grange'. Not long after one reads in the disbursements for the year,

Srende [shroud] for Umphry Carwardine	6/6d.
Coffin	13/6d.
6 qts.Ale	1/6d.

Among the Whitfield Estate archives are many leases which illustrate the way farms changed ownership. Occasionally the names of under-tenants are given. A few years before Humphrey Carwardine was elected to live in an almshouse he was farming a small amount of land, possibly a few strips, in the area of Kipperley common field and the parish paid his house rent of £1 for some time before his moving to the alsmhouse. Possibly he had become too infirm to work his land and gain a living.

The 'mansions' today differ greatly from the way they appear in an old photograph taken at the turn of the century. It shows the roof level was much lower and must have been altered previous to the main restoration in 1962 when the fishing rights that went with the land were sold to enable proper kitchen, bathroom and toilet facilities to be installed.

When the Charity Commissioners investigated the various charities throughout the country in the 1830s, they found that the Kingstone almshouses were in good repair. Sir Hungerford Hoskyns of Harewood End had reported that they were in a ruinous state and scarcely habitable and that timber worth £40, felled from the Byefields, had been sold and the money devoted to repairs of the houses 'as far as it would go'. The commissioners were not pleased to find that three of the dwellings were not occupied by poor men as elected but had been let by them to others, while they lived elsewhere. The commissioners commented, 'This is an abuse of the charity, and at variance with the intention of the donor...'. William Hoskyns would certainly not have approved.[1]

On the other hand, he would be agreeably surprised if he could see the almshouses today. In 1986 another full-scale modernisation was carried out. Damp courses, central heating and emergency alarm systems were installed at a cost of some £35,000. When the latest work was completed many local people thought the houses were 'little palaces' so perhaps the original description of mansions was not so out of place after all.

Mrs. F. Podmore, the oldest inhabitant, 103 years of age in 1995.

What would William Hoskyns have thought if he could have been present at the sale in 1981 of the land he bequeathed? The sale was decided upon by the trustees when it was realised that the cost of re-fencing the land for a new tenant would be prohibitive in relation to the rent that could be expected. The Charity Commissioners were scrupulous as to the way in which the proceedings were conducted. They set the price the land should fetch and this was conveyed in a sealed letter to be opened at the auction in Hereford. Had this figure not been reached, the land would have been withdrawn.

The original inscription stone on the almshouses had weathered considerably over the years and a new stone of slate, a faithful copy both in style of writing and wording, has now taken its place ensuring that the name of William Hoskyns is commemorated for many generations to come.

> This Hospital was built, endowed and given by William Hoskyns Esq., in trust to Sir Hungerford Hoskyns and Joseph Clarke, Esq. A.D.1712 for ye maintenance of 4 poore men, two of Doore and two of Kingston forthwith with ye rent of the Byefields and the Stenders.

REFERENCES

[1] Report of the Commissioners for Inquiring concerning Charities. 1837. Hereford Record Office.

Extracts from Kingstone Parish Records. Book commencing 1739. Hereford Record Office.

18 THE PRIMITIVE METHODIST CHAPEL

The Primitive Methodist chapel, which stands mid-way down Green Lane, is today a pleasant private dwelling with its plaque still indicating its original use. Through the Methodist Archives in Manchester, trade directories and the reminiscences of older inhabitants it has been possible to trace a little of its history.

Before the chapel was built preachers from the Hereford circuit visited the village to conduct services. Later on superintendents of the circuit came to live locally and preached at meetings held in their homes. In 1852 the superintendent was Mr. S. Tillotson and he was followed by a Mr. Smallman. These two men made quite an impact and 'the cause prospered, sinners were converted, and the congregations increased'. All efforts to procure a suitable site on which to build a chapel failed, since 'the clerical influence was strong, and was exerted to crush the infant cause, they failed; but earnest prayer continued to be made to God for this object'.

These are the words of William Guillim, the superintendent in 1856. Since he was living in Kingstone, he determined to purchase the cottage and garden in which he lived, hoping to build there if no better site could be found. However, since his cottage was close to the church, he felt it was not prudent to do so as it might have 'nourished hostile feeling'. His cottage was the old Green Cottage, later demolished. It had belonged to a family named Powell, and in 1871 was bought by James Capel Croome who told Edwin Wathen, who rented Green Court Farm from him, to pull it down. Edwin Wathen then used it as a garden for some years and it later became the site of the house now known as Caradoc.

By this time the little band had made an impression in the village. They began to gain support for their cause including that of the rector, Archdeacon Wetherell. He used his influence with Mr. J.S. Gowland, owner of Kingstone Farm, now known as Whitehouse Farm, to lease a piece of land for 300 years at one shilling per annum on which the chapel would be built.

Mr. Guillim describes it thus after its construction in 1857:

> 'We have a neat comfortable chapel, it is a brick building covered with the best blue slate, 27 feet long by 19 feet wide, and is 12 feet from the floor to the ceiling, a boarded floor, oak joists, well ventilated; the aisle is flagged; it has four sash windows, and one swing ditto, with iron gate, and palisades in front; altogether it has a neat appearance, and is the only dissenting place of worship in the neighbourhood'.[1]

The first service was held on 22nd November 1857 with Mr. Guillim preaching in the morning and the Rev. T. Hobson of Hereford in the afternoon and evening. The congregations were so large that many could not gain admittance. What an event it must have been. The collections amounted to £5 15s 6d which was thought to be excellent in view of all the fund raising that had gone on before.

The minister commented that society was composed chiefly of the labouring classes, and that they had contributed to their utmost for this object, and yet were still anxious to commence 'begging' so that they would have a good sum in hand before the land was secured. The amount they had in hand was some £67 including the opening collections. The rest of the money had been raised by donations, including £3 from Mr.Guillim himself, and by tea meetings. A Miss Buck had organised these and given several sermons which had realised £15. The total cost was expected to be about £120 but the figure of £143 is mentioned in a copy of the Hereford Journal of 1924 given to me by the late Mrs. G. Weeks whose family had worshipped there from the very first.

Mr. Guillim went on to record his thanks to the farmers who carted nearly all the materials gratis and to all friends who assisted in the undertaking. 'We are also happy to record that the Lord is watering our Zion with the dews of his Holy Spirit, and thirty sinners have recently been converted to God'.

By 1867 the minister was a Rev. R. Bowen and in the 1890s a Rev. G. Annakin was residing in Rose Villa. The Rev. J.H.C. Rogers was resident for some time before 1920, possibly in the Manse. At that time the circuit covered Cobhall, Cagebrook, Madley, Shenmore, Vowchurch, Dorstone and Ploughfield, quite a large area which had been even wider. In 1924, the minister was the Rev. William Mason with Mr. Enoch Christopher, a newsagent from Madley, as one of the stewards and a lay preacher, while Enoch's sister was the organist. The Christopher family had relatives living in Kingstone and were one of the mainstays of chapel life in the village. Ephraim played the organ and had two brothers, William and Enoch.

A Methodist Chapel Collection Journal dated 1934/44 has a few entries which show that in June 1934 there were fourteen members, and that a quarter's collection money amounted to £3 13s 0d with class and ticket money amounting to £1 3s 6d and 'love feast' collection of two shillings. I assume these amounts were for Sunday school collection and for a special outing. The chairman was a Mr. William Softley. Edith Christopher had written out an account for expenses amounting to about 17s for four gallons of oil for the lamps, one cwt. coal and two lamp glasses. By 1943 the collection money for one quarter had dropped to £1 18s 3d.[2]

This little building, representing the culmination of much earnest prayer and hard endeavour, finally closed its door to Methodist worship in 1976 by which time its dwindling congregation was joining others in the main church in Hereford. It was sold at public auction in the Bull Ring Inn, and realised the sum of £1500.

Kingstone Primitive Methodist Chapel, now a private dwelling.

REFERENCES

[1] Methodist Archives. John Rylands University Library, Manchester. Primitive Methodist Magazine, 1858.
[2] Methodist Journals, 1830s/40s. BC.20. Hereford Record Office.

Details of the ministers from Herefordshire trade directories.

19 EDUCATION: PRIMARY SCHOOL

The first reference to local education appears on the benefactions board in Kingstone church. George Powell, a stonemason residing and working in the village, died in June 1721 and in his will left 'Eight pounds of lawfull money of Great Britain for a stock for ever to put a poor child to school of the parish to learn to read English, which Eight pounds shall be delivered unto the Minister and churchwardens and overseers of the parish of Kingston to be put to Interest for the aforesaid use, and the Minister...shall elect and appoint ye said poor child and put it to schooll and when one child hath learned to read English tolerably well that shall be taken from schooll, and another who cannot read be put in the room thereof, so that there shall be allways one kept at schooll by the interest of the said 8 pounds'. He signed his will with his name, not a mark, so it is likely he was able to read and realised the value of being able to do so.[1]

The poor law records give many instances of children being 'put to school' with widows in their cottages. Mary and Jane Williams at the Barrow featured regularly, being paid 4s half yearly. There is one item mentioning 'Widow Williams allowed to buy books for ye children by ye parish consent 1/6d'.

The Hereford Journal, in an article dated 5th April 1924 about Kingstone, mentions that there was formerly a private school conducted by two old ladies in an old cottage. The article further states that the cottage in question was, at the time of the article, lived in by Dr. W.R. Forster. In later years he lived at the villa next to the old school but this could hardly be termed 'an old cottage'.

The first practical steps towards building a school were taken in 1845 by the non-resident lord of the manor, William Croome. He conveyed a parcel of land amounting to nineteen perches which formed part of the 'Farm at the Church Stile', known today as Green Court. The land was conveyed to the Lord Bishop of Hereford, the Archdeacon of Hereford and the Vicar of Kingstone as follows:

> '.....to permit the said piece or parcel of land and buildings erected or to be erected to be for ever hereafter appropriated and used as and for a school for the education of children and adults or children only of the labouring, manufacturing and other poor persons in the Parish of Kingston with Thruxton aforesaid and for the residence of the Teacher or Teachers and for no other purpose whatever which said School shall be and always be united to the National Society.......and shall be under the management of the said Vicar for the time being...'.[2]

The National Society was founded in 1811 and by 1830 some 346,000 children were receiving an elementary education in church schools run by them. The school was opened in 1846 with a grant of £90 from the government through its Committee of Council. The National Society contributed £30. Local subscriptions amounted to £165, of which £100 was donated by the rector, Henry Wetherell, £20 by James Martin, owner of the Arkstone Estate, £10 from the Dean and Chapter of Hereford and ten smaller amounts.[3] The cost of the schoolroom and the teacher's accommodation which was attached to the schoolroom was £361 14s 8d made up as under:

Original contract	281.	15.	0.
Additional bedroom	32.	0.	0.
Fence in front	6.	10.	0.
Cost of well and pump	7.	2.	10.
Back kitchen and stone wall	15.	0.	0.
Sheds and coping	8.	14.	3.
Iron Spouts	2.	5.	0.
Sinking the site and levelling yards	7.	7.	7.
Book case	1.	0.	0.

The final account showed a deficit of £42 9s 9d which was met by the Bishop of Hereford.

The original plans show that the school comprised the large room called 'the schoolroom' measuring 34ft by 20ft, a smaller classroom measuring 12ft by 10ft 6ins together with the living quarters for the teacher consisting of a small sitting room, kitchen and two bedrooms above.[4] There is no indication of toilet facilities. The school was to accommodate thirty-five boys, forty-five girls and twenty infants, a total of 100 children.

For many years little attention appears to have been paid to the state of the buildings since no comments appear in any reports. The 1872 inspector's report does make the following recommendation:

> 'New offices with separate approaches are necessary and should be built immediately. One of the sets at present in use might be used by the Master and his wife who at present have none other but those of the school. Every school which is attended by scholars of both sexes above the age of infants, must be furnished with separate offices having separate approaches from the schoolroom'.

The first record of any alterations does not appear until 1890.

ADMINISTRATION AND FINANCE

Any school grant-aided by the National Society had to be run according to the society's dictates. Pupils were instructed in the liturgy and catechism of the Church of England and the vicar was to superintend the religious and moral instruction of the pupils. He was the chairman of the school managers, which comprised the churchwardens and other prominent church members. At this time the rector lived at Thruxton while his curate usually lodged in Kingstone. Either would open the school in the morning with prayers and the log books record that often both would visit the school again later in the day. It was not unusual for four different clergy to visit within the course of a week, often taking charge of lessons. They would examine the classes in general knowledge and would hear the children read, in addition to teaching scripture and arithmetic.

The creed, catechism, various prayers and the old and new testaments were learnt, and each year a diocesan inspector visited the school to test the children. In addition there was an annual visit by a government inspector.

The National Society records show that when the school was opened pupils paid twopence a week or two shillings a quarter and that the school commenced with a mistress whose salary was £30 per annum. By the end of 1846 there was a resident master and mistress with a joint salary of £38 per annum.

An old school account book covering the period 1856 to 1873 exposes the very limited financial means on which it existed. Prior to the appointment in 1862 of John Jarrett who was certificated, no grants were made. The Council for Education did not give grants to any school in the charge of an untrained teacher. The only income was derived from the voluntary contributions of local landowners and the school pence.

This pattern continued for a few years. The landowners appeared to be disenchanted with the whole procedure. Their contributions dropped noticeably and there were fewer of them to contribute. Archdeacon Wetherell had to make up the deficit on many occasions. The school pence figure was made up of payments by the parents who, in the rector's words on a grant application form, 'assessed themselves according to their rank in life'. The payments ranged from sixpence down to one penny.

In 1860, although there was a deficiency in income, there was a payment of £1 for the hire of a harmonium, no doubt to accompany the teaching of hymn and psalm singing. Later accounts show a slight improvement once grants were received, some years actually showing a small balance in hand. The following extracts show the type of expenditure made:

Prayer Books	6. 0.
Hymn Books	3. 4.
Ink Pots	1. 0.
Chalk	10.
New door	2. 5. 2.
Register Books	13. 10.
Slates	2. 0.
Brooms	4. 0.
Desk	11. 6.
Bench	6. 0.
Coke, Coal and Hauling	12. 3.
50 Faggots (bundles of wood)	3. 6.
Ventilators, Benches and House Repairs	4. 2. 3.
Shed and Privies	2. 18. 0.
Blacksmith for stove	3. 6.
Cricket and Playthings	7. 9.
Carriage of Forms for School Feast	1. 0.

The Elementary Education Act of 1870 was passed in order to provide education for any parish where no school existed. Kingstone school managers issued a letter to all parishioners pointing out to them the need to maintain the school which would occasionally necessitate levying a small rate. Since the trust deed would not allow the buildings to be used by a non-sectarian school board, the alternative would have been the provision of a new school resulting in a heavy rate being imposed on all ratepayers. The parish accepted this recommendation and the old accounts show the occasional levying of a voluntary rate.

Grants paid to the school were calculated as follows:

'4/- per scholar based on average attendance
2/8d. for each pass in Reading, Writing, and Arithmetic
6/6d. for infants under 6 years of age without examination provided they were present on that day'.

If pupils had attended more than 200 times in the year a grant of 8s per child was added. Kingstone never achieved such results in the early years. Copies of form 17a, which set out the results of examinations, are few in number and end in the 1870s, so there is no way of telling how later grants were calculated.

Kingstone and Thruxton National School.

TO THE PARISHIONERS OF KINGSTONE AND THRUXTON.

The Managers of the National School of these Parishes desire to call the attention of the Parishioners to their position with respect to the Elementary Education Act of 1870.

The Act is to provide the means of Public Elementary Education for every Parish in the Kingdom where such provision has not already been made.

In this Parish sufficient accommodation already exists, and may be continued under the present management if the contributions of the Landowners and others are supplemented by a small Voluntary Rate from time to time. It is in order that you may see that the present plan of conducting the School is the more expedient, that we submit a short statement of the probable working of a School Board, which the Government will oblige us to elect if our present School is not supported.

A School Board is composed of not less than 5, nor more than 15 Members, to be elected by the Votes of the Ratepayers, and is subject to the control of the Government Education Department. They have power to appoint paid Officers, such as Clerk and Treasurer, and certain Officers to enforce the Bye Laws of the Act, and to compel the attendance of children at School, and in default to summon the parents before the Justices. The Management of the School is in their hands, and all expenses are defrayed by them. To provide for this they have the power, by means of the Poor Rate Assessment, to levy a rate for all their expenses, such as Expenses of Election of the Board—Salaries of Officers—Office Expenses and Correspondence--Law Expenses which they may incur in carrying out the provisions of the Act—the payment of School Fees of poor children, and the Building and Maintaining of suitable Buildings.

Under such a Scheme as this the Landowners and others, who at present contribute the greater part towards the expenses of the School, would not be required to give anything—the whole expense would fall on the Ratepayers.

The terms of the Title Deed of the present School Property will not allow the Trustees to transfer the Buildings to a School Board for Secular Purposes. The Parish, in the event of having a School Board, would have, in all probability, to erect new Buildings.

The Managers hope, therefore, that each Ratepayer will do his utmost to maintain the present economical School by subscribing to a small Rate when required, and also by inducing and facilitating the attendance of children at the School. By an increased attendance, not only are the children of the Parish benefited, but the Government grant is increased, and the expenses of the School thereby reduced. The Voluntary Rate which has been asked to supply the deficiency in the Funds of the School for the last year only amounted to 1½d. in the Pound. We estimate that the rate under a School Board would not be less than 9d. in the Pound for the Maintenance of the School.

Signed T. THISTLETWHAITE SMITH, GEORGE WOOD, T. W. WATHEN, W. H. HOBBS, } Managers.

Kingstone and Thruxton National School, November, 1872.

Circular letter concerning Kingstone and Thruxton National School.

ATTENDANCE

Although the school was built to accommodate 100 children, attendance was irregular. There were many causes for this as instanced in the log books.

> 'Several left in the afternoon, owing to the attraction of a feast at Madley and a tea at Hungerstone'.
> 'Very small attendance owing to sickness'.
> 'Smaller still owing to Miss Clive's wedding'.
> 'Many away gathering potatoes'.
> 'Ascertained that several had left for winter'.

The latter reason for absence was due to many children having to walk up to three miles along muddy roads and fields to reach school. Coupled with dark mornings and evenings and inclement weather, parents were not prepared to send them to school, particularly when some were not well shod.

> 'Attendance low in consequence of many of the children staying away to make cider'.

Other reasons given for absence were reaping, gleaning or leasing, field work, thinning turnips, carrying bark, minding house for parents to attend May Fair in Hereford, cricket matches, gardening at home, minding pigs, ploughing matches, birdscaring, setting potatoes, tea parties, hay making and gathering apples. Chilblains and bad weather were the most common causes. One unusual reason which recurred throughout the early log book was the following:

> '21st December 1865. St.Thomas's Day. Many of the children away, gathering corn'.

This sounds rather a strange happening at such a time of the year, but a local book on folklore explains the significance of St.Thomas's Day.[5] 'This was called "gooding day". A sack of wheat was placed at the door of each farmhouse, and from it a quartern measure of wheat was given to every woman who called for it, to be added to what she had gleaned after harvest. More would be given to those who had families. It was usually ground by the miller free of charge'.

Acts passed in 1876 and 1880 made it compulsory for children between the ages of 5 and 10 years to attend school. Employment of children under 10 years of age was illegal and those between 10 and 14 could only be employed if they had attained certain educational standards. Although this led to improved attendance, it could not be strictly enforced because there were exemptions for children with long distances to travel. Children were also allowed up to six weeks absence to help with agricultural work. It was from this time that the appearance of doctors' certificates became far more common to explain absence, usually for coughs and colds. Scarlet fever and measles often caused school closures for up to four weeks.

STAFF AND CURRICULUM

The early years saw the most frequent changes of staff. There were fifteen head teachers from 1846 to 1885. There may well have been more since the first recorded head is J. Sanders whose name appears in a trade directory of 1851. He is recorded in the 1851 census as living in the schoolhouse and a parish magazine of 1900 records that he died at Stourport aged 91 years. The only evidence available as to the state of the school prior to the first log book and the later school managers' minute book is a small file of documents dating from 1857. The first inspector's report in 1857 comments that the school is 'imperfect, and the master and mistress untrained and very deficient in professional skills'.

As the years went by there was little improvement. Writing was poor, copy books were dirty and badly graduated, arithmetic bad to pretty fair. Indeed, 'fair' appears to have been applied to almost everything except needlework which was often taught or supervised by the wives and daughters of the local gentry.

In 1869 came the signs of an upward turn. The report commented: 'The school has made creditable progress, and is in a very fair condition. Arithmetic requires most attention, and Geography should be taught. Mr. Bennett will shortly receive his Certificate'. Mr. Bennett had commenced at the school in June 1868 and left in September 1872. His wife taught needlework. Their four years at Kingstone were to be full of tragedy since two of their children died, and Mrs. Bennett's health was such that she had to go away for a while shortly before the death of their second child. The school accounts show '£1 donation to the master on the illness and death of his child' which seems paltry under the circumstances. The children's grave is close to the path leading to the church door.

There are several instances in the inspectors' reports which show that some 120 years ago they were probably far more in tune with methods which have been advocated in recent years than might have been thought. There were comments that the desks should be arranged in groups instead of along the walls, that the methods used in arithmetic were too mechanical and the blackboard too much used.

As the years progressed, paid monitors were allowed and pupil teachers were added to the staff. The latter had to serve five years and were given one and a half hours instruction by the head teacher each day. The head received an extra £5 a year and the pupil teacher was paid £10 per annum rising by annual increments to £20.

The curriculum was laid down in accordance with the standards by which every scholar was to be examined for grants. Arithmetic was a vital part of the examination. Dictation was given first on slates and then on paper. Geography lessons were given to the top standards on land and water, Europe, Hereford and adjoining counties, boundaries of England and rivers. Object lessons were given to the top classes on copper, sugar and tea, and to the whole school on wild and farm animals. The children could probably have taught the teacher a thing or two about the latter. Grammar lessons included much work on the alphabet, capital letters and punctuation.

The only reference to sport came in 1864 when we learn that 'the boys formed a cricket club and started practice today'. There was very little playground space adjoining the school and, in 1866, the vicar was in correspondence with the Ecclesiastical Commissioners for permission to use a small piece of land as a playing field at a nominal rent. He stated that the children were forced to play in the highroad, complaints being made of the dangers to the passers-by as well as the scholars. The land was leased for a playground and, eventually, a new school house built on part of it.

Music was a necessary part of the timetable. In addition to the examination in religious knowledge, the diocesan inspector would listen to hymn singing and the saying of prayers. What would today's children make of the following additional songs that were taught? *Stay little Blackbird*; *Pretty painted Butterfly*; *The Fox's Journey*; *Labour's strong and merry children*; *All Hail, Gentle Spring*. The age of admittance varied greatly; at one end of the scale a 15 year old, at the other a 3 year old.

The school's instability was to end after the fifteen changes of staff in the first forty years of its life, years of much poverty. The influence of the church was to gradually diminish in the decades that led up to the outbreak of the second World War in 1939, culminating in the decision to pass over control to the Local Education Authority in October 1939.

THE MIDDLE YEARS

By 1885 the succession of good, bad and indifferent teachers had caused a blistering report from the inspector: 'I have very great hesitation in recommending any Merit Grant as so little is shown to deserve it, but the school has no doubt suffered from 4 changes of teachers during the year'. The managers appointed Mr. Charles Edward Bullock, a certificated master, and his wife, Lucy, on 30th April 1885. Mr. Bullock was expected to assist in the Sunday School and to play the organ in church when required. They were to remain at the school for many years; Mr. Bullock until the end of his career in 1926, Mrs. Bullock until 1909 when she retired due to ill health.

School group with Mrs. Lucy Bullock about 1900.

Their coming was to herald an era of increasing stability, an ever widening curriculum, excellent inspectors' reports and a great improvement in the facilities of the school building, together with the provision of a good teacher's house.

The average attendance by the year 1889 had risen to eighty children, but the cramped facilities of the building led H.M. Inspector to comment forcefully on its shortcomings.

> 'The premises are very unsatisfactory; there is no lobby for hats and coats. The classroom is quite unfit for its purpose, the offices are not in good order, the Teacher's house is wretched, and the playground also wants draining. I should suggest that the master's house be converted into a class-room, though it is hardly larger than the present

classroom, it would be loftier, and that the main room be carried the whole length of the building. Accommodation for the teacher might probably be provided not far off'.

The inspector concluded that in view of the conditions under which the Bullocks were working the results, particularly in the infant section where space and air were so lacking, were worthy of merit grant. This really proved the spur for immediate action. It was decided to approach the Ecclesiastical Commissioners for a site to be given directly opposite the school, adjoining the ground leased nearly thirty years earlier for the boys playground, on which to build a school house.

The commissioners agreed to give the site but no money, and ordered that the managers were to be responsible for providing the walling around the land. The site was adjacent to the dilapidated church tithe barn. It was stipulated that the tenant should take down the old barn, use the timber and thatch and leave the stone for work in connection with the new school house. What a pity that this was long before the period of popular photography. It is the only reference to the tithe barn and its location I have found.

The school improvements consisted of hat and cloak lobbies for boys and girls, new toilet closets and the extension of the main schoolroom to the whole length of the building, doing away with the small infant classroom at one end and the schoolmaster's living room. Instead, a new infant room was to be added which appears, from later comments, to have had some type of gallery, but no plans exist to show just how this was constructed. The plans were drawn up in August and finalised in November 1889. The schoolroom was licensed for divine service at this time since the church was undergoing an extensive restoration.

The final cost of the school improvements amounted to £611 3s 6d and it was through the support and generosity of Lt. Col. the Hon. G. Windsor Clive, who donated £400, that it was possible to carry the project through. He had always been supportive of the school as were the whole Clive family for many years afterwards.

When the same inspector, Mr. J.C. Colvill, visited in 1891 he commented, 'the school has been much enlarged and improved since last year, and is now eminently satisfactory. The work of the school is thoroughly good throughout, and reflects great credit on both teachers'. His scathing criticism earlier had produced the required effect. Very little alteration was ever made again and this was to be the reason for its eventual closure in 1952.

The schoolhouse must have seemed a mansion to Mr. and Mrs. Bullock after living in the cramped quarters attached to the school. It had a parlour 15ft x 11ft, a kitchen of the same size, a scullery and three bedrooms all of good size.

As soon as the Bullocks were appointed new teaching materials had been purchased as suggested in the inspector's report. A harmonium was purchased not rented, poetry books were ordered, new slates and kindergarten toys were received, together with a new set of infant reading books. The object lessons given by the new headmaster in the first six months had quite a different character: Elephant, Honeycomb, Butterfly, Human Body, Lion, Leather, Whale, Sugar, Ostrich, Apple, Cow, Sheep, Child's frock, Coal, Hose, Straw, Giraffe.

From 1891, pupils were entered for drawing examinations which attracted an extra grant paid to the headmaster. In 1896 he commenced a course of carpentry as an instructor under the county council's Technical Instruction Scheme. The school had a headmaster who was able to broaden the curriculum as well as achieving a good standard in the three R's, while Mrs. Bullock's work in the infant school was always much praised in reports.

Needlework was still a very important part of the curriculum since many of the girls went into service on big farms and estates. A copy of the needlework scheme in Mr. Bullock's hand, presumably drawn up by Mrs. Bullock who was responsible for the subject, lists the work to be done in every quarter by each standard throughout the school. Standard 1, which commenced with hemming strips of material 18 x 2 inches with coloured cotton in the order, black, red and blue, also covered knitting, pleating, making pinafores and overalls, darning on canvas, patching on flannel, buttonholes, darning and patching in calico to mention but a few of the skills. Prizes for the best drawing and needlework were for many years given and presented by the resident owner or tenant of the Whitfield Estate.

ATTENDANCE AND DISCIPLINE

Mr. Bullock was to prove a strict headmaster with regard to both attendance and discipline. By 1890 school attendance officers called every week 'for a list of irregulars' and Mr. Bullock kept a sharp eye on any pupil who appeared to be truanting. In the log book Bullock notes that, after questioning one lad, he was assaulted by the father the following morning. School was 'unsettled all day' following this incident. After attending the local Police Court at Abbeydore to prosecute, he writes, 'The case was brought into Court and decided against Gwynne, but the fine imposed 5/- was ridiculously small. The magistrates were a very weak-kneed trio'.

On another occasion he notes:

'Gilbert Smith warned in presence of the other scholars that if he answered me back again when I was scolding any of the other children in such a way that I was unable to hear exactly what he said, and then refusing to repeat it, he would receive a caning and be sent home. This is not the first time he has done this,and the effect of it on the other scholars is bad'.

Nevertheless, he was fair in noting when poor attendance was justified. Very wet weather, causing flooded roads and snow, made it impossible for children with long distances to travel to get to school. There was a clothing club run by the vicar into which people could pay throughout the year. Every Monday money could be paid in at the school at midday and, at the end of the year, interest at the rate of twopence for each shilling up to 15s was added by the charities fund.

There were cases of children truanting in order to earn money and these were also noted in the log book. Often children were engaged as beaters for shoots at nearby Whitfield. It was to Whitfield that the children were taken for Christmas treats and summer feasts, and it was there that gifts and prizes for good work were awarded. This did not deter Mr. Bullock from commenting on 10th November 1898, 'John Hopkins, John Rogers and William Nash are illegally employed by Mr. Bates, Whitfield, today'. Mr. and Mrs. Bates were tenants from 1897 to 1908 and were frequent callers at the school. In later years, the practice of beating for the estate appears to have been regularised: '1st and 2nd December 1903. No school on Dec. 1st and 2nd, the boys being employed beating by Mr. Bates, Whitfield'.

Although sometimes at variance with parents over poor attendance, and who can blame a teacher for that, Mr. Bullock seldom resorted to the cane, which is confirmed in this comment in the inspector's report for 1926, 'The discipline is amazingly good, yet not oppressive'.

There are notes in the log book of a pupil teacher who, when nearing the end of her five years, appeared to be rather slack as regards her duties. She was repeatedly late, although living nearby. Mr. Bullock's comments show that he lived up to the old adage, 'a place for everything, and everything in its place'.

'1901. I had occasion to speak to Miss Jones this morning. On Wednesday afternoon she left the rod for opening the ventilator out of its place, and had to be asked to put it back. She neglected to put the room in order for the girls for needlework. She kept the infants and Std. 1 writing from 2.35 to 3.40 p.m.'.

'1901. Miss Jones came to school this morning at 9.10 a.m. Class room not in order. No lines drawn down the room'.

Presumably lines were drawn to denote the positions to be occupied by various standards.

The school in this period was increasingly used for parish activities. Magic lantern lectures, harvest dances, concerts and carpentry classes all took place in the schoolroom. Mrs. Grethead, the widowed sister of Mr. C.M.B. Clive of Whitfield, took great interest in these activities. A Penny Savings Bank was opened at school in 1892. School fees were still being charged in 1891, some being paid by the local workhouse guardians. No accounts exist for this period but such payments were noted in the school log book.

HEALTH AND SANITATION

The school suffered the usual closures for whooping cough, measles, scarlet fever, diptheria and mumps. There was an outbreak of smallpox in 1888 which caused the death of one adult and the closure of the school for two weeks. No children were recorded as suffering from the disease. Exclusions as a result of school medical inspections were rare but eczema, ringworm and dirty heads were the usual cases reported. Just before the end of the first World War a severe influenza epidemic hit the county causing the closure of two-thirds of its schools including Kingstone. By 1919 the School Medical Service was working well enough to ensure that regular inspections were carried out in all schools, and the results were presented regularly to the Education Committee of the county council. A county council minute of 30th September 1922 records the setting up of a clinic for the treatment of children suffering from minor ailments which dealt with eye and skin complaints, anaemia, debility, goitre and the most common ailment of all, enlarged tonsils.

The sanitation of the school remained unchanged after the alterations made in 1899. An inspector's report of 1907 drew attention to the fact that 'there are no lavatory arrangements on the premises!', and the managers decided at their next meeting to 'provide lavatory arrangements as recommended by H.M.I.' but nothing was done.

By the 1930s the School Medical and Dental Service was extremely thorough and regular inspections were made in addition to those carried out by district nurses. The School Milk Scheme was introduced in 1935 and prior to that Mr. Bullock's successor, Mr. Edwards, organised a lunch-time drink of Horlicks malted milk at twopence per week. The School Meals Scheme commenced in 1946.

School group taken in 1924.
Back Row L to R: Edith Williams, Brenda Stratton, May Preece, Edith Colcombe, May Christopher, Flossie Jones, Milly Roden, Edith Mutlow, Phyllis Gilett, Hilda Payne, Clara Jones.
Second Row: Eva Powell, Marjorie Miles, Ruby Morris, Vera Stratton, Ivy Pugh, Elsie Thomas, Ena Powell, Peggy Williams, Molly Colcombe, Gladys Preece.
Third Row: Doris Brown, Florence Powell, Phyllis Reece, Irene Jones, Hannah Phillips, Gladys Hughes, Mary Williams, Norah Thomas, Irene Williams, Phyllis Brown.
Bottom Row: Doris Brown?, Marjorie Jones, Evelyn Davies, Violet Phillips, Cissie Taylor, Phyllis Payne, Nancy Price, Frances Harrison, Violet Harris, Vera West.

THE LATER YEARS (1926 onwards)

The school at the time of Mr. Bullock's retirement in 1926 was well taught and disciplined with a firm foundation laid for its future. But no one could have foreseen the population explosion and the consequent upheaval which was to occur as a result of the building of a R.A.F. station in Kingstone parish in the early 1940s.

Mr. T. Rees Edwards succeeded Mr. Bullock in 1926 and broadened the school's activities still further. Girls were now taught drawing; there were more physical training activities; school gardening, weaving and basketry were on the timetable; and school reports commented on the active participation of pupils in oral work. Empire Day was celebrated, medals being distributed by a member of the Clive family. Armistice Day was observed and after the two minute silence *The Supreme Sacrifice*, Kipling's

Recessional and *God Save the King* were sung. In 1938 the log book records that the children listened to the radio broadcast of the armistice service. The school's attendance remained good and half-day holidays were given as a result. Holidays were recorded for royal weddings, for the silver jubilee of King George V, and school outings were made to Barry Island, South Wales, the nearest seaside.

Reasons for non-attendance became far less varied than in the early years due to the gradual use of more sophisticated farm machinery. Children were away for fruit picking and, as Christmas drew near, they were kept home to dress poultry. The Local Education Authority would allow a week's closure for hop-picking, usually the last week of September. When the second World War started, and agricultural labour became scarce, children were taken to the nearby pea fields for instruction and, later, to help with the picking. The same applied to potato picking and hay making.

Although the school continued to be a Church of England school, by this time various education Acts had altered the way it was administered. The vicar was correspondent to the managers who were all connected with the church, but the local authority was responsible for salaries, equipment and certain repairs and renovations. The managers remained responsible for certain maintenance.

By 1934 it was patently obvious that the building was sub-standard. The sanitation was the main worry, together with the provision of a proper supply of drinking water. The managers could not cover the expense involved and pointed out to the authority that the building was now unsuitable due to undivided classrooms, poor lighting, bad ventilation and inadequate playground facilities. They further stressed that the increased traffic was proving a hazard since the school was so close to the road. They suggested that a new school should be erected on a different site.

Although the latrine problem was dealt with, the problem of a water supply was still outstanding, water being pumped from a house nearby. Having decided to clean out the existing well at the school, and to recondition the pump, another problem presented itself. The school floor was in a poor state, the likely cost of repair being in the region of £126. The local authority was prepared to pay a proportion of this but the funding of the balance was a different matter. The condition of the building was such that the expenditure was not felt to be worthwhile. It seems such a small figure by today's standards but in those days was sizeable. The managers decided to hand over the school to the local authority and a report by the special committee sent to view it stated:

> 'After a thorough inspection the Committee beg to report that the School has nothing to commend. It is situated on a dangerous bend

on a very cramped site, and the buildings require extensive alteration. The ventilation is poor throughout, and the sun never shines in the main room..........The Special Committee recommend that they do not accept the transfer to them, and that the L.E.A. build a new Council school for infants and juniors and that steps be taken at an early date to secure a site'.

This was a sad end after almost a century of progress, albeit at times somewhat faltering. The school had provided learning some twenty-five years in advance of the 1870 Act for compulsory education, at which time it was reasonably up to standard. The site was the factor which hampered its development. It was only an eighth of an acre sandwiched between two dwellings with orchards. Although it was part of Green Court Farm, it was of little use agriculturally which may have influenced its choice. When the lord of the manor, William Croome, gave the land he would not have considered the need for more playground space or the dangers of proximity to the road. He was providing the means whereby children would be able to acquire the basic skills for a working life which offered little opportunity for the majority. In 1845 it was adequate but with the coming of the motor car and more emphasis on sport and leisure it was quite the reverse a century later.

The outbreak of war in September 1939 prevented the building of a new school and, although the school passed out of church hands on the 2nd October 1939, it had to remain in the old building. It became known as Kingstone and Thruxton Council School.

The R.A.F. Training Establishment which had been built in 1940 was vacated in 1947, only to be re-occupied by families from many parts of the country who were without homes. Many of them were poor and unused to country life. The 'huts' as they were called, although strongly built, were bitterly cold and conditions were spartan.

Mr. Edwards, who had been in charge for over twenty years trying to cope in a building which had been condemned, even with lower numbers, was now having to cope with rapidly rising numbers. He was the only qualified teacher on the staff and, by April 1948, he had 107 children in the school, seventy-three of whom were in the main room. Three months prior to this thirty-four children had been transferred to the secondary modern school housed in part of the old R.A.F buildings, which he was also trying to supervise. It is little wonder that he suffered a nervous breakdown, was away for a while and died shortly after his return at the end of 1949. The inspector's report refers to him as '...a devoted and conscientious teacher of long service here, whose failing health should never have been subjected to so heavy a strain as this, even physically

School group with Mr. T.R. Edwards in 1938.
Top row L to R: K. Winney, F. Stewart, H. Bevan, B. Morgan, V. Stewart, G. Lloyd.
Second row: ——, G. Colcombe, M. Williams, B. Davies, S. Williams, B. Harris, J. Randford, C. Phillips.
Third row: M. Randford, D. Lippet, B. Phillips, E. Preece, E. Evans, M. Preece, G. Ruck, O. Williams.
Front row: D. Winney, I. Bagley, T. Griffiths, E. Evans, S. Ruck, W. Postans.

The fleet of buses which brought children to Kingstone secondary and primary schools in the 1970s.

considered, involved'. He must have been a true village schoolmaster in every sense of the word. He was very strict. Some pupils remember being sent on occasion to cut hazel from the hedgerow to replace broken canes but there are many in the village today who remember him with great affection.

It is often the case that tragedy has to take place before action. It was but four weeks later that two classes of junior children were transferred to the huts leaving only the infants in the old school almost a mile away. During this time the log book records incidents of broken windows and the stealing of coal and items of school equipment.

By 1954 the numbers on roll had risen to 222 and the original plans for a new school, drawn before war started, were shown to be hopelessly inadequate. The school continued in these makeshift buildings until 1972, some twenty years after the old school had been finally vacated. Even then, the new school, which was sited a short way off, was built with only four classrooms to accommodate juniors while the infants were moved close by into yet more of the old R.A.F. huts. It was not until 1991 that the building of an infant block completed the final phase.

Since 1950 the school has been in the charge of four experienced and dedicated headmasters who have given the necessary guidance required to absorb the many educational changes that have come about. The four years of Mr. T.G. Angwin's charge were to see the establishment of the school in four buildings comprising assembly hall, dining hall, eight classrooms, staff room, kitchen, etc. The adaptation of the old R.A.F. buildings caused much disturbance but was successfully achieved by 1954. Set against this was the growing realisation that, with such a rapid influx of population, there was a very wide range of ability with many youngsters only able to work at a very slow pace. Many of the newcomers had little learning opportunity due to frequent moving about and poor housing. Mr. B.A. Williams (1954-1968), Mr. E.J. Coleman (1968-1978), and the present head teacher, Mr. J. Pullen, have seen the development of, firstly, a remedial class, followed by the setting up of the first Slow Learner Unit in the county, violin and cello classes, swimming instruction, chess classes, educational visits and holidays at home and abroad, participation in athletic and sports galas and the many activities which are available. This was in addition to maintaining a business-like approach to the basic subjects which were, in the early years of the old Kingstone and Thruxton National School, the be all and end all of the school curriculum.

My husband, Eric Coleman, had to oversee the building of the new primary school and the moving from the old buildings, while the infants moved from one section of nissen huts to another section adjacent. This was a formidable undertaking since it was to involve assisting the builders in translating the plans from the old imperial measure into the new metric system which had just come into force. The building, although outwardly very spacious and modern, had also been designed as open plan meaning there were no doors on classrooms, which was soon found to prove difficult in many teaching situations. As is so often the case, those who were responsible for the management of the school and the teaching were not consulted until it was too late. This problem was later remedied when Eric's successor, John Pullen, was appointed. He was able to convince the authorities of the problems, particularly the noise factor, and doors were added, together with walls and extra storage room which could double for teaching small groups. The final phase was completed in 1991 when the new infant block was added. This is a really delightful, custom-built area linked to the main building by a bright corridor, which can be used for a reception and display area and also houses the school library. The infant classrooms are separated by doors! Enough said!

New School (old huts nearby), 1977

In September 1995 a nursery class was started in another hutted-type building. This was a milestone for the school and for the children who will have the early grounding that will give them such an advantage in their school life. The move to promote state nursery education appears to be gathering momentum. I only hope that one day, not too far distant, it will be possible for every primary school to have a class to cater for dyslexic children at the top of the infant school range. This would be invaluable to dyslexics as, like small children, they need to be helped from an early age.

In the old days of the payment by results system, as it was known, the vice-president of the education department, Robert Lowe, made an oft-quoted comment on education. He said, 'If it is not cheap, it shall be efficient; if it is not efficient, it shall be cheap'. The old school at Kingstone at its most efficient was never over-financed judging by its problems. Likewise today, those responsible for the financing of education always seems to be lacking in true knowledge of the problems faced by those actually teaching.

The original school built on William Croome's piece of land has taken on a new lease of life, literally, since a long lease was granted by the trustees to the Boy Scouts Association who are slowly improving it by providing new flooring, a mezzanine storage area, together with kitchen and toilets.

This was possible due to William Croome's last direct descendant, William Iveson Croome who died in 1967. He was active in leading and supporting the Diocese of Gloucester as chairman and trustee of its many committees. Much of his estate was left to that diocese. Through them the old school was offered to Kingstone for a nominal sum, although there was still the problem of repairs and unkeep. This has now been happily resolved by the lease to the scouts, while the church has the use of it for special occasions.

When visiting Cirencester and North Cerney in search of the Croome family, I had a long talk with the late Canon A.J.C. Turner who had been a great friend of William Iveson Croome. He was most surprised to hear of the Herefordshire connection and, since he was writing a short history of the Croome's achievements, we were able to exchange notes. North Cerney church and Cirencester church have many memorials to the family. The wording of the deed for the school house made it clear that in the event of it being no longer required for its original purpose, should it be sold, the proceeds must be put into an educational trust to be applied for the benefit of Kingstone and Thruxton. The educational charity was signed and sealed by the Charity Commissioners on 28th August 1991 when the property was sold and the proceeds were duly invested with them. The six trustees are the rector of the benefice of Kingstone, Thruxton, Clehonger, Eaton Bishop and Allensmore, the head teachers of both Kingstone schools and of Clehonger school, and a member from each of Clehonger, and Kingstone and Thruxton Group Parish Councils.

The trustees can draw on the interest from the capital and applications are invited twice a year for consideration. The income is to be applied for the benefit of any person living in the benefice or who has a parent or parents living there. It must be used to promote education, including social and physical training and education in the doctrines of the Church of England.

To date grants have been made to the scouts and guides for tents and camping equipment, to the Aikido club for mats, to children in need of finance for school trips or activities, for hymn books at the high school, and towards text books, travelling expenses and admission fees for older students on training courses. The fund generated by the sale of the old school house is being sensitively and sensibly used as laid down by the trust guidelines.

The school house was regarded as a palatial dwelling by those who dwelt there first in 1890, even if they did have to cross the road to get their water from the pump in the old school yard. In more recent years it did not come up to the standards that most people now expect. What, no central heating? Today it has had a remarkable transformation, and how surprising to find that the old school garden was sufficiently large to allow another sizeable dwelling to be built alongside. It was always shrouded by very tall trees and now the corner has a surprisingly mature aspect. The reader will recall that the plot was originally the site of the old tithe barn and the tithe map records it as barn and hopyard, while adjacent was Pigeon Close. No doubt the rector had his pigeon house or dovecot there as well.

The old school plaque dated 1845. The site was known as nursery land, part of Pit close.

REFERENCES

[1] Hereford Deanery Wills. Hereford Record Office.
[2] Trust Deed 4th February 1845. Hereford Record Office.
[3] National Society Records Office, Westminster, London.
[4] Copy of Original Plan. Hereford Record Office.
[5] *Folk-lore of Herefordshire*. Ella Mary Leather.

Kingstone & Thruxton School Accounts Book 1856 to 1873. Miscellaneous correspondence, H.M. Inspectors' Reports, etc. School Log Book, commencing 1863. All at Hereford Record Office.

20 EDUCATION: HIGH SCHOOL

Separate secondary education in Kingstone commenced on the 5th January 1948 in three of the huts vacated by the R.A.F. At that time the old school was overcrowded and thirty-four children were transferred together with other pupils of secondary school age from Bredwardine, Preston and Blakemere, Madley and Clehonger. The school roll was 131 with three qualified assistants, one student, and Mr. T.R. Edwards, formerly headmaster of the village school, who was appointed acting headmaster.

This was a time of great austerity. New furniture, equipment and text books were non-existent. John James, who was in his final year in the old school, remembers helping Mr. James Perkins, who taught at the school for many years, to carry desks and chairs to the new classrooms. These were the old instruction blocks divided into four rooms about 30ft square with two pot-bellied coke stoves in each room. Long tables which had been used by the trainee wireless operators and long benches were in use for some weeks, together with the stacks of message pads which had to take the place of exercise books until supplies arrived. Other schools were contacted for text books which, on arrival, were found to be of little use in most cases.

Mr. N.K. Tillotson, a permanent supply teacher in the county, was appointed acting headmaster in May 1948 when the health of Mr. Edwards finally broke down after such pressure of work. A permanent domestic

Part of the original secondary modern school housed in the R.A.F. buildings.

science teacher and a woodwork master were added to the staff and a further hut was taken over to house these activities. A year later Mr. A.G. Snook took over for a while as acting head.

The school had its first permanent headmaster in September 1950 when Mr. G.L. Hall took charge. Although still housed in unconverted huts, work was in hand to convert twelve huts into a temporary school which would eventually draw children from a much wider area. A metal-work master had been appointed but, as there was no room available for him, he served for a considerable time as a class teacher.

Geoffrey Hall was to stay for just over four years. In that time his administrative abilities rapidly became apparent since the numbers on the roll rose to 263 and he had to cope with piecemeal conversion of twelve more huts into classrooms. Soon after his arrival part of one hut was in use for serving school dinners which continued to arrive in hot containers from a central kitchen in Hereford. It was not until 1951 that a school kitchen was completed in yet another block and dinners were cooked on the premises. Does anyone recall, I wonder, that school meals were increased to ninepence in 1953?

Two huts were converted into six flats for staff, Mr. Hall and his family occupying part of one which was situated on the present primary school playground. Gradually, rooms for art and craft, music, needlework, woodwork and metalwork were added, together with a domestic science room and flat, science laboratory, gymnasium (partly equipped from the R.A.F.), library and assembly hall. Alongside all this had to be the provision of adequate cloakrooms and toilets.

While all this work was taking place two classes of junior children had moved into the upper part of the site, to be followed finally by the infant classes in 1952. Both headmasters commented frequently that the few paths that existed between classrooms were often impassable because of mud and that electric cables were lying exposed due to the delay of the builders in covering ditches. Senior pupils were now being transported to school in a fleet of buses from Abbeydore, Ewyas Harold, Wormbridge, Much Dewchurch, Kilpeck, Allensmore and Eaton Bishop. The catchment area was eventually to cover twelve primary schools.

It was not until January 1952 that Mr. Hall was able to record in the log book that two playgrounds had been completed and were in use for the first time. There must have been heartfelt sighs of relief from staff and pupils alike. The dining hut had temporary electricity installed in December 1950 which was later extended to the rest of the school. At the same time the comment is made that a cleaner had been engaged to relieve the caretaker of some of his duties, which included the lighting and supervision of twenty-three tortoise stoves and a boiler. It was necessary for some of the boys to assist in the removal of four tons of coal which had to be unloaded in the school garden because the lorry got stuck in the mud. Photographs taken then portray a miserable picture of grubby looking buildings below a swirling smoke-filled sky, reminiscent of industrial slums rather than a rural school.

The headmaster and staff, several of whom served the school for decades, created an environment which surmounted these physical difficulties and it is due to them that the school has progressed so well over the years. Continuity in those early years has paid a handsome dividend and many old scholars remember with affection and nostalgia their time there.

Staff group in 1953.
Back row L to R: R. Jones, A.G. Morgan, E.J. Coleman, J.E. Perkins, J. Watkins
Front Row L to R: Miss M. Hawkyard, H. Watkins, Miss E. Delahay, G. Hall (headmaster), Mrs. J. Morgan, R.G. Aston, Miss U. Davies.

The curriculum was always forward looking and visits to the cinema, theatre, ballet, South Bank Festival and Three Counties Show, to name but a few, became a regular part of educational and cultural provision. There were very few cars and most of the teachers had bicycles or travelled by bus. For pupils living in out of the way districts, these visits opened up a world that few of them had been able to share and enjoy. The first school trip was to Colwyn Bay in 1952, the year the first school pantomime was performed. *Cinderella* played to an audience of 200 which included Mr. M.L. Edge, the Director of Education for Herefordshire and Mrs. Dawson, H. M. Inspector of Schools.

The four houses of Windsor, Tudor, Stuart and Hanover were introduced, together with school uniform and the school badge designed by Mr. J. Perkins, showing the letters for Kingstone County Secondary intertwined in gold on a royal blue background. The school football team played its first home game on 15th December 1951 on ground at Dunswater Farm. No playing field was available for another two years when the hockey team played its first home match on ground adjacent to Huff Cap cottages where the present day playing fields are situated. The hockey posts were in use for the first time, being made in the woodwork class, and football was also to be played there for a while before the old R.A.F. 7 Site became available. House cricket matches commenced in 1954. Cross-country runs were held every year.

Assembly in the school hall in 1948.

The school began to reach out into the community by running evening classes at the end of 1951. These comprised dressmaking and woodwork and were very popular. A few years later I joined the dressmaking class, my first real introduction to the intricacies of a sewing machine. The variety of garments from pinafore dresses to a very lovely little girl's fur trimmed cape, completed most professionally, were very eye-catching. The school took over the R.A.F. cinema block and my husband, who was rural science master at that time, used to collect films from Wyeval in Hereford which he projected on Friday evenings to the village to boost a school fund. This also made it possible to screen shows for both schools on special occasions.

By the end of the summer of 1954 the school had emerged under Geoffrey Hall's guidance into a well organised, happy and disciplined community. It was staffed by teachers who identified both with the children and the rural background from whence they came, which fortunate state of affairs has continued to the present day. Geoffrey Hall left to take up a larger headship in Bristol at this time, four other members of staff also leaving. Mr. R.G. Aston and Miss E. Delahay took up headships in Herefordshire and Devon, Mr. R.E. Jones went as music master to Gillingham Grammar School, and Mr. J.G. Watkins, who had charge of metalwork, took up a similar appointment in Monmouthshire.

Mr. John Reed took up the reins of headship in January 1955. During the twenty-three years of his charge he was to see the school roll climb steadily, the school eventually being re-organised in 1973 to become a comprehensive high school for pupils aged 11 to 16 years. The five years from 1973 to 1978 saw the building, in two phases, of a completely new school.

Mr. Reed introduced a special course for General Certificate of Education (G.C.E.) Ordinary Level examinations which created a fifth form and, in 1962, a second course was introduced for pupils who wished to take the Certificate of Secondary Education (C.S.E.). John Reed was the longest serving headmaster, deservedly earning great respect and affection in all his dealings with colleagues, parents and students. It was a great shock to the community when he died suddenly in December 1978 so soon after his retirement.

A fine oak lectern, made by a local craftsman, was commissioned in his memory. It bears his name engraved on a brass plaque salvaged from one of the original war time horsa huts. It was used for the first time at the annual speech day and prize giving on 8th November 1979.

One of the finest examples of the way a practical curriculum was applied was in the planning and building of a learners' swimming pool which was built through the combined efforts of pupils, parents and staff under the guidance of the late Mr. J.H. Watkins, woodwork master for twenty years. The pool was officially opened on 10th July 1959 by Alderman L.J. West, 'Jack' to many, school manager, farmer, county councillor and local councillor, who lived at Kilpeck and was always ready to take up any cause which might adversely affect education. Unfortunately, the pool had to be dispensed with when the new primary school was built.

The transport of pupils from so many distant villages, many of them in isolated areas, was often a problem when weather was inclement. The log book entries for December 1960 tell of torrential rain with the Wye Bridge and approaches being under water; of buses from Bredwardine, Eaton Bishop, St.Weonards and Garway unable to run; of staff being stranded; and of the Eaton Bishop pumping station being flooded to a depth of twelve feet. The school was closed for three days, no water being available. In those days of hutted classrooms, there were always problems with sanitation if it snowed and the temperature dropped severely. Toilets would freeeze, pipes would burst in various classrooms, ice would form on floors, and temperatures would plummet to little over freezing. Children from hilly areas would be sent home after dinner and often did not return for days because buses were unable to get through snow drifts. Mr. Reed mentioned that floors 'reek with damp' and he praised the caretakers, Bill Martin and Jack Munn, for their efforts in keeping the fires constantly stoked. The early days of 1963 must have taken heavy toll of the buildings which were only one brick thick with no insulation. On several occasions the drifts of snow in the grounds were up to three feet high and children had to be kept in the hall until paths had been made.

When it was not wintry conditions that made problems it was summer, particularly hot and breezy days, which made school life difficult. At the end of 1962 Sid Wright Ltd. proposed to use some huts on their land adjacent to the staff flats and to some classrooms for piggeries. For the next four years the smell from these was at times unbearable, particularly for the staff living on the premises. Classes had to be moved, it was unpleasant to have games nearby, and staff threatened to move out. The many log book entries refer to the smell as 'nauseating, quite overpowering, horrible, appalling', etc. In later years rats were reported in cloakrooms, in the domestic science room , in drains and on roofs of the flats, together with infestations of flies. At times these were intermixed with anthracite fumes from the stoves, so that it seems hardly surprising that the headmaster recorded 'a great number of children ill with stomach upsets and sickness'. Dr. Chandler remembers writing many letters of protest on behalf of the school and of the infant welfare clinic which was situated very close to the piggeries. The matter finally resolved itself at the end of 1967 when the Local Education Authority purchased the land belonging to Sid Wright Ltd. and relinquished the old 7 site which had been used as a football pitch for some years.

These peripheral and frustrating problems did not prevent the establishment of a yearly prizegiving ceremony attended by prominent people in many fields of Herefordshire life. Mr. Hall returned to present prizes in 1963. My husband was invited to perform the same duty and it was a great tribute to the school to observe the quiet, efficient and courteous way in which the head boy and girl, together with form prefects, shouldered much of the responsibility for the arrangements at this and other such events.

Music and drama have always played a prominent part in school life. *As you Like It*, *Wizard of Oz*, *Snow White and the 7 Dwarfs*, *Toad of Toad Hall*, *Tobias and the Angel*, *Androcles and the Lion* and *Alice in Wonderland* are but a few of the ambitious and successful productions performed. The school hall is fully equipped with a large stage, curtains and lighting, together with a baby grand piano, making it a venue suitable for many other purposes. Having opted to manage its own budget in accordance with the present government recommendations, there is a music centre which operates in and out of school time enabling pupils to have specialist tuition on an instrument of their choice.

In the 1950s and 1960s the domestic science curriculum included the chance for pupils to experience 'living' in the school flat which was so planned as to allow them to bring in a younger member of the family for a few hours. This was a really down-to-earth approach which, with the need to cover so much more in today's timetable, has now been abandoned. Cooking in the early days was carried out on paraffin and solid fuel stoves which was what many children were used to at home.

Needlework was a particular strength in those days and a dress show was a traditional yearly event in the school. When Denise Wall was one of very few to win through to the finals of the European Stylemaker Contest, a coach load of supporters travelled with her to Bristol. Claire Winney was twice runner up and won the Fashion and Dress Making Section at the Royal Show, Stoneleigh.

Clubs and societies were encouraged and, because the scattered nature of the school population made it difficult to hold meetings out of school hours, one period a week was set aside for boat building, art, photographic studies, table tennis, first aid, cycling, cabinet making, style and grooming, etc. The Duke of Edinburgh's Award Scheme and outdoor pursuits were undertaken and one of the first gold awards in the county was to Peter Smout, later to be a R.A.F. Flight Lieutenant and leader of the Falcons, the free-fall parachute display team. He was later awarded the Air Force Cross, the R.A.F.'s highest peace-time award.

Fostering of agricultural pursuits was naturally given high priority in a rural area and a school farm was set up. The school had its own flock of sheep and entered it in the Three Counties Show winning many awards.

The Clun Society helped with the purchases while the Ryeland Society loaned a ram. Ewes were bought out of money from the rural science budget. Various crops were grown and two goats were presented by an appreciative parent. The school P.T.A. purchased a sheep-weighing machine. One year the pupils took part in a field trial to help the Ryeland Flock Book Society. This involved crossing rams loaned by Ryeland breeders with a variety of ewe breeds and crosses, the object being to obtain information on the breed as a fat lamb producer. The progress of the ewes, their rations and injections, any loss of condition, lambing difficulties, weight of lambs at birth and so on was faithfully recorded. In recognition of the help given to them the Ryeland Flock Book Society elected the school to honorary membership in 1984.

The 1980 top award by the National Farmers' Union was to Paul Griffiths, a former Kingstone pupil at the College of Agriculture. Two further awards went to Keith Lawrence and Angus Wiggins. Sun Valley Poultry declared Ian Cheshire 'Apprentice of the Year' and another former pupil, James Apperley, helped to design some of the computer systems on the space shuttle. It is always invidious to single out particular names and I only do so as a tribute to the staff who throughout the years have given unstintingly of their talents to produce such results. There are many others who have achieved much in their adult lives as a result of their time at the school.

Throughout the years sporting activities have increased. Today there is a large playing field with ample space for rugby, soccer and hockey in winter. Summer time activities are catered for with a full-sized athletics track, a cricket square (including an all weather strip), a rounders pitch and four asphalt tennis courts.

The new craft block was added in 1986. There are now four science laboratories, four technology areas, a computer laboratory, two art/pottery rooms, together with a separate modern building for rural studies including a large greenhouse.

School visits are regularly made abroad. The first visits were to Belgium in 1966 and Austria in 1968. Today's pattern involves exchange visits from students and families which does so much to foster a better understanding between ordinary folk in Europe.

When John Reed retired the school had begun its transition from old buildings to new. His successor, Mr. L.E.J. Powell, arrived at a time when, although the number on roll was 670, the rolls were falling and creating the need to re-locate staff. He had to plan for at least twenty-four subjects to be taught to examination standard and to press for greatly increased resources to cope with the introduction of the General Certificate of Secondary Education while trying to get essential repairs carried

The high school today.

out since maintenance at the school had dwindled due to the financial climate. He was very concerned at the lack of space allowed for buses arriving and departing which was becoming dangerous, and repairs to wire netting which had been neglected by the authorities. The school files contain several photographs which show the wire to have been full of jagged holes 'sufficiently large for a man to walk through'. It must have been most frustrating to have to devote time to such problems when G.C.S.E. was of such importance. However, his personality and enthusiasm were such that these problems were eventually resolved and numbers increased rather than decreased. His twelve years at Kingstone left a strong foundation and sense of order in addition to the excellent facilities already mentioned, many of which were obtained through dogged perseverence against budget cuts.

Dr. G. Bedford succeeded Mr. Powell in the autumn of 1989, remaining until July 1993. The faculty system, which enabled subjects to be linked under several specific headings instead of many separate departments, was introduced. 1991 saw the opening by Mr. Tim Eggar, minister of state at the Department of Education and Science, of the new dining/activity area instigated by Mr. Powell. The dining area is built to an innovative design, as is the craft block, and serves as a multi-purpose building being used by the community for receptions, parties and keep-fit classes. The view of the surrounding landscape from its windows must

J.L. Reed, headmaster from 1955 to 1978.

L.E.J. Powell, headmaster from 1978 to 1989, speaking from the lectern dedicated to the memory of J.L. Reed.

be among the finest in the country.

The school badge has been up-dated and was designed by one of its former art teachers, Miss S.C. Elliott. It recalls, by the inclusion of a crown, the village's Saxon origins since Kingstone was in the King's possession before the Norman Conquest. The symbol below the crown is a molinet or stone. The first headmaster, the late Mr. G.L. Hall, gave the school its motto, Achievement through Endeavour, which has served it well as it approaches its first half century of life.

The present headmaster, Mr. M. Bride, recently appointed, has inherited a fine tradition and building with a teaching staff of thirty-four full-time and two part-time teachers. What a transformation it has been! I hope he will enjoy many years of achievement and endeavour as did his predecessors.

21 R.A.F. MADLEY

The R.A.F. Training Establishment was situated partly in Madley and partly in Kingstone adjacent to the ancient Roman way named Stone Street, the parish boundary. Today British Telecom occupies part of the site for its communications centre which deals with telecommunications throughout the world.

The building of the 'drome', as it was known locally, commenced in 1940 shortly after the outbreak of the second World War. The bulk of the work was done by the building contractors Mowlem who brought in as many as thirty-six busloads of workers every day, many of them ex-miners from South Wales. They were on site by 7 o'clock in the morning and worked until 6 o'clock at night, seven days a week. The building was completed within a year. Hard-core was brought by rail to Vowchurch Station, then loaded on to waiting vehicles employed non stop conveying the foundation material to the various sites scattered over a wide area. Local farmers were hired to assist with their tractors and trailers at a rate of 5s 6d an hour.

The establishment was divided into twenty-one separate areas from Batcho Hill on the Peterchurch road across to Great Brampton House on the west, to Meer Court and Arkstone Court on the east, with sites adjacent to Hanley Court, Gooses Foot, Whitehouse Farm, Bridge Court and Turners House to the south of the Hereford road, while the instructional site was spaced on the northern side of the same road from Coldwell to Coldstone Cross and Dews Corner. Behind these buildings, close by the Hartley's jam factory and Webton Court, was the access road to the aerodrome and technical site. A sewage waste disposal works had to be built as well as a huge electric power unit to generate sufficient light for the whole camp since mains electricity was not available in the village at that time. It was said that the power unit was identical to that of the Cunard liner Queen Mary but, be that as it may, it certainly had to generate sufficient power to distribute over a very large area.

The various blocks of buildings comprised barrack huts and nissen huts, together with 1, 2 and 3 Wing Mess sites. In addition there were the Headquarters Mess Site, W.A.A.F. Site, Instructional Site and the Sick Quarters Site. The latter was situated on the corner of Stone Street, fronting on to the Peterchurch road at the foot of Bacho Hill. Many of these sites are remembered today by people who will refer to 'over by 2 Wing', or 'back of 3 Wing' quite casually in their conversation. When looking through some documents recently I noticed they had been witnessed by someone living at No. 12, 6 Site, Kingstone.

The population of Kingstone in the 1931 census was 292. During the war years it rose to around 5000. R.A.F. Madley, planned as a school for wireless operators, was originally known as No. 4 Signals School. It aimed to train 2800 ground and 1200 aircrew wireless operators. When opened prematurely on 27th August 1941 there were insufficient eating and sleeping facilities so the men who were sent to open everything up had to be billeted at R.A.F. Hereford, Credenhill some twelve miles away.

The impact on the village does not seem to have been very great since there were special buses provided to ferry the men into Hereford for their off-duty hours. The headquarters mess site at Gooses Foot was equipped with a cinema, squash court, gymnasium with a church annexe, a grocery and local produce store, tailor, shoemaker and barber's shops and a N.A.A.F.I. canteen. There was a demand for good laundering services, however, and several women in the village carried out this work. Mrs. Eveline Powell remembers that in the early days there were many Free French trainees and their shirt collars were very difficult to cope with. The collars were much stiffer and higher than on normal shirts and ironing them was not easy. Her mother used to wash for six airmen and found the best solution was to mix a very thick starch for the collar, place it round a pudding basin, and dry it off in the oven. One of the young men she looked after was killed in a flying accident on the Brecon Beacons. His death caused much grief in the village as he was a more familiar figure than most. Sometimes the men brought socks for darning along with their laundry.

The medical staff from station sick quarters, in addition to their normal duties, were called upon to attend aircraft crashes and to deal with casualties which occurred from time to time due to the proximity of the Welsh mountains. Training in mountain craft became part of their everyday life and, by 1943, a properly equipped mountain rescue party was set up which was competent to deal with such eventualities. There were two crashes in 1944, one of a U.S. Navy Liberator in August, and a Wellington in November, both of which proved fatal. One of the medical staff was a young R.A.F. doctor, Douglas Chandler, who at the end of the war remained in Kingstone as partner to Dr. Oliver Cotton and is still resident in the village. He recalls that the hospital site was very well equipped with two wards of fifty beds each plus two isolation wards, an operating theatre, dispensary, an ambulance depot and kitchen facilities.

The airfield was grass-covered until October 1943 when it was reinforced with Sommerfield Tracking, the work being carried out by an R.A.F. Airfield Construction Flight. The hangarage consisted of three rare, pre-war Hinaidi types, dated around 1927, and two Callender-Hamiltons, later joined by thirteen Blisters. This information is definitely for those who understand such things. I am indebted to David J. Smith, who details these facts in his book,[1] and to the R.A.F. who kindly pointed me in the right direction. The Hinaidi hangars are still in use today on the area used as an industrial site.

The planes provided for training were sixty Proctor IV's and eighteen Dominies with a small number of Lysanders used to train local army personnel and, at different times, a Tomahawk, Hurricanes and Mustangs were attached for short periods. Mr. Ernest Griffiths, who lived with his parents at Huff Cap Cottages on the perimeter of the airfield, remembers that the wing of a Halifax training plane protruded over their garden hedge. He has pleasant memories of men and women stationed there sitting round the fire chatting with his mother. One day, to show their appreciation, they made her a gift of a wireless set which they had made.

It was not until after the war ended that local people heard that Rudolph Hess, Hitler's deputy, had been imprisoned locally since 1941 after landing in Scotland. The fact that he was transported from Madley in a Dominie to face his prosecutors at the 1946 war trials in Nuremburg, however, was front page local news.

When the radio school was disbanded after the war the huts were left. They were scattered over a vast area. Some of those on farm land were soon dismantled as land was reclaimed but many others remained, some still furnished. These were soon taken over by the homeless and by returning servicemen whose homes had been destroyed by air raids, or who had married during the war and had no place of their own. The huts were to remain until the late 1950s when they were replaced with council housing. The main area of the drome reverted to its original use of farming and market gardening until the 1980s when the Post Office Earth Satellite Station arrived. Parts of the land today are in use for the training of HGV (heavy goods vehicle) drivers, by a firm engaged in recycling of plastic products and as a permanent council site for travellers.

Apart from the old hangars and the memories of the older parishioners, there is little to remind one of its original use but many young people were trained there in the vital work of radio transmission and navigation. Sadly, there must have been many who departed with postings to different sectors of the conflict from which they never returned.

REFERENCES

[1] *Action Stations*. Vol. 3. David J. Smith. Patrick Stephens Ltd.

22 MADLEY COMMUNICATIONS CENTRE

The Madley Communications Centre is now an accepted and welcome part of the villages of Madley and Kingstone, straddling the old Roman road of Stone Street. A great deal of its acreage was part of Street House Farm which was within the parish boundary of Madley, while its administrative buildings and some dish aerials are built on the medieval area of Coldstone Common in Kingstone.

It was in 1973 that the possibility of the Post Office (as it was then) siting its Communications Centre in the area became known. Many viewed it with some misgivings, mainly due to lack of information and the fear that the landscape would be impaired. A public meeting was held at Madley Parish Hall on 4th December 1973 at which the facts were well presented and from then on the project gained momentum. We learned that the site was chosen because of its perfect geographical location. It is largely protected from high winds, an obvious priority since it could affect the operation of the dishes. Also, it is an area free from industrial and electrical interference which would guarantee quality transmission. The location ensured that satellites covering the Atlantic and Indian Ocean regions, taking in Europe, North America, India, Africa and the Middle East, could be seen. The final factor, which was vital, was the quality of the sub-soil which had to support the first 300 tonne dish. This was nearly twenty years ago. Today's building materials are very different. A modern dish weighs in the region of two tonnes. The only other communications centre is at Goonhilly Downs in Cornwall. This was opened in 1962 and the original dishes there weighed around 1000 tonnes.

By September 1975 planning permission had been granted. Eric and I, as Kingstone parish councillors, well remember many meetings at which different aspects of the building programme had to be discussed. In the early days concern was expressed at the design of the radio relay tower. Permission had to be given for a small stream running across the site to be diverted slightly so that it could be dammed to provide a pond for fire fighting purposes, while the colour schemes for the dishes also had to be considered. A suggestion for the latter was bright blue which had originated from seeing empty plastic sacks of a similar colour used by the farming community on land adjacent. I also recall some years ago, when there were proposals to erect street lighting on the Coldstone Cross estate, the comment was made that 'they get enough light from the satellite already' which was quite true.

Planning permission was given for six more aerials in 1983 and today there are eleven dishes with more planned. The members of local parish councils were all invited to a special visitors' day in June 1987 and

Aerials at Madley Communications Centre. *BT Corporate Pictures; a BT photograph*

it would be fair to say that it was a most enjoyable experience but one that left us with the realization of how little most of us know and understand about the world of science and technology.

I am not qualified to write in depth about the centre but its work, which was originally to transmit and receive international phone calls, has widened to embrace Fax messages and television programmes. The orbit of the first communication satellites launched more than twenty-five years ago was so low that they would skim across the sky from horizon to horizon in less than twenty-two minutes when contact was lost for an hour and a half. This is why one had to book international calls in advance. Today's technology ensures that the satellites are in orbit above the earth at such a height that they can be accessed twenty-four hours a day. This enables us to dial our international calls and to be connected within a few seconds. How often when we do this do we make the comment 'I can hear you as clearly as if you were in the room'? This remarkable achievement of top quality transmission is due to the dishes at Madley and Goonhilly being automatically re-aligned to follow any slight movement which the earth's gravity exerts on them.

We all have some knowledge of the fact that flights can be changed if one misses the slot into which they are due to take off or land. The B.T. centre, by adopting specialised computing technology and by entering into partnership with several other satellite earth stations around the world, has adopted a similar procedure with its international phone calls. Their research discovered that people only speak to each other for 40% of their time on the phone, the remaining 60% being taken up with listening and natural pauses. Science took over and developed a computer which searches for the pauses and fills the gaps with up to four other conversations on the same circuit. This has led to reduced international phone call costs.

The television transmissions that pass through Madley travel on satellite circuits leased by different broadcasting organisations. BBC programmes are sent all over the world. Those for the Far East are sent to Hong Kong and distributed from there. Likewise, programmes for other areas of the globe are sent to a link country which passes them on.

News coverage is another vital part of the centre's transmissions. Cable News Network leases a permanent circuit from B.T. Their news goes uncut via Madley to its studios in London where it is processed and returned to Madley who then send it on to America to be broadcast around the world. Other bookings are made on an occasional basis if there is airtime available. These might be taken up by broadcasters getting crisis news through or sporting events such as Wimbledon and the Olympics.

The centre employs local labour, indeed B.T. ranks as the fourth highest employer in Herefordshire. Madley has its own caterers, cleaners and a highly trained work force which, in addition to secretarial staff, has to control computers, ingoing and outgoing television material, maintain and overhaul dishes, control air and water cooling systems and maintain generating systems in the event of any interruption to the main electricity supply. Many of these folk have moved to Herefordshire from different parts of the country and those I was privileged to speak to have settled very happily into the area. One of them commented that he is always glad when his obligatory visits to London are over and he is on his way 'home'.

There are links with the two villages and the surrounding area which have resulted in playgroups and schools visiting the centre and grants are regularly given to secondary schools both locally and in other parts of Herefordshire. A donation of £500 was given to Kingstone Sports Association in 1985 when it purchased the old R.A.F. 7 Site playing field. Kingstone High School has excellent science facilities and at speech day in 1979 Mr. Ken Owen, a past manager of the Earth Station, presented the school with a handsome trophy in the form of a dish aerial which is now known as the Madley Science Trophy. This is awarded annually for achievement in science. Mr. Owen told his audience:

'Few people realise that Britain really is a world leader in international telecommunications. The possibilities are endless, and the Post Office will need scientists and engineers of a high calibre. Some might even go into space to carry out maintenance on satellites. Some of you might be among them'.

The Madley Science Trophy presented by BT to Kingstone High School.

The dishes are now an accepted part of the Madley-Kingstone scene. By day they merge happily with housing, field and hedgerow and by night, well, they become something quite different. Silhouetted against a frosty night sky, glowing with light, they become an impressive sculpture and a memorial to the technological age in which we live. The old straight course marched by the Roman soldiers from Kenchester to Abergavenny, the Stone Street, which takes one to the entrance of the communications centre, is a memorial to the age of communication by the process of civil engineering. Both are timely reminders that change is inevitable and ongoing.

23 HEALTH CARE

The village has for many years been fortunate in having caring doctors and staff living in its confines. Today it has the best possible provision since it has a conveniently placed surgery and dispensary, together with an excellent range of community care facilities which can be reached through the administrative side of the practice, hospital provision being within easy reach in Hereford city. The practice has about 4000 patients, two full-time partners with two part-time assistants, a part-time practice nurse and six staff. There is a happy co-operation with the community who on several occasions in recent years have, through donations and fund raising, enabled the purchase of equipment not otherwise available. Such aquisitions have allowed treatment of patients in the home rather than their having to undergo wearying visits to hospital, especially the elderly or terminally ill.

The first doctor I have found in Kingstone is recorded in an 1867 trade directory. He was Dr. John Brunton, described as a surgeon and medical officer to the Dore Union. He would have attended at the Abbeydore Workhouse when required. Unfortunately, no address is given but the 1876 Hereford trade directory lists David Evans, L.R.C.P., M.R.C.S. as residing at Kingstone Villa. He died in 1897 and is buried at Kingstone together with his wife who died a year earlier. He was 53 and she only 37 years of age. The name of their daughter, Ethel Ruby Evans, also appears on the stone. She died in 1916 aged 34.

Dr. John Kingdon Frost was most likely practising in the village before Dr. Evans died. His little three-year-old son was buried at Kingstone a few months before David Evans died. Dr. Frost lived at Green Court. He appears to have had a partner, Dr. Frederick Edward Bissell. Both are listed in a trade directory of 1902.

Then follows Dr. William Revely Forster about whom many a tale is told by older Kingstone folk. He was an extrovert, a humorous and respected character. Resident at Kingstone Villa, he traversed the parish on horseback and also owned a trap. Village boys were often seen holding his horse when he was on a call or grooming and cleaning both horse and trap in the old barn which was adjacent to the villa, now demolished. He was fond of a drink, particularly gin (people smiled very broadly at me when I mentioned this), and on occasion was wont to tell a patient, 'there's not much wrong with you, that a little whisky won't cure' and would wave them off with a coin to purchase same. Another incident which makes one's hair stand on end was when a patient who had put his arm out of joint was tended by Dr. Forster, quite effectively I am told, but presumably there was no suggestion of anaesthetic. The job was completed with two men sitting on top of the patient! Since he was a naval surgeon who had seen service in the China Seas, this was probably commonplace to him. It was also said that if one needed minor surgery, it was a wise precaution to visit the Bull Ring first!

Dr. Forster would turn out in all weathers to deal with a sick child and could be seen trudging up the Cockyard road with a hurricane lamp in the middle of the night to deliver a baby. This would often involve cutting through the woods to Kilpeck and returning home on foot in the early hours of the morning. He was known to have woken up Tom Morris at the Masons Arms at 3 or 4a.m., on his way home, to ask for a nip of whisky. No doubt he was in need of something to keep warm. There are still a few alive today who remember him with respect and affection. He died in 1931 aged 74 and is buried at Kingstone. His wife Alice and younger daughter Jessie outlived him some twenty years and are buried with him.

From the end of the 1800s to the 1930s it is possible through school log books and medical inspections to gain some idea of the illnesses which affected children. These have been mentioned in the chapter dealing with the primary school. By 1919 the school medical service had been set up and routine inspections began to make a noticeable difference to the old problems. Clinics were treating children suffering from minor ailments but tuberculosis was one of the scourges which attacked all ages. There was an instance in 1936 when the school had to be closed for two weeks due to an outbreak of conjunctivitis (pink eye). Prior to this Mr. Edwards, the headmaster, had been told by the medical officer whom he called in to examine the children to administer a boracic eye wash to each child twice a day.

In the early 1900s the services of a district nurse were available due to the generosity of Mr. and Mrs. Bates, tenants of Whitfield. Her name was Nurse Akers and, in 1902, she was resident locally. Mrs. Ruby Meats remembers a Nurse Meadows who was a midwife living in part of Rose Villa or the Tin House (her grand-daughter taught in the old school). She also told me that people could contribute monthly to the Cresswell Penny Fund which entitled them to care in Hereford's General Hospital. Miss Ockey from Thruxton was the secretary and the collector was an E.M. Davies. In 1911 there were nineteen people paying contributions; some paid for the whole year one shilling, some for six months, and some every three months. In 1911 the parish magazine makes mention of the Rev. H. Knight purchasing a wheel chair which could be obtained from him for use in the parish on application. Prior to 1939 there was a district nurse/midwife who served the Kingstone, Madley and Clehonger area and was employed by the county council.

In 1931 Dr. O.J. Cotton moved into the village and was to practise there for thirty-two years until his tragic death in the bitter winter snow and ice of 1963. For the first few years he lived at Caradoc close to the church, using the dining room as a waiting room. In 1937 he moved to Mill Orchard, custom-built and incorporating a surgery, waiting room, consulting room and a dispensary which accommodated an examination couch and a filing system. From those very early days he associated himself with many aspects of village life, taking a keen interest in the church, the school and the parish council.

There are memorials to both Dr. Forster and Dr. Cotton in the parish church, subscribed to by their patients. Dr. Forster's reads:

> 'In grateful memory of the life and works of W. Revely Forster, M.B. - C.M. of Kingtone Villa who for 21 years laboured in this neighbourhood. A true philanthropist and friend of the poor. This tablet was erected by his patients and friends. A.D.1933.'

Dr. Cotton's memorial states:

> 'Remembering with love and admiration Oliver John Goode Cotton, M.A. M.B., B.CHIR. doctor and friend to many in South West Herefordshire, 1931-1963'.

Before the coming of the National Health Service in 1948, patients were required to pay for medical treatment. This was within the means of those who had work and were well paid and these became known as 'panel' patients. For the lower paid or unemployed the possibility of illness was something to be dreaded since they were often unable to pay. To help these families Dr. Cotton devised a scheme by which they paid regular amounts to the doctor, which then paid for any treatment required by them. There was a scale of charges, and for a family with three or more children 3s per month was collected.

By 1941 R.A.F. Madley was developing fast and some of the personnel were bringing their families to live in the village. Since the station medical officers were responsible only for R.A.F. personnel, Dr. Cotton became responsible for the N.A.A.F.I. (canteen) staff and the Womens' Land Army stationed at Blakemere. He was also the police doctor and was sometimes required to conduct post mortem examinations. It was becoming increasingly difficult to manage without qualified assistance so he engaged Miss Muriel Ballard as his dispenser/secretary/receptionist. She had qualified in dispensing in 1935 and worked in Bristol and Kent before coming to Herefordshire. She worked devotedly at Kingstone, in the early days dispensing, collecting monies, and dealing with all the administrative problems while, in later years, her knowledge was to be invaluable in phasing in all the different changes that came about in the health service. When she retired in 1976 a presentation was made to her at the village hall in recognition of her thirty-five years service. She can remember, in the days before the introduction of antibiotics, that many illnesses, particularly infections of the ear, nose and throat could only be treated palliatively as was the case with chest and wound infections.

Like his predecessor, Dr. Forster, it was quite typical for Dr. Cotton to stay up all night with a pneumonia patient to see him or her through the crisis. The hurricane lamp was still in use in isolated areas. On one occasion Miss Ballard had to take to Moccas an item that Dr. Cotton needed and was told to look for a lamp hanging on a gate which was where she was to stop.

The population of the village rose dramatically during the war years and Dr. D.A. Chandler, who had been a medical officer at the R.A.F. camp and had been assisting Dr.Cotton by doing locum duties for him, was invited to become a partner in the practice after his 'demob'. He and Mrs. Chandler came to live at Bryn Tirion where they still reside in retirement. Kingstone has been fortunate to have had doctors who were, dare I say it, good old fashioned GPs who always had time to listen. Mrs Chandler was a qualified nursing sister and able to assist in many ways in what was becoming a much larger and busier practice. They have always been fully involved in all aspects of village life.

A big step forward was the starting of an infant welfare clinic in 1948 at Mill Orchard surgery. It was later moved to one of the old R.A.F. huts, long since gone, adjacent to Huff Cap Cottages. The area is now part of the new high school playing field. Dr. and Mrs. Chandler were prime movers in this scheme. I remember taking my young son there regularly to receive orange juice and cod liver oil and to be weighed, etc. We used to have a rota for making teas and fund-raising activites were undertaken in order to purchase small items of play equipment for toddlers waiting to be examined. It was a happy place and, although it was only a hut, it was clean, bright and cheerful. Many of the young mothers attending were living in difficult conditions in the huts. The children of those days were nowhere near so well dressed and healthy looking as they are today. When the new building programme commenced at the high school the hut housing the infant welfare clinic was demolished. The village hall was being renovated at this time and the clinic moved there on a temporary basis which lasted several years. It now meets in the surgery.

The infant welfare clinic played a very important role in helping newcomers to the village to gradually become assimilated into a life which was very different from what many of them had been used to. One can understand that there were occasions when the locals must have wondered how life was going to be with such an influx of population. Clashes of varying temperaments could have caused problems but the common bond of the children and their welfare touched everyone's lives. The welding together proceeded through educational and social activities and, no doubt, will continue equally amicably in the years to come when the newcomers who are now the locals will absorb still more changes.

Dr. Chandler recalls that it took him some time to find his way around the narrow roads and winding lanes of the sizeable rural practice some fifty years ago. Miss Ballard was required to navigate. It was not uncommon to have to move stock off the lanes and on one urgent late night call he had to deal with a bull which showed little inclination to move. The primitive, crowded housing contributed to a widespread epidemic of measles in 1950 when Dr. Chandler and Dr. Cotton worked round the clock for weeks in an effort to contain it. Sadly, it was not uncommon to visit a child in the morning only to return at night to find it had died. Tuberculosis was rife and polio was still a potential killer. The increasing use of protective injections at an early age has been one of the great medical landmarks of the second half of this century.

The need for larger surgery accommodation was the next thing to be dealt with and a specially designed surgery was built in the grounds of Bryn Tirion, with Miss Ballard residing in her own rooms in the new surgery until eventually moving to Clehonger.

The present practice consists of Dr. R.S. Terry who arrived in 1963, his partner Dr. J.D. Sleath who joined him in 1991, with Dr. B.H. Smallwood and Dr. E. Donovan as practice assistants. Dr. Sleath now occupies Kingstone Villa which was the old home of Dr. Forster. At one time it was known as the Malt House. Although I am no longer resident in Kingstone, the parish magazine contains abundant evidence that the present partners keep up the tradition of parish involvement, which seems admirable when one realises the pressures put on the medical profession today. I well remember when I was a member of the parish council that it was always Dr. Terry who undertook to mend swings or to fit new ones on the Coldstone Cross play equipment.

Prior to the coming of the Health Service, drugs had to be ordered and paid for out of a small capitation fee for panel patients or from the monthly payments already mentioned. When sulphonamides and penicillin were introduced these were claimable from the government, as were some injections. Then in 1948 everything changed, as we all know, and with it came the need for meticulous administration to cope with form-filling. As the years have gone by different allowances have been given to pay for ancillary staff and other items. Paper work increased greatly and the computer age arrived. The use of computers has now become very much a matter of routine. So, in the ever increasing pace of medical and technological change, the patients of the Kingstone practice can rest easy in the knowledge that their surgery is keeping up with current trends and they have their GPs living in their midst.

24 HOUSING AND LOCAL INDUSTRY

The population of Kingstone in the 1931 census was 292. By 1951 it had risen to 1161, when the village was listed by the county planning office as a key village, capable of expansion because of its facilities and geographical location. There has been no change in parish boundaries or place names, although new road names have been added, but the community has changed from a rural agrarian base to an amalgam of agrarian-industrial-commuter base.

The old Dore and Bredwardine Council built two estates, Green Lane in 1954 consisting of forty-four houses, followed in 1956 by eighty-eight houses at Coldstone Cross. A further fourteen houses and six bungalows were erected at Highland View, near Coldstone Cross, in 1961 and ten houses and four bungalows at St. Michael's Close were completed in 1973, with a terrace of three more houses on land once occupied by the village hall. In addition a number of private houses were built including small developments at Orchard Close, Barrow Common, Yew Tree Close and Coldwell Road, followed in 1973 by a large development of fifty houses adjacent to Whitehouse Farm, from whence the name Whitehouse Drive was taken.

The most recent developments have been ten houses on a small estate named the Denes, and the Mitch Place complex of smaller homes for older residents, aptly named from the tithe map, plus several detached homes 'in filling' in various parts of the village. There is the prospect of fifty new dwellings to be built on Mill Field in the near future. It has become commonplace to see many of these attractive properties without chimneys since central heating, in some cases of the ducted electric variety, is now the norm, while the coal fire is a rarity. While admitting the convenience factor, it is surprising how many people on entering a room with a 'proper' fire make the comment 'what a lovely fire, I wish we had one' or 'I wish we hadn't done away with ours'.

The village has two main industrial estates, Gooses Foot and the Dene Industrial site adjacent to Webton Court part of which is the old Hartleys site. The first factory to be built at Gooses Foot was under the joint ownership of Mr. B. Burns, Mr. and Mrs. C.J.L. Hunt and Mr. G. Farndon and was known as Claude Hunt Ltd. Later taken over by the Dickinson Robinson Group and known as Wye Plastics, it has now been bought by Mr. John James who also owns the adjoining unit of James and Williams. Golden Valley Plastics, as it has been aptly re-named, specialises in injection moulding and metallising mainly for the motor trade. James and Williams specialise in funeral furnishings, patenting many of their own designs, and have built up a thriving export business. Mr. and Mrs.

Industrial units at Gooses Foot on the site of the R.A.F. cinema and gymnasium.

Whitehouse estate in the 1970s.

James live in the village adjacent to their first business, started in 1970, which deals with plating on plastics, metals and glass. Their businesses employ twenty local people.

At Gooses Foot English Estates have built small factory units which are occupied by businesses of a diverse nature. The largest company, Flavex, now owns the four-acre site. It is engaged in the manufacture of ingredients and products for the pharmaceutical industry including cosmetics, homoeopathic medicines and toiletries based on botanical extracts. In addition, they manufacture flavourings, extracts and colourings for the food and drinks industries. Flavex employs approximately thirty people.

The smaller businesses are DeW Systems, Instrumentation and Control Services and Aconbury Sprouts. DeW Systems specialise in the production of ultrasonic and magnetic particle inspection equipment which is capable of detecting defects in iron and steel components and which would normally require rigid and tedious physical inspection, and in the testing of pistons. Over three-quarters of their output is for the export market.

Instrumentation and Control Services manufacture prepared kits of wires, sleeves and cables for the electrical industry. Agricultural milking parlour equipment and timer kits also form part of their output.

Aconbury Sprouts produce a range of seeds and pulses which are marketed by retail and through wholesalers. These are for use in sandwiches, salads and cooked dishes and, since they are low in calories, and rich in protein, vitamins and fibre, are in popular demand. These smaller units provide work for another twenty people.

The Dene Industrial site comprises five units at the present time, all occupied by small companies who have found a niche in today's competitive market. HPD Joinery was set up three years ago by Dave Rowberry who decided to take the plunge and start his own business. The making and supplying of staircases, conservatories, etc. for new housing keeps him and two employees busy and he too has found an export market.

System Enclosures employs seven people to make control panels and rack mounting systems for the electronics industry, together with plastic moulding of items like rawlplugs. Also on site are Saffron Selection who deal in fancy goods, brassware, flower containers, etc. and an Auto Service which deals specifically with Morris Minor repairs.

The old Hartley's site at Webton is now occupied by a small car and body repair yard and two haulage businesses; that of Brian Phillips, who also does lorry repairs, and the family business of W.H. Andrews who has two sons to drive these huge vehicles all over the country.

There remains at Webton the business of Seating Contracts who store many thousands of seats in preparation for transporting, erecting and dis-mantling at major events in this country. They have provided 16,000 seats for the British Open Golf Championship, the Benson and Hedges Snooker Event, R.A.F Air Shows, open air concerts and V.I.P. visits.

Close to Whitehouse Farm is another small factory, also started by Mr. and Mrs. Claude Hunt, originally dealing with vacuum metallising and named Cyclops. This now houses the pine furniture making business of Goldcrest Furniture.

A unit of Sun Valley Poultry Farms is situated on the road to Gooses Foot. The huge poultry houses are set out on a nicely landscaped plot with two well-built, modern bungalows available in the grounds for employees. This is a highly intensive venture and only two regular staff are employed.

Another employer in the village is the County Council Education Committee who employ caretakers, groundsmen, cleaners and catering staff for both schools. There are about twenty-five people, some part-time, working on the campus, in many cases the same families having handed on their jobs to younger members over the years. They form a very close-knit group and have a special rapport with staff and children which makes for a caring and happy environment.

Visiting the industrial sites proved to me the great flexibility there is among people who have to work and plan efficiently to create businesses that will give employment to others as well as themselves. The number of skills that have been mustered is amazing. It seems to me that Kingstone has unobtrusively managed to merge its agricultural past into an ever widening and demanding technological age very successfully indeed.

Coldstone Cross estate in the 1970s.

Early sixteenth century Rose Cottage, the almshouses and the new Mitch Place development beyond.

25 PARISH LIFE THROUGH THE AGES

For many centuries past, right up to the present day, churchwardens have attended an annual meeting to present completed forms relating to the maintenance of the church buildings and valuables. A great many of these visitations, as they are known, have survived the centuries and form a valuable part of the archives of the cathedral library in Hereford. One of the earliest relating to Kingstone is dated 1397. It is a very long entry and, whereas many parishes complained of broken windows, of vicars selling churchyard trees for their own profit, winnowing corn in the belfry and keeping sheep in the churchyard, what appeared to worry Kingstone folk was the loose living of its inhabitants. Couple after couple were named for misdeeds and it was suggested that marriages were taking place between people too closely related and contrary to the church code. This points to the fact that communities were very closed, people did not travel far, and maybe the clergy who officiated at such marriages were not sufficiently local to know very much about their parishioners. Such matters show the darker side of village life.

There was a lighter side, at least to the researcher if not to those involved at the time. When the heir to an estate was of age to inherit, it was necessary to have proof of his entitlement and, since most folk were illiterate, it was necessary to rely on memory. Local people would attend the sheriff's court to quote their recollections as evidence. The following extracts from such proceedings make one wonder how much was true, how much was loyalty to the young squire and, dare one suggest it, how much was it worth? The date of this inquisition, as it was called, was 1375 in the reign of Edward III and the young man hoping to gain his inheritance was Thomas Dansey.[1] The sheriff was informed that:

'Thomas is 21 years of age and more, having been born at Kyngeston on the eve of St. Laurence, 27 Edward III (1354) and baptized the next day by William Muleward, chaplain in the parish church there.

William Hobyes remembers because he was in the church and saw the baptism, and on his way home a horse struck him on the leg and broke it.

William Gorewy says that he went after a chaplain to baptize the said Thomas, and the chaplain hit him on the head with a stick so that he was ill for a long time afterwards.

Walter Hayward says that he carried water to the church for baptism, and in taking it from a well he fell in, and so remembers'.

Among the other recollections were births, a marriage and deaths, not to mention a sudden fire which burned up a whole house. That day the village must have been in chaos which may explain why the chaplain was not in the best of tempers. It would seem he had been on permanent call. While it is not unknown for most of us to remember a particular happening by something quite amusing or inconsequential, one cannot help wondering at the number of remarkable events and occurrences that day.

Thomas Dansey did inherit his estate which was that of Webton Court. The Danseys were in possession for almost another 400 years, marrying into the Morgan family of Arkstone and the Parry family of Bacton.

The parochial life of Kingstone rumbled on with the occasional excitement of weddings, the prospect of doles being handed out to the poor at the church door after the funeral of worthies who wished to be remembered after their passing, together with the quarterly mass or communion collection which was also given to the poor, and the celebrating of the special holy days. These church festivals must have enlivened the monotonous routine of rising at dawn and retiring early to bed when the fire died down. The need to save valuable candle wax was as important as the risk of fire to homes of wattle and daub and, more often, plain stick and thatch.

Holy days could be likened to a calendar which marked the passing of the year, since very few could read. The distribution and blessing of ashes on Ash Wednesday, the lighting of candles for Candlemas, the veil on the altar at Lent, the distribution of palm branches prior to the sorrow and joy of Easter were followed by the blessing of fields at Rogationtide, probably coupled with a perambulation of the parish so that the young were brought up to know the boundaries (beating the bounds was another way of expressing it). Then came the blessing of the loaf at Lammastide, the first fruit of the harvest, and the warmth of the Christmas festivities signifying the passing of the old year with the promise of spring in addition to the birth of Christ. These were all red-letter days both in the prayer book and in the life of the village.

When there were special duties to be undertaken for the lord of the manor and for the whole community, the time limit given was always a saint's day or festival day and the notices were given out in church. Even the illiterate would be familiar with the holy days of the church calendar.

As far back as 1532 it was the churchwardens' or overseers' duty to pay for the killing of vermin. Anyone bringing live or dead hedgehogs, foxes, moles, wild cats, crows, rooks or choughs, magpies, jays, young owls and unbroken eggs was entitled to payment from the parish rate since these creatures were considered to cause damage to crops and live-stock. Wild-cats were commonplace in the area during the 1700s. The following entries from the accounts are typical:

Killing a fox 1/-
Paid a man with 3 live foxes 2/-, catching sparrows 6/7½.
Paid a man for killing a wild catt in Morehampton Park 6d.
Paid a man for diging an old bitch fox and four young
ones and a wild catt 2/-

How one would have liked to travel beside the many clergy who wended their way round the parish. Certain it is that in those early days they travelled on foot, later on horseback, still later by horse and trap until the coming of the bicycle and motor car. Two men were in charge of the parishes of Kingstone and Thruxton for over sixty years. They were Christopher and Zacharias Whiting, father and son, residents of Thruxton who died in 1709 and 1742 respectively.[2] Christopher Whiting's will, written in his own hand, indicates that he was an educated man and very concerned that his worldly goods should go to his wife, while provision was made for his children and grandchildren by way of monetary bequests. Zacharias Whiting was rector of Thruxton and vicar of Kingstone from 1709 to 1741.

After the Whitings came the ministry, from 1742 to 1796, of the Rev. Richard Vaughan and his son Thomas. The latter took over for five years from 1787 to 1792. They left no wills but there are memorials in Thruxton church to the family. The Hereford Journal of 1st February 1776 mentions that a James Edwards of Thruxton was sent to gaol for stealing corn from the granary of the Rev. Richard Vaughan and, in a book of excursions in Hereford by J.P. Malcolm published in the early 1800s, there is mention of the writer visiting Thruxton and Kingstone to meet the Rev. Thomas Vaughan, his brother-in-law.[3]

His comments give just a glimpse of life at that time. 'We walked to Kingston the day after my arrival; and in the short distance of two miles everything inviting in rural life arrested my attention, and excited admiration.' Possibly he was a town dweller, since he refers to Kingstone as an 'inconsiderable village'. Malcolm tells how Vaughan went to the belfry of the church and rang the tenor bell with such fervour 'as served to discompose the silence of the hamlet, and introduce a number of enquirers to the churchyard; who eagerly demanded why the summons was issued'.

Another interesting observation refers to 'the purity of the atmosphere,which forced itself upon my notice at every breath I inhaled; but the following fact establishes, beyond dispute, the superior advantages enjoyed at Kingston. There are FIFTY gravestones in the whole circuit of the cemetery; twenty two of those record ages upwards of seventy. The remainder, 28 in number, are not remarkable for premature deaths'. When the churchyard memorials were recorded in 1988 by the Hereford Family History Society, the total number of graves was 345, not including those memorials in the church. As the years have gone by so has it been possible for more families to afford memorials, apart from the fact that the village population has greatly increased.

After the visit to Kingstone they walked to Dore Abbey. The Cockyard road is described thus:

> 'The valleys were filled with perfumes, and the grass contended with the wild flower in rapidity of growth; the forest trees extending their branches, formed canopies of new leaves, bright from the hands of Spring; the hedges closed again over the narrow road, and shaded its steep banks'.

The extremes of misery and poverty that existed did not escape Malcolm who described them thus:

> 'But the foreground of the picture is the labour of misery, and the fruit of the industry of the wretched peasant. "What are these huts", I exclaimed, "on each side of the road? Can it be possible that those cases of wood which emit smoke are chimneys? What must be the fire that moulders in them, and consumes them not?" '

He found the makeshift homes were constructed with fragments of branches stripped from thickets, inverwoven something in the manner of baskets and imperfectly filled or coated with clay which fell into dust when dried by the sun and shaken by the wind. Through the cracks could be seen broken stools, rough tables and straw mattresses. The crude dwellings were built on the waste bordering the road, sometimes grazed by a cottager's sheep or cow. In a small area at either extremity of the huts vegetables were planted. The occupants were able to live rent and tax free since it was public ground, but Vaughan says that he had known a plough team driven against the huts to pull them down when the occupants could not pay forty shillings per annum.

The Hearth Tax Assessments for 1664 show that Kingstone had forty-nine dwellings, of which twenty-six were exempted from paying due to poverty, while of the remainder fifteen had only one hearth, two had four hearths, three had three hearths and one had seven hearths. The latter must have been Arkstone, preceeded by Dunswater, Kingstone Grange, Hanley Court, Whitehouse and possibly Marsh Farm.[4]

The name Cockyard may have originated from the fact that the sport of cocking was carried out in the vicinity, but there is mention of 'Cotghete' or 'Coeghere' as far back as 1239.[5] There are suggestions that the cockpit was behind the Cockyard Farm, while an advertisement of 1793 in the Hereford Journal proclaimed that 'On Whit Monday a Main of Cocks will be fought at the Bull Ring in Kingstone, and on the following Tuesday will be fought at the Red Lion in Madley'. This was a source of entertainment for those who were able to find the cost of a mug of ale which, no doubt, enabled them to watch the proceedings.

From 1804 to 1857 Henry Wetherell was rector of Thruxton and vicar of Kingstone. Towards the end of his life his health was such that he was frequently granted permission to be absent from the parish for long periods, while providing curates to take services and maintaining the glebe houses at Thruxton. Mrs. Wetherell was the sister of the Rev. Archer Clive whose family had bought the Whitfield estate. Archer Clive and his wife spent much time at Whitfield although his living was in Solihull. Henry Wetherell later became Archdeacon of Hereford and was a generous benefactor to the village church and to the school. Judging from the diaries and family papers of Mrs. Archer Clive, he was a kindly man whereas Mrs. Wetherell was a difficult lady to get on with. She could be

Whitfield, Allensmore.

very sharp of tongue and was possibly jealous of her brother. The stained-glass east window behind the altar in Kingstone Church was placed there through her bequest in memory of her husband. A small orchard running alongside the Whitfield to Thruxton road near the Grithill is still known today as Wetherell's Orchard.

Copies of the *Kingstone and Thruxton Almanack*, started by the Rev. Reginald Bird (1885-1907), still survive and are very helpful in providing evidence of parish activities. By 1886 the population was 437 and there were 105 houses in the parish. A Clothing Club and Boot Club were run and the collection from the holy communion service held on the second Sunday of the month was shared amongst church, parish and clothing club expenses. Interest of twopence in the shilling on savings up to 15s was added at the end of the year. Mrs. Bird played the organ at Thruxton Church and a silver paten was presented by the parishioners after her death in 1907.

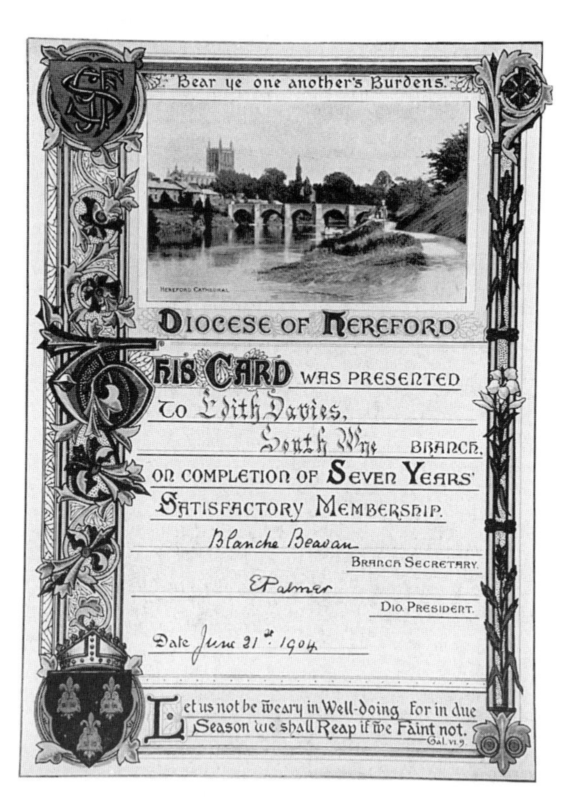

"Bear ye one another's Burdens."

Hereford Cathedral

Diocese of Hereford

This Card was presented
To Edith Davies,
South Wye Branch,
on completion of Seven Years'
Satisfactory Membership.

Blanche Beavan
Branch Secretary.

E Palmer
Dio. President.

Date June 21st 1904

Let us not be weary in Well-doing for in due Season we shall Reap if we Faint not.
Gal. vi. 9.

Girls' Friendly Society card measuring 9 x 12ins and printed in blue, red and gold. Edith Davies later became Mrs. Tom Morris.

The old school was the place where dances, concerts, teas and lectures were held. The classes consisted of bee-keeping, wood carving, gardening, carpentry, veterinary science, poultry keeping and cider making. Mothers' Meetings were held at Bridge Court and a course of cookery

Ted Colcombe with the Rifle Club shield.

Thruxton church.

classes was commenced in 1891 under the management of Mrs. Grethead, the Rev. Archer Clive's daughter. She was a widow and, in addition to five children of her own, looked after the five children of her widowed brother, Mr. C.M.B. Clive, at Whitfield. For many years up to 1895 she organised outings and teas for the children of Kingstone, Thruxton and the Whitfield estate. A favourite game at parties was the Snapdragon. On consulting a book of Victorian customs I discovered that a fiery spirit such as brandy was poured into a bowl followed by the throwing in of sultanas. The liquid was set alight whilst everyone would try to retrieve the fruit before it snapped and, presumably, before they got burnt! It sounds a risky business. The church magazine mentions that the materials had been donated.

Theatricals and a fête were held at Whitfield in aid of the big church restoration of 1890 and Queen Victoria's Jubilee was marked with festivities to which many were invited. Mrs. Grethead rented a house in Kingstone so that reading and recreation rooms would be available for men and boys under fifteen. Newspapers and games were provided and a charge of one shilling a quarter or a penny a week was made. When her nephew Percy Clive came of age in 1895 the church almanac records Mrs. Grethead's departure from Whitfield which was 'sincerely regretted by her many friends in the parishes'.

The Girls' Friendly Society was another organisation run by the church. We are told it was to encourage purity of life, dutifulness to parents, faithfulness to employers, temperance and thrift. When a girl went away or into service she was to inform the vicar's wife and, if her employer gave her a good character after a year, she received a 5s reward. Going into service, either in a home or a shop, were the only real outlets for girls at that time.

A football club was established about 1897 when a supper and smoking concert for the members was held at the Bull Ring Inn. Games were played on fields loaned by local farmers. A library service commenced in 1906 thanks to the Bishop of Hereford who offered two large boxes of books. Miss Wathan of Bridge Court acted as librarian. Books were borrowed at one penny per volume, although later on the loan was free. The presentation of a rifle by Captain P. Clive in 1909 led to the setting up of a Mens' Club which met three evenings a week in the school.

Harvest was celebrated with tea taken in a large tent erected in the Mitch Meadow followed by a concert and dancing in the schoolroom, while the Coronation of George V and Queen Mary in 1911 must have been a great occasion. A string band was arranged, mugs were bought for the children, sports and a baby show were held (nine babies were entered) and a meat tea was provided for all. Dancing took place in the evening in the field behind Turners House. The bill for all this amounted to £35 5s 7d.

Meat Tea	12.16. 4.
Mugs	3. 7. 3.
Band	3. 0. 0.
Flags and badges	2. 4.11.

Weddings were events in which all the village participated and, when John Wathen of Bridge Court married Maude Farr of Arkstone in 1912, even the school children had a half day's holiday and arches were erected in the road bearing mottoes and flowers. The old custom of 'chaining the bride' was also carried out. The children would spread a rope across the gateway to prevent the happy couple leaving until some coins were thrown over it to gain release.

Some five years later, in 1916, it was necessary to employ a firm to clean the church and the accounts record that Lindsey Price of Hereford charged £10 2s 0d for that service. It also gives a brief glimpse of the days when horse power still reigned supreme.

70 hours at 8d. hr. 3 men.	7. 0. 0.
Lodgings for 3 men	12. 6.
Journey each way with ladders,materials, horse hire, man's time with horses	1. 4. 6.

The horror of the first World War was to take the lives of many local men, among them Lt. Col. P. A. Clive. In 1915 the Rev. H. Knight gave a lecture sponsored by the Daily Mail entitled 'How British Soldiers Fight' illustrated with pictures shown on the magic lantern by Mr. Bullock. Proceeds were donated to the Prince of Wales's fund. Mrs. Knight held regular knitting circles at the rectory to make socks and woollen hats, and organized regular egg collections which were packed there and sent to London for distribution to the wounded in France.

Mrs. Clive took over the supervision of the estate and continued to play an active part in village life. Charlie Powell who worked at Whitfield as a boy, remembers being told that Mrs. Clive wished to speak to him and wondering anxiously if he had done something wrong. She told him he had been there long enough and it was high time he was apprenticed to a trade. She arranged for him to be apprenticed to a plumber in Hereford which he is quite sure he would never have done of his own accord.

Life in the 1920s and 1930s still revolved around agriculture. Most farms had several teams of horses and some people had their own traps to

Thruxton rectory.

Mrs. Bethell with daughters Netta and Laura outside Coldwell Cottage in 1910.

travel to market. There were no buses but a Mrs. Gilbert, who had a shop in Church House, ran a horse brake to Hereford twice a week on Wednesday and Saturday. This was an open vehicle in which about six passengers sat back to back. Seats had to be booked and the journey commenced at nine in the morning, dropped the passengers at the Black Lion by the old Wye Bridge, returning at four in the afternoon. The mother of Reginald Jones who kept the post office, which was at Gladstone Villa in those days, also took a cart to Hereford twice a week.

Many people had bicycles, a few had cars and Charles Edwards, the master of the bell ringers, had a motorcycle. He was such an enthusiast, being willing to travel for miles to conduct ringers, that the Hereford Guild decided to provide him with this vehicle out of their funds. What a lovely gesture that was and what pleasure he must have gained from owning it. Bicycle repairs were dealt with by members of the Christopher family who had a workshop behind the cottages which were demolished to make way for the Yew Tree estate.

There were the two public houses that remain today. The Bull Ring, we know, was the meeting place centuries ago of the manor court. In this century it was home to the May Fair which stopped for three days, erecting swings and roundabouts in the orchard behind the inn. The front yard used to be fenced in and, to the left of today's front door, there used to be a shop. The Mitch Meadow was also used on occasion for the May Fair.

The Bull Ring Inn with shop early this century. Mrs. Davies, the licensee, and her family.

The Masons Arms is described in the old directories as a cider house. The landlord for thirty-five years, until about 1948, was Tom Morris whose daughter Mrs. Ruby Meats was born there. She has many memories of village life in those days, and says the great treat of the year was the visit in her father's horse and trap to the Christmas pantomime at the old Kemble theatre in Broad Street, Hereford. Both public houses were popular with the farm workers for their lunchtime pint. Summer and hop picking time also saw an increase in custom. In the war years from 1939 to 1945 public houses were often unable to open for more than an hour in the evenings since supplies of beer and cider were very difficult to get. The Bull Ring was a tied house and certainly found it difficult while Tom Morris at the Masons Arms, being a free house, was able to contact more brewers. He would be on the telephone early in the morning to see what was available and often ended up at Symonds Cider Mill at Stoke Lacy where he would load up, no doubt, with great relief!

The Masons Arms in the 1930s with Mrs. Tom Morris and her daughter Ruby.

Apart from the post office and stores, which were run by the Jones family for some forty years, there was the original forge where horses from the local farms were taken to be shod. Close by was the Corner House, demolished in the 1930s. In the early 1800s the forge and corner house were owned by the Baugh family. William Baugh was the blacksmith there in 1747 and his son carried on the business until his death in 1805. The next blacksmith was William Harper, then a John Davies whose sons, Amos and Charles, were also blacksmiths. The blacksmith who followed the Davies family was William Lewis who was resident at the forge at the beginning of the century. Another was Tom Phillips and then Bob Havard who was one of the last of the long line of craftsmen who had once been such a necessary part of rural life. Mules kept for pulling carriages at Brampton were shod at the forge in the late 1920s. Bill Stone, then working at Bridge Court, remembers that it cost £1 for a set of shoes including fitting.

The Corner House was occupied from early in the nineteenth century by the Bennett and Powell families. The latter were shop-keepers in Kingstone. Then the Berrow family owned it until the above-mentioned William Lewis bought it at the 1884 auction held in the Bull Ring. The last occupant was a Mrs. B. Wilding, a widow. Ted Colcombe who lives on the Barrow Common nearby told me 'she was a bit of a tartar! Folks used to shelter against her wall out of the wind for a bit of a gossip, and she would throw out the slops over them to get them to move'.

Adjacent to the forge, often the case since the two trades complimented each other, was the wheelwright's shop which today is known as Rose Cottage. This is probably one of the oldest buildings in the village. It is thought that the workshop at the back was at one time the hall of a much larger residence, possibly early sixteenth century. It has been added to and much altered, carpenters' marks indicating the late seventeenth century. The adjoining almshouses were built in 1712 and the alterations could have been of similar date. Rose Cottage was owned in 1830 by Thomas Preece, a wheelwright and carpenter. On his death it passed to his wife Mary who in turn passed it to her daughter and son-in-law, Elizabeth and George Griffiths, who lived at the Stone cottage adjacent. The next wheelwright was Thomas Powell, the occupier in the 1860s, but by 1893 it was tenanted by George Morgan who lived there until 1933. In that time it ceased to be a wheelwright and carpenter's shop and became a bootmakers. George Morgan was a popular cobbler because he always had a fund of funny stories, so the late Mrs. Grace Weeks remembered. The wheelwrights that are remembered today are Thomas Meyrick and Enoch Christopher. Rose Cottage has also been used as a butcher's shop and a sweet shop.

There was a cobbler living at Dene Pool named Bob Smith who was crippled from birth. He would travel around in the bottom of an old pram pulled by his dog. He was a very popular figure in the village and during the war some of the R.A.F. personnel, who used to chat with him in the Bull Ring, clubbed together to raise money to buy him a wheel

The Three Horse Shoes, Allensmore. Note the different forms of transport.

The old forge next to Rose Cottage, home of the wheelwright, and the almshouses, with limber well loaded outside the Bull Ring in 1927.

RCHME Crown Copyright

Bob Smith the cobbler with his faithful dog.

Bob Miles of Barrow Common.

chair, such was their regard for him. Dr. Oliver Cotton also tried to persuade him to try one out but it was no good. Bob did his best for a few weeks but the wheelchair was abandoned in favour of the old pram. He ended his days in a residential home near Kington.

There was another Bob who was a real village character. This was Bob Miles who lived on Barrow Common. He had lost both legs when young as a result of an accident with farm machinery. Even so he was extremely agile, moving around on specially made shoes fitted to his stumps. Reg Powell remembers many happy hours rabbiting with him. While Reg would be pushing through undergrowth looking for burrows, Bob would be way ahead of him and, because of his size, he didn't have to bend down and would be putting nets over the holes with a minimum of disturbance. As a lad Reg would work with him at Arkstone cutting the bands of the sheaves and Bob would feed them into the threshing machine. He could climb a ladder as well as anyone and was always cheerful and full of fun.

There were few people with cars in the early part of the century. Allan Watkins at Dunswater had a French car. John Wathan at Bridge Court had a Humber and he insisted that Bill Stone, a working pupil or, in effect, a farm apprentice, went with the family to Madley or Kingstone to church once a month. There was little leisure time but Bill did go to the old school for whist drives where they played on the old desks, clumping into the building in hob-nail boots and leggings. Dances were held on a Saturday night, when the entry fee was sixpence and the music was provided by a Miss Wood on the piano and Percy West on the drums. In later years it was usually a three piece band!

The routine at Bridge Court in the 1920s was probably very similar to many other sizeable farms. They made their own cider, the workmen being allowed one gallon a day, worth about ninepence. The higher quality cider for the house was made from Kingston Black and Fox Whelp cider apples grown specially in the orchard and was bottled with wired corks. The cider house would store twelve to fourteen hogsheads every year, each hogshead holding about 54 gallons. At Hanley Court a horse was used to pull the huge crushing wheel around. Apples were carted from Bridge Court to Ridler's Cider Farm near Clehonger church, where they also had fifty pigs and used to have 100 litters per year. Mrs. Doris Meek remembers that a travelling cider mill used to visit the village from Eaton Bishop to make cider for those who required it.

Ted Colcombe's father was a waggoner at Hanley Court. There were eight or nine workers on the farm which in the 1920s included the Bigsty farm. Hanley Court had seven shire horses while Dunswater had five. In those days it was common practice to drive cattle into Hereford, starting out at seven o'clock in the morning. In 1925 a stockman would work a 60 hour week including Saturday and Sunday and would get the same wage as a waggoner, 36s a week. Workers who did not work at weekends were paid 31s 6d.

At that time the shepherd Amos Williams lived at Turners House close to Bridge Court and was a regular bearer at funerals. He would sport a bowler hat which looked 'a bit green around the edges' and would be paid 5s and given the rest of the day off. There would normally be eight bearers since coffins often had to be carried for quite a distance and this enabled the men to change part way to get a rest. This would certainly have been the case when the Ross family lived at the Bigsty. Ted Colcombe remembers when Mr. Ross died his coffin had to be carried through several fields and down the footpath through the Mitch meadow to church, a distance of more than a mile. He also showed me the account for his father's funeral in 1932 which included eight pairs of gloves for the bearers at a cost of 12s. This age-old tradition lived on for centuries in Kingstone and other areas.

Two workmen attached to Bridge Court farm lived on Coldstone Common, namely Jim Poyner and the waggoner, John Edwards, who had to be up at five in the morning to get the horses ready for work. The waggoner's job was of great importance since horses and carts were needed for all manner of work. When wheat was sent to the Bath Street Flour Mills the carts had to climb up the steep pitch at the Bowling Green, Clehonger on their journey to Hereford. It was necessary to put special fittings on the brakes to prevent the horses slipping with heavy loads on the return trip. Bill Stone remembers, as a young lad in his teens, bringing back one such load when the horses ran away with the wagon. He decided to jump for it after doing his best to control them. Bill said he thought Mr. Wathan had not known anything about it. Mr.Wathan kept his counsel at the time but teased him about it quite a while later. The poor horses had to be schooled very thoroughly with the waggoner's special black snake whip and it never happened to Bill again. Charity coal was fetched from the Barton Yard in Hereford by farmers in turn. In earlier days it had been brought from the Forest of Dean to Tram Inn.

A travelling threshing team would visit the farms when required. Sometimes they had to be tracked down in the local pubs which they would visit when a job was completed. Threshing was the separating of the grain from the husk and straw. At Bridge Court they would need to use six bays of the barn to deal with the harvest. It was a heavy and dirty job. The team would look a pretty rough lot at the end of it but it was all part and parcel of the farm year. At Turners house the barn was filled with harvest corn and threshed during the winter. Today it is a private house but it was a different scene in the days when Reuben Hughes would come along with his steam tackle to start the ball rolling.

The forerunner to tractors and mechanisation was the traction or steam engine. These were a familiar sight and Reuben Hughes, who lived at Green Villa now known as Yew Tree House, was the local contractor. He had his own steam traction engine which was used as a power unit for all manner of jobs including threshing. It was used to help with road making, together with two trailers which would carry dhu stone delivered from the Clee Hill quarry. Sometimes it would be fetched direct, sometimes hauled from Tram Inn Station. The stone was pushed off the trailers by hand. Occasionally Irish labourers, who had long handled hammers with which they would knapp the stone to egg size, were employed. The horse and cart hauled stone, chippings and water for the steam engine. A coarse layer would be put down first, then chippings would be sprayed with water and the steam-roller would be used to roll them. On top of that would be one or two more layers of small stone. Roads surfaces were still very poor. This was the cause of sometimes fatal accidents when people were flung out of their traps after horses slipped or wheels were caught in potholes. Dunswater Pitch was a notorious spot, several people being killed there. Reg Powell recalls that when Jackie Price from the village used to drive the Rev. Harrison to and from Thruxton Rectory, he used to whip the horses to get up sufficient speed much to the rector's annoyance.

Although the village had a post office the post was delivered via Clehonger. The postman had the use of a hut where he could rest before proceeding on his journey. It was situated inside the Mitch Meadow and he would blow a whistle on arrival. His round was done on shanks's pony and, no doubt, he was glad to rest. One of the first postmen was Claude Lock whose round took him through to Whitfield and Wormbridge. In later years he set up in business as Lock's Garage which still prospers today and is run by the Powell family of Willocks Bridge. The post office had its own plant to generate electricity and people used to get their batteries charged there. When the postman's hut became obsolete Mr.Johns at High house kept it as a store for petrol in two gallon tins. It would not be permitted today.

The first hint of industry came in the early 1930s when Mr. T.E. Davies of Ledbury Preserves purchased Webton Court farm with its land and hop fields. He had hop kilns on the premises then and, later on, started a jam factory which was bought in 1941 by Messrs. W. P. Hartley. They added a canning line and made marmalade which was supplied to the forces. The hop fields were situated either side of the road leading from Kingstone to Brampton and Madley. Tony Griffiths remembers when, as a young boy, his family were out from dawn to dusk with the pickers. His father was in charge of the hop yard and the cutting of the vines but there was no favouritism shown to Tony because of that. They all had to take their turns at different jobs. Sandwiches and drinks would be eaten sitting down between the rows.

Mr. Davies was a very strict man but fair. He would always do the bushelling himself, usually dressed in plus fours. The hop yards were kept tidy, no refuse was left on the ground. Tony remembers picking into an open umbrella, making sure there were no leaves, and then the gathered hops would be emptied into the long canvas bag, supported by sticks at each corner, called a crib. The hops would be put into a measuring basket, paid for by the bushel, the going rate being four bushels for one shilling. At the end of the day the pickers' hands were stained dark brown to black. The pickers who came from further afield slept in farm buildings near Webton Court or in tents. In the evenings a grocer from Peterchurch would come down and open up a shop for them to buy what they needed. He told me that Ledbury Preserves bottled for royalty and had a black van with 'by appointment to His Majesty' emblazoned on it. They also used special fluted jars for their produce.

Miss Gladys Addis worked in the office at Hartleys for eighteen years, until the business was closed on 22nd December 1961. She recalls

Three generations at work in the hopfields at Brampton in 1948: Mrs. Matilda Brookes, Wilfred Williams (Morgans Bus Conductor), Mrs. Elsie Brookes and young Brian Brookes.

W. P. Hartley Ltd. The girls are wiping jars prior to labelling.
L to R: N. Bucknell, M. Redmond, M. Young, M. Behan, ———, J. Watkins, B. Saunders, A. Powell.

W. P. Hartley Ltd. The area where fruit was brought in and conveyed to the boilers.
L to R: R. or D. Maguire, B. Norman, J. Lewis, N. Buckland, ———, L. Price, A. Clayton, N. Evans, L. Bethell, S. Williams, F. Jones.

many local people were employed in the factory, sorting, washing, canning and labelling, while the fruit fields which extended up the Bacho Hill beyond the village were teeming with pickers in the season. The pickers were paid on the field. Later on, peas were added to the factory output. Farmers were paid to grow them and deliver them by tractor, after which they passed through a thrashing box, down the conveyor belt into the factory where they were sorted, washed and canned. Blackcurrants and raspberries were grown locally but strawberries were brought in from Wisbech. The jam was made of pure fruit and did not have any swede or rhubarb added.

Tony Griffiths was often in demand for odd jobs like many lads in those days when labour was getting scarce due to the war. Mr. John Wathan from Bridge Court would sometimes call in at the school to ask permission from the schoolmaster, Mr. Edwards, for Tony to be released for a half day's work on the tractor. When he finally left school in 1941 he was offered a job at Bacton Station. This little station on the beautiful Golden Valley line, long since closed, was a very busy place. Farm machinery and tractors made by Allis Chalmers were shipped from Milwaukee to Southampton, then sent by train to Pontrilas and on to Bacton, where there was a workshop, offices and stores. The huge crates were lifted off by crane, unpacked, the machinery assembled and despatched all over the country. Allis Chalmers also took over the vacant Abbeydore Workhouse for offices. Later on Tony went to Hartleys where he served his apprenticeship as a fitter.

Alongside Hartleys was the longer-lived market gardening business run by Mr. Tom Morris (Masons Arms) and his son. This comprised, at first, some thirty acres adjacent to Coldstone Common called Coldstone Gardens and, later on, some fifty acres of Street House Farm was added when Mr. Morris Jnr. bought it in 1955. Street House farm had previously been a poultry farm but, under the Morris family, became a successful market garden and pig farm. Many tons of potatoes, cabbage, cauliflowers, sprouts, peas, beans, carrots, beetroot, marrows and lettuce were grown to supply markets in South Wales and Hereford. The land was sufficient to grow sugar beet, barley, wheat and mangolds to feed the pigs which were reared for pork and bacon. All potatoes were graded by hand, the small ones put aside for pig swill. Breeding sows were housed in wooden sties which were moveable and placed in the fields after the crops were gathered. Pig meal and pig nuts were processed from the cereal crops on the farm. Corn was kept in silos and ground up as needed while the straw from wheat and barley was used for pig litter which became manure and was ploughed back into the land. It was a good example of modern intensive husbandry on a relatively small acreage and was, basically, organic farming. Use was made of everything without recourse to the buying-in of fertilisers. There was a permanent work force of about fifteen which could increase in the summer months to between thirty and forty people. Today the eighty acres forms part of the Madley Communications Centre.

Agriculture in the 1920s and 1930s was not as profitable as it was to become in the latter half of this century. Rents tended to be on the increase while there was over-production world-wide and, although farms employed more manual labour than today, all the members of a farmer's family would take their share. This would often mean the agricultural worker having to move when the son(s) of his employer became old enough to work. Many jobs had tied cottages which meant moving home as well as job. When Ted Colcombe's father worked for Hanley Court the family lived in a small cottage named The Thatch. Ted remembers his mother and other women from the village walking up after breakfast to Nell's Wood, on the outskirts of the parish, to gather wood for the fire and the boiler. There was not enough money to buy coal. Most cottages had a large metal wash container which was set in a brick surround with a recess underneath in which a fire was kindled to heat the water. The party of women would return carrying bundles of wood on their heads in time to get the mid-day meal.

Washing was put out to dry on hedges and bushes. I was told that on one occasion when the nurse called to 'lay out' a recently deceased parishioner, she asked if there was a clean shirt available. This caused

The Thatch on Barrow Common in 1927. *RCHME Crown Copyright*

some confusion since it was explained, 'they be all drying on the hedge, us can't put them on him, he'll catch his death of cold'.

The Thatch fell into decay many years ago but, fortunately, it was photographed in 1927 which gives one an idea of the buildings that still existed in the village at that time. Ted's father changed jobs from Hanley Court to the nearby Dunswater Farm so the family moved to another cottage on the Barrow Common. Dunswater Cottage became home for them. At one time the cottage had been a butcher's shop tenanted by a Mr. Thomas Vale who also lived at High House. The shed attached was the slaughter house. In the 1950s the cottage was lived in by Mrs. Tabb, a staunch member of the W.I., and I remember that there were traces of lettering across the front of the building indicating that a shop of yester-year was licensed to sell 'tea, coffee, tobacco and snuff'.

There was another black and white cottage on Barrow Common called White House, now demolished. It was occupied by James and Mary Phillips, a brother and sister who were sexton and cleaner for many years at the church. Ruby Meats recalls that her mother often called to see Mary Phillips who, being an excellent wine maker, always expected her guests to sample a glass.

The house known today as Barrow Cottage was known as White House Cottages and comprised three small dwellings. Ted remembers the three men who occupied them. Dick Cook was a mole catcher who always sported a moleskin coat while, next door, was 'General' Roberts, possibly so-called after the well-known Boer War soldier. He was living there as a young man with a family of five children in 1891. Then there was 'Tiger' Jones, a dab hand at rabbiting, as were Mrs. Ross and her daughter Ginny who, when Mr. Ross died, moved from the Bigsty to the Upper Jury Farm in Abbeydore. With a farm of 100 acres they had a full time job. Ginny, incidentally, ran the annual flower and vegetable show held in the field behind Turners House before the war.

Behind Barrow Common was the Barrow Pool, mentioned previously in the court rolls. This was a sizeable pond surrounded by trees which provided Ted and others with many a meal of moorhen's eggs. What a pity it has disappeared.

In those days before the coming of mechanised cutters, hedges and verges were kept in order by use of the scythe and long handled bill hook. Joe Prosser who lived in Yew Tree Cottage on Barrow Common was a familiar figure on the farms with his scythe. He also kept the churchyard tidy. I remember he disliked being photographed but if he was assured that it was only the scythe you wanted in the photo, that was quite alright. Ted would be paid two shillings per 100 yards to tidy the verges and banks on the Cockyard near Barrow Common and this included the topping of

KINGSTONE AND THRUXTON

GYMKHANA
: FLOWER SHOW :
AND SPORTS

to be held in

THE MITCH MEADOW,
HANLEY COURT :: KINGSTONE

(By kind permission of J. H. Bevan, Esq.)

on SATURDAY, JULY 16th, 1960

Commencing at 2-0 p.m.

MOTOR CYCLE RACES

Run under Rules by the Wye Valley Auto Club

ADMISSION TO FIELD:

Adults 2/- Children 6d. Car Park 2/-
Motor Cycles 1/- Bicycles 3d.

Hon. Secretary : Mrs. E. Watkins, Meer Court, Clehonger

Hon. Treasurer : Mr. R. Vincent, 20, Council Houses, Kingstone.

Chairman : J. H. Bevan, Hanley Court, Kingstone.

THE SHIP PRESS, ROSS ROAD, HEREFORD

Programme of Gymkhana, Flower Show and Sports in the summer of 1960. In earlier times this was held in the field behind Turners House.

the hedges.

The Whitfield Estate provided a great deal of employment as already mentioned but for Ted Colcombe, at the tender age of five years, it was a wonderful day out. He told me he would walk up the Cockyard to the Prill cottage by 6am where Mr. Symonds, the head keeper, would give him a steaming hot cup of coffee. 'I had never had coffee before in my life, it was a luxury, and it had a lovely taste', he recalls. Then he would start his day's work of 'tapping in' which was to tap the ground with a stick round the outside of the woods to keep the birds inside until the shoot was ready. They would go round the Treville wood to Wormbridge, then to Kilpeck and as far as Marlas Mill. At noon Charlie Powell (the

Joe Prosser of Barrow Common busy hedging.

apprentice plumber) would come along in a horse and trap with food. Ted would be given a bottle of pop, a big hunk of bread and cheese and a piece of cake. At the end of the day he was paid a shilling. His sturdy young legs were very weary as he trudged back home but I expect the money in his pocket made up for that.

With the passing of the years the number of people working at Whitfield has decreased due, in great part, to the mechanisation of agriculture and forestry. The estate still owns Dunswater, Hanley Court and Kingstone Grange, and Mr. George Clive and his mother, Lady Mary Clive, continue to show great interest in and support for the life of Kingstone and the surrounding area. In this age of change continuity is rare but the old parish of Kingstone and Thruxton, as it was, has been fortunate in getting the balance about right.

REFERENCES

[1] Inquisitions Post Mortem. Edw.III. Hereford Record Office.

[2] Hereford Deanery Wills. Hereford Record Office.

[3] *First Impressions, or Sketches from Art and Nature.* J.P.Malcolm. London, 1807.

[4] *Herefordshire Militia Assessments of 1663.* M.A.Faraday. Royal Historical Society, 1972.

[5] *White Monks in Gwent and the Border.* David H.Williams.

26 VILLAGE ORGANISATIONS TODAY

THE VILLAGE HALL

It was not until the end of the second World War that Kingstone acquired a village hall. Prior to that time the old church school had been the venue for social gatherings. Meetings, magic lantern shows, lectures and dances had all taken place there. The R.A.F. training establishment comprised many different wings made up of groups of nissen huts placed throughout the parish. The gymnasium block at Gooses Foot was used for a while by the old youth club when the war ended.

The W.A.A.F. (Women's Auxiliary Air Force) quarters were situated in the area around Green Lane and the present village hall was part of the W.A.A.F. Sergeants' dining room and institute. At the end of the war when the site was abandoned, it was decided to purchase this building which already possessed a stage. The parish council bought the building from the Air Ministry in 1954/55 for £100.

When I first visited the hall as a member of the Womens' Institute in 1953 I remember it as being quite large, very cold and in need of decoration. The building consisted of a hall connected by an entrance lobby to another smaller room which had a counter at the far end to separate it from the kitchen area. Off the small room was a toilet area. The heating was from overhead strip heaters and fan heaters. The roof was lofty and any heat travelled up and usually stayed there. The floors were concrete and very cold. The building flooded on occasions.

Christmas in the old village hall in the 1950s.

This was Coronation year and, when the festivities were over, the surplus of £40 which remained was donated for the acquisition of thirty new chairs and eight card tables which left a balance of 9s 4d. Well, it was forty years ago!

When the parish council became the owners of the freehold a trust deed was set up appointing trustees to run the hall. After an interim period a management committee consisting of a representative from each of the various organisations in the village was to be elected annually. It was difficult to find anyone willing to take on the responsibility. Various hard-working people tried the usual activities of whist drives, dances, tombola and jumble sales, while there was a youth club and the W.I. using the hall on a regular basis. By 1965 there was still no properly appointed management committee and the parish council remained responsible for the maintenance of a building which was far from ideal for its purpose.

During this time the kitchen, cloakroom and toilet facilities had been improved and 100 chairs were bought for £75 in 1961. There was no electricity and, although it arrived in 1957, it was late 1961 before the heating system was installed at a cost of £318. Dances were held with music provided by the Moonrakers, Marlasaires, Terry Phillips and the Melody Makers; names which will stir memories for some folk. Dancing competitions took place as well as sports days but the problem of overall participation and responsibility for administration remained.

In 1967 a serious outbreak of foot and mouth disease took a toll not only of animals but also of social events. The hall more or less closed down for months and it was not until October 1969 that a properly constituted management committee was eventually elected. It was realised by this time that the hall was in need of improvement and that few people wanted to make use of it. No grants could be obtained to make any changes until the trustees had formally handed over to this committee. This was duly done and the Charity Commissioners gave the hall its necessary charity status.

This was the era of the blossoming of the Playgroups Association and several young mothers in Kingstone were anxious to see a group functioning in the village. This was perhaps the start with regard to a fuller interest being taken in the care of the hall. Before a licence could be issued for a playgroup it had to be shown, quite rightly, that it met in suitable premises. A group of us got together scrubbing, sweeping, painting and polishing to give the required face-lift. A huge jumble sale was held to get the necessary funding for the venture. This did very well and the authorities, after their inspection, granted a licence. The playgroup met three mornings a week during the school year. This was to be financially helpful to the management of the hall as well as creating another organisation which embraced new faces and fresh ideas.

It was common knowledge at this time that the Dore and Bredwardine Council intended to build more houses in Kingstone. They had built two estates after the war and there was a scheme to build more adjacent to the hall. The idea that they might be persuaded to buy part of the hall site to add more houses to their scheme was one that would make major improvements,or even a new hall, a viable proposition.

The years 1971, 1972 and 1973 were eventful. The parish council, which owned the freehold of the hall, were willing to approach Dore and Bredwardine who in turn agreed to buy. The Charity Commissioners were agreeable only if the Department of Education and Science approved and so it went on. The land had to be valued independently with a district valuer acting for the council. Approaches for grant aid were made to the county council and to the Department of Education. We were led to expect grants of up to 75% if we could find the other 25%.

Estimates for a new hall proved to be far beyond what had been expected and it was decided to go for full-scale renovation, a complete outer brick skin, making the original into a cavity wall, and a lowered ceiling. The one rectangular building to be retained would be completely rebuilt inside with stage, toilets, small committee room and kitchen. The final estimate was in the region of £7500.

There were moments of panic when the government decided to freeze grants for some months, then re-instated them on a much lower scale. The amount that we had hoped for was more than the total the government was offering to be shared amongst three new halls, two of them in other villages. It was through the good offices of the late Lord Gibson-Watt who, as David Gibson-Watt was then our MP, that the county allocation was increased from £2300 to £6000. Fund raising commenced in earnest with a fête at Arkstone which raised £300. The Hereford Amateur Operatic Society gave its services for a concert, donations were received from many sources and interest free loans were offered and gratefully accepted.

The final grant aid fell short of what had been promised. This last hurdle was eventually resolved by the parish council who took over responsibility for the shortfall of £1500 by a county council works loan which was paid back over ten years.

When the rebuilding commenced, the chairman of the hall committee, Bill Burley, felt it would be better for a younger person who was used to all the complexities of such a project to take charge. Such a person was Peter Meiklejohn, a civil engineer, then resident nearby at the Manse. When the work was completed Bill took office again. The village owes much to them both and to Roy Vincent who was treasurer for many years.

The painting of the hall was done by the committee in order to save money and a sponsored knit-in raised £181 to buy twelve tables and fifty-two linking chairs to conform with fire regulations for concerts.

In 1975 the car park area was levelled, fencing erected and tarmac laid at a cost of £1658, increased over the original estimate by the addition of VAT. When checking these details memories that one has forgotten flood back such as the purchasing of two Calor gas heaters in 1973 due to the energy crisis, and the fact that the cost of a second order for chairs was nearly 15% more because of the increase in the price of oil.

The cost of rebuilding the hall, improving the car park, together with furnishing, curtains, china, floor polisher, etc. was in the region of £10,500. The sale of the land, the catalyst which set the project on its way, realised £1350, leaving a vast figure still to be raised. We must be thankful that the project was achieved in those days when costs were more realistic, although when the will is there, all things are possible.

In 1977 extra storage provision was added at a cost of £1700. Alterations were made to the small committee room and a new heating system installed which has recently been renewed.

The hall re-opened in 1973 with a dress show. I remember it had to be arranged with due respect to the, as yet unsealed, wood flooring which was duly covered up. A coffee evening was given for all those involved. There were many people who, alas, are no longer with us today who were always willing to lend a hand with all sorts of jobs and gave willingly of their time for meetings. One remembers in particular Bill Burley, chairman for many years, Marilyn Terry, Mr. and Mrs. Ernie Watkins, Bill Weekes and R.J. Field of Shelwick who undertook the virtual re-building of the hall. There were not many contractors who were willing to take on work which involved a lot of hassle over funding since grants were never easy to achieve. There were problems but it was a job well done.

Today, twenty-three years later, the hall has maintenance problems. With the opening of the nursery class at the primary school there is now no need for a playgroup and the high school has excellent all-round facilities for functions. These factors affect the number of bookings for the village hall and reduce the income available for running expenses. Having had a great deal to do with its progress over the years, I hope and trust it will continue to provide a happy meeting place for the village.

KINGSTONE WOMEN'S INSTITUTE

Kingstone Women's Institute was started under the auspices of Mrs. M.A. Clive at Whitfield in 1919. When the Golden Jubilee was celebrated in 1969, three of the founder members were in attendance; Mrs. Annie Gillett, Mrs. Ivor Rogers and Mrs. Grace Weekes, all of whom, sadly, have since died. Mrs. Weekes was the only founder member still living in the village at that time and it will be remembered by many that she was, even then, a very active participant in village life. She remembered travelling with other members up the Cockyard in a light cart with Mrs. Wathen of Bridge Court and, for some while after that, meetings were held in a wooden hut erected in Mitch Meadow. The heating was from a primitive tortoise stove and the members were often smoked out. In later times they met in the old school lit by oil lamps. This must have been a familiar happening in many Herefordshire villages at that time.

The members, from then to the present day, have always been willing to help in village projects while following their traditional role of preserving and improving the lot of the country dweller. Delegates attend county meetings in Hereford, the annual general meeting at the Albert Hall, the yearly county picnic, etc. and used to take part in various courses and entertainments away from the village. In Kingstone they would organize their own concerts. The W.I. has taken an active part in the running of the village hall through representation on the management committee. They provided the first curtains and many other items needed at that time. When in 1977 the National Federation of Women's Institutes decided to record the changes in the countryside that had occurred during the first twenty-five years of the Queen's reign, Kingstone members put together a very worthwhile contribution, now in Hereford Record Office, a valuable asset to future local historians. Today, as with so many other organisations, it has fewer members but is still a valued part of the community.

KINGSTONE SUNSHINE CLUB

Kingstone Sunshine Club is another organisation which exists very happily with its village counterparts. It was formed in 1972, Mrs. Doris Watkins having been president for most of that time. The fellowship amongst its members makes for a pleasant couple of afternoons every month, while in the past there was a yearly county produce show for all senior citizen clubs which used to generate much enthusiasm and some splendid exhibits. Kingstone used to do very well in the way of cups and prizes. Although this is no longer held the club still has its own show every September. Over the last twenty-two years there have been some very resourceful outing secretaries, notably the late Mrs. C. Godwin, the popular village postmistress for many years. For the elderly, sometimes living on their own and without transport, these coach trips to the many beautiful and interesting venues in the locality provide much pleasure and many happy memories.

Sunshine Club outing early 1970s.

Other groups in the village include Brownies, Cub Scouts, Scouts and Venture Scouts, whose activities are familiar to all. The Scouts have been able to take over the old school on a repairing lease, providing them with a home base while allowing the church to use it when required. They have thus been able to make some worthwhile changes which would have been very dear to the heart of Miss Irene Lee Warner who worked tirelessly for the Brownies and Guides for many decades prior to her death in 1975.

Another organisation working with a special aim in mind is that of the Kingstone Senior Citizens committee which devotes its efforts solely to raising sufficient funds to provide an excellent Christmas party for the elderly every year, which would do credit to many larger and better known charities.

There is a Keep Fit Club and an Aikido Club meeting regularly, in addition to the Kingstone Rovers Football Club, affiliated to the Kingstone Sports Association which has the responsibility for maintaining the six-acre playing field acquired at a cost of £20,000 in 1985. They were fortunate to be able to acquire old sports field equipment consisting of two ride-on mowers, a gang mower, lime markers, etc. for £700 from Painter Bros. in Hereford, enabling association members to do the work themselves. Although they obtained good grants, there are still loan repayments to be found, for which a yearly grand fund-raising effort is made by a sports meeting or fun day. A youth club has recently been re-formed after many years of inactivity, and it is to be hoped it will receive the necessary support and commitment for it to flourish.

WORMSIDE AGRICULTURAL IMPROVEMENT SOCIETY

This society was established in 1844 by farmers on either side of the river Worm, hence its name. It was formed to provide a day of competitions to show the skills needed in horse ploughing. Hedging, ditching and root classes were added later. Nowadays visitors can enjoy sheep dog trials, poultry and ferret shows, together with handicrafts, cookery, wine making and horticultural exhibits, photography and classes for children. It was not until 1951 that a ladies' committee was formed. How did they manage without them for so long?

The ploughing match is held at a different farm every year so that the whole area has a turn and, since it takes place on the first Saturday of October, there have been times when the weather has been less than kind. However, people still come and a good time is had by all. The first meeting was held at Whitfield in 1844 and the 150th anniversary was also celebrated there. Old photographs, utensils and 'implements of husbandry' were on display and in addition to prize money and trophies, commemorative tankards and horse brasses were awarded. The parade of shire horses

A ploughing match at the turn of the century.

with their gleaming harnesses and the pleasure of watching the old horse ploughs in action again attracts young and old alike. The original format has been widened, but not too drastically, to embrace the ever-changing face of agriculture.

With so many organisations functioning today there are difficulties in raising funds. One hears the oft quoted phrases, 'it's the same ones doing all the work', 'they're always asking for money', and 'people don't turn up to things like they used to'. Cheer up, it's not only Kingstone that has these problems. But we all know what they mean. Perhaps we should be a little more thankful for, and thoughtful about, all the advantages which are available to us. Should we not be prepared to do a little more to help those who shoulder community responsibilities? Villages like Kingstone are good places to live in. They will only stay that way if the inhabitants, whether new to the area or old residents, show support for and interest in what goes on.

The Wormside Agricultural Society committee in 1951.

THE PARISH COUNCIL

The Local Government Act of 1894 provided for the setting up of parish councils to replace the parish vestry which, as we have seen in the working of the poor law, did many duties which today are undertaken by different departments of local government.

In the early days the councils had little money and little power. By the mid-1940s Kingstone council were to be catapulted into much activity by the departure of the Royal Air Force from Madley. The huge complex of huts was deserted and with so many men and women returning from the forces, many newly married, some with families and nowhere to live, however poor the conditions of the dwellings they provided somewhere to settle. By June 1948, the Rev. D. Ellingford, then vicar of Kingstone, was chairman of the parish council and it was reported that the huts were in use for housing. The situation was giving cause for alarm and the local M.P., J.P.L. Thomas, later to become First Lord of the Admiralty, was asked by the parish council to inspect the site. He saw huts with no partitions, lighting, water or cooking facilities. The roofs were leaking, the walls were damp and windows were broken. There was no refuse collection, no resident policeman and rents of ten shillings per week were being charged.

Ten shillings was a considerable sum of money in those days. The average agricultural wage was between £4 and £5 for a 60 hour week, with cleaning or shop jobs bringing in about £2 per week. In today's money, 10p would take one to the cinema, 3p would buy ten cigarettes or a pint of beer.

Following the MP's visit, the Ministry of Health made an inspection after which things started to move. Lavatories were to be installed at once, brick work in the huts, to enable them to be made into flats, was to be put in hand but the cost was not to exceed £250 per flat. Water taps were to be installed in the open for use of residents in the interim. Number 7 site was to be cleared and disposed of through the Ministry of Works. It was acquired by the county council and used as a school playing field.

In 1949 electricity was installed in the buildings taken over for the new Kingstone Secondary Modern School. The village was not connected until about 1955 and then not fully completed.

The parish council minute books tell of an age-old problem of blocked drains and flooding on the Barrow Common and in the Dene Pool. This was causing a great deal of 'aggro' in 1948, just as it was forty years later when I was on the parish council. It was even mentioned in the Kingstone Manor Rolls in the seventeenth century so perhaps it's a case of 'man proposes and nature disposes'.

By Coronation year in 1953, while making arrangements for a fancy dress, sports, sideshows, tea for all, a dance and fireworks, and gifts for pensioners, silver spoons and mugs for the children, the council were at the same time battling with the deterioration of the huts and proposals from the old Dore and Bredwardine Rural District Council to build 100 houses. Eventually, since Hereford City Council were able to re-house some people at that time, this number dropped to the forty-four houses built on Cook's Lane, known then as W.A.A.F. Lane (the W.A.A.F. huts were adjacent) and now known as Green Lane.

In 1954, the parish council were responsible for buying the old W.A.A.F. Entertainments Institute, as it was called. The land on which it stood was sold to the council for £50, the building for £100. There was a, presumably rather unsightly, water tower on the site and, since by this time the Coldstone Cross housing scheme of eighty-eight houses was under way, it was suggested the tower could be taken down to provide rubble for the builders. However, the builders did not appear to be interested so Mr. Ernie Watkins of Meer Court, a parish councillor for many years, did the job himself.

Problems with housing, roads, sewage, public paths, rights of way and maintaining a playing field at Coldstone Cross, in conjunction with overseeing the running of the parish hall, as it was then called, were all part and parcel of the council's brief. The Local Government (Financial Provisions) Act of 1963 allowed councils to raise a rate of one fifth of an old penny which gave them more scope. This was followed by another change in 1972 which allowed a 2p rate to be used for anything that was of benefit to the community.

The new grouping of parishes became law in 1972. The council was from thenceforth to be known as Kingstone and Thruxton Group Parish Council. It held its first meeting on the 21st June 1973 under its new chairman, Mrs. Sylvia Chandler. An important addition to its work was the need to peruse and discuss applications for planning permission and to ensure that any person likely to be interested was informed. Whenever there was any likelihood of a problem the site was visited by members of the council.

This was an eventful time for the area since 1973 saw the proposal for an earth satellite station to be built in the parishes of Kingstone and Madley. Much time was devoted at many meetings in the succeeding years to planning applications relating to the station which has steadily increased its aerial provision. At one time it seemed likely that the rates from the station would go to Madley since it was partly in Madley parish, and is so named, but Kingstone has a sizeable rate from the undertaking which has helped the council budget greatly.

By this time the council were dealing with provisional speed limits at junctions and accident blackspots, playing areas, litter bins, street lighting, street signs, regular hire of skips for rubbish, grass cutting and car park inspections. With regard to the latter there were often instances of cars being abandoned or being repaired by people who were not resident.

Planning consent was also discussed with regard to advance factory schemes at Gooses Foot which are now in being and working well, while a pleasant minute book entry of 1977 tells of the decision to give all children up to 16 years of age a commemorative Jubilee crown coin.

The parish council are to be congratulated on their decision to assist in the formation of the Kingstone Sports Association when the opportunity to purchase some six acres of the 7 site playing field offered itself. It was due in great measure to their support that this project was successfully completed. The land is to remain for recreational purposes in perpetuity, its siting particularly fortunate since a new estate of some fifty houses is proposed to be built on the opposite side of the road. A scenic green area will provide a welcome change of landscape.

One entry in the council minutes, which is perhaps a sign of the changing times, was the application to open a post office counter at Lock's Garage, Allensmore in place of the old post office at Thruxton. The post office, and the forge before it, were a very important part of life there at one time.

End of an era. Mrs. Betty Wilding retires in 1985 after 28 years as postmistress for Allensmore and Thruxton. *Hereford Times*

The parish council has completed its centenary year of 1994. The first councillors would see a very different village from that of 1894. The main difference would have to be the number of dwellings: Green Lane, Coldstone Cross, Highland View, St.Michael's Close, Yew Tree Close, Whitehouse Drive, the Denes, Mitch Place. To these various estates would be added the additional separate dwellings in all parts of the parish. The provision of public amenities of all kinds and the increase in population would see the council of 1894 shaking their heads in disbelief. The present parish councils have a far more complex role to perform than their predecessors. They have worked very conscientiously for the benefit of the area, more so than perhaps people realise.

REFERENCES

Information from Parish Council Minute Books. Kingstone.

27 FOLKLORE AND LEGEND

Much of the folklore of Kingstone has been recorded in Ella Mary Leather's classic book, *Folk-lore of Herefordshire*, in which quite a portion emanates from the tenant of the Grange. When the calendar was changed in 1752 it resulted in the loss of eleven days from September 3rd to 13th inclusive. At the time it was bitterly resented by many people who thought that their lives had been shortened by that amount of time. The change-over had been brought about by Pope Gregory XIII. It took Britain 170 years to follow suit, while Russia and Greece waited until the 1900s. Apparently the old farmer at Kingstone Grange still insisted that the 'real' Christmas was the old Christmas Day, namely Twelfth Night, January 6th.

He celebrated in fine style and, for the twelve days of the feast no work was to be done, apart from feeding the stock presumably. At the Grange it was said that a tree was drawn into the kitchen by two cart horses and, when it had almost burnt through, a small piece was taken away and kept to start the yule log the following Christmas. This was a common happening because it was thought that it was a lucky charm and would keep the occupants safe from fire and lightning. The log was usually lit on Christmas eve.

Another story from Kingstone Grange was that this same old gentleman would bleed his cart horses, together with the oxen he used for ploughing, on St. Stephen's day, 26th December, and they would not be worked until after Twelfth Day.

Twelfth Night was celebrated by a custom called wassailing when farmers and their friends and servants would gather together in the arable fields where twelve small fires would be lit around a central and larger fire. Everyone would form a circle and shout greetings which would be heard over the fields and answered by others doing the same thing. At Kingstone the central fire was made of straw round a pole and was called Old Meg. The meaning the fires had was explained in different ways, some maintaining they represented the twelve apostles with Judas the traitor in the centre, others that it was the Virgin Mary surrounded by the twelve apostles. It was said that the Holy Thorn would blossom on Twelfth Night (it certainly used to do so at Orcop when the tree flourished) and the cattle would go down on their knees at twelve o'clock in remembrance. At Kingstone it was done only by the seven-year-old oxen, the same age as those in the stable at Bethlehem.

Another custom already mentioned since I came across it by chance in the school log book, was that of 'gooding day' when corn was given to those who were in need, in addition to what they had gleaned after harvest. At Kingstone so many of the children were absent in 1865 that it was noted that they were 'absent gathering corn'.

People at Kingstone and Thruxton, on the eve of May Day, used to put trays of moss outside their doors for the fairies to dance upon. One of the farms on the Whitfield Estate had a tall pole of birch with branches erected outside the door. The Rev. Archer Clive's wife, Caroline, commented that the church at Thruxton was dressed with yew and ivy for Easter and oak and ash for Whitsuntide, and that she felt the people 'retained more primitive customs here than elsewhere'. Lady Mary Clive mentions that one of the farms still had a maypole in 1940.[1] Yew was considered to be a guard against evil and was often used in other villages for decoration at festivals.

Very weird stories are told of cures. The one ascribed to Kingstone for teething makes one shiver. Twenty-one woodlice were sewn up alive in black ribbon and placed around the baby's neck. Poor little mite! Another cure was for whooping cough for which it was considered beneficial to pass the sufferer nine times under an arch of briar while eating bread and butter. After this was done, the bread and butter was given to a bird or some other creature (not a Christian), the receiver would die, and the cough be cured. A Kingstone woman recalled that she once got into trouble for supposedly causing the death of someone's duck in this way.

Another legend I have heard recounted was that of the huntsman of Arkstone who, in the time of the Parrys, was engaged to look after the pack of hounds kept there. One night he heard a terrible howling coming from the animals and went to find out what was causing it, taking his whip with him to calm them down. He did not come back and, when he was searched for, all that could be found of him were his boots.

It seems a lovely link with the village's past to realise that nearly all the stories told to Mrs. Leather were recounted first to the Rev. Reginald Hereford Bird, rector of Kingstone and Thruxton from 1885 to 1905. He was interested in history and folklore and thank goodness he was, otherwise we might be none the wiser.

REFERENCES

[1] *Caroline Clive. From the Diary and Papers of Mrs. Archer Clive (1801-1873).* Edited by Mary Clive. Bodley Head, 1949.

CONCLUSION

The Kingstone story, as I have tried to relate it, spans nine centuries and soon the village will be entering into the second millenium. The pace of change in the last century has outstripped anything that went before. At the present time this is particularly noticeable in the field of agriculture.

Today the land is used more and more for potato production. The rich red soil of Herefordshire is ideally suited for this crop; indeed the county is now renowned together with Lincolnshire for its potatoes. The demand is increasing from wholesalers supplying the ever growing number of supermarket chains all over the country. The fields have grown larger, more hedges have been removed to make way for one-way ploughing justifying the purchase of the large and expensive machinery which does the job. The precision drill has been a big labour saver; seeds are planted 6" and 8" apart, sprayed with weed-killers and watered regularly which has done away with many hours of field work 'singling out'. Even this has been computerised to enable the farmer to estimate the likely yield.

The pallet loader took a lot of backache and hard labour out of sack handling but, with regard to potatoes, the new process involves little or no bagging. After raising the potatoes, they are graded with an automated grading machine which sorts out the dirt and stones. This requires a minimum of labour, possibly two workers. The potatoes are then put in wooden boxes which hold one ton, and these can be moved four at a time by a special loader. They are then stacked in huge environmentally controlled sheds which are kept at a constant temperature a few degrees above freezing point. This involves electricity being operated twenty-four hours a day for many months, and a hefty bill. The buyer deals with the bagging and distribution.

The small farm today could not undertake production on the scale that is demanded in order to realise the huge investment needed to purchase the machinery. A large acreage is required, often leased from different places, and a hard-working labour force to harvest the crop. Two decades ago five acres a day would be good going, today double that is necessary when dealing with a big acreage.

The sight of round bales has now become a familiar sight. The black plastic protects the hay cut green for silage and keeps it airtight, while the lighter weight netting type is often used for the traditional animal feed. The rotary mower did away with the need to employ labour for filing knives and blades and these are now capable of cutting an 18ft swathe. Bulk corn dryers are still used, loading being done with a bucket on the front of the machine, tipping one ton at a time.

The introduction of quotas has led to very little milk production on the village farms, and there is also less meat production, due possibly to the increased demand for white meat and the proximity of Sun Valley Products in the area. Sheep farming is still carried on and the bigger farms still have large arable acreages, but the imposition of a two per cent reduction on land for cultivation means the farmer has to do his sums very carefully these days, hence the introduction of computers into the farm office. Sugar beet is still a main crop but orchards are a thing of the past.

Farming today is a stressful occupation and, in many ways, those working our land could be thought of as industrial craftsmen since they have had to adapt to handling machinery and ideas every bit as demanding as those in technology and industry.

When one looks at the pastoral beauty of the land that is Kingstone, I find myself thinking that the common fields of long ago probably did not look so different from the huge areas we see today, devoid of hedges and stretching for what seems to be miles. When travelling down the Cockyard to Kingstone in my mind's eye I can see William Popkin trudging behind his team of oxen and his plough into the Adder Pits, and Francis Clarke keeping a close watch on his tenants working the strips in Kipperley and Christfield. I can imagine the Rev. Mr Vaughan trotting along the lane from Thruxton Rectory past the bounds of Kingstone Grange, which the white monks were at such pains to establish, to meet William Baugh and others gathered in the church for the parish meeting which would adjourn to 'ye Buldring'. This is what comes of knowing a village for some forty-three years and having the opportunity of being privy to so many of its secrets. I hope that this journey through the past will give as much pleasure to the reader as it gave to the writer.

APPENDICES

APPENDIX I THE MANOR OF KINGSTONE in WESTON-UNDER-PENYARD, HEREFORDSHIRE.

The Domesday Book for Herefordshire shows the small manor of Kingstone in Weston-under Penyard listed as 'Land of the Church of Cormeilles'. It is placed under Bromsash Hundred in the southern part of the county. Since both villages had connections with the Abbey of Cormeilles, this has given rise to some confusion because, at that time, they were in different hundreds from those known today. Bromsash later became merged with the hundred of Greytree and was known by the latter name, while the old Stretford hundred merged with Dinedor and became known as the Webtree hundred.

The Kingstone in Weston-under-Penyard entry reads:

> IN BROMSASH HUNDRED
> St. Mary's Church of Cormeilles holds 2 hides in Kingstone; they pay tax and do service in Gloucestershire, but the men who live there come to pleas in this Hundred to give and receive right.

The Cormeilles connection made it necessary to check the Abbey's English possessions so as to be absolutely sure to which Kingstone various references referred. This was particularly so when it came to entries in the bishops registers when Newent came under the jurisdiction of the diocese of Hereford.

The Abbey's possessions in this area were catalogued in the surviving cartularies of the Priory of Newent, of which there are two, dating back to the thirteenth and fourteenth centuries. A microfilm copy of one is available in Gloucester County Record Office, while the other is in the British Library. Since both were in Latin it was necessary to commission a translation of the one in London. A copy of the cartulary at Gloucester was also obtained and after making slow and sketchy headway myself, Miss Sue Hubbard of Hereford Record Office came to my aid and, with her usual patience, cheerfulness and skill enabled a clearer picture to emerge.

When the index mentioned a 'List of farming utensils, etc. and their valuation, being stock received by the bailiff of Kingstone, co. Heref.' and 'Customary of the Priory, stating the rents and services due from the tenants of Kingstone', I have to admit to wild expectation that it would be Kingstone near Hereford. My hopes were soon to be dashed as I realised the names of the tenants and their holdings did not correspond to the information I already had. In fact, to my great disappointment as I progressed the names of Le Brut and Boletre established without doubt that all this information related to Kingstone in Weston-under-Penyard. The De Brett, Britte, Brut family were lessees of the manor of Weston, while Bolitree is the estate on which the finds of Roman coins in the 1800s marked it as the site of the old Roman town of Ariconium.

There are many mentions of Ysabel Boletre, Adam de Boletre and John de Boletre as tenants of lands held by Cormeilles. The Register of John de Trilleck records that Richard le Brut of Kingstone was granted a licence to have mass celebrated in the oratory of his house there, while a dispute over tithes in 'Kingston' was amicably settled between the Rector of Ross and the Prior of Newent. Sounds familiar!

The two hides of land mentioned above were given to the abbey, whereas in the other Kingstone the whole tithe of the manor was given with some land and one tenant. Kingstone was a subordinate manor to several other manors in Weston-under-Penyard and today is little more than a charming hamlet. From the rent roll of the Priory of Newent the two hides of land, which would have been at least 240 acres, was shared into many holdings varying in size from nine to twenty-four acres.

The names of the tenants, the size of their acreage, the duties they had to render to the lord of the manor in addition to their rent, give a remarkable insight into the lives of the people who lived there. This would not be very different from other manors and for this reason a few examples are set down here.

> William de Weston holds 1 messuage [dwelling] with a curtilage [yard or enclosure], 1 virgate of land and a water mill for which he pays 32s. per annum at two terms, viz. Michaelmas and the Purification by equal portions. He does suit of court every three weeks. He owes three hens and three halfpenny loaves at Christmas.
>
> Adam Haralt will plough for two sowings and will harrow, and on the last days ploughing he will have 1d.
>
> William Zeli holds 1 messuage and 18 acres of land.... He owes per annum 3s. at the terms above mentioned. Ploughing twice a year, once for rye and once for oats. And if he ploughs with a complete team he will have 1d. for food and drink. He will give three hens and one capon at Christmas, and owes reaping in autumn for 8 days. And if he sells or buys a horse or mare he shall give the lord 2d. as a toll. He is to pannage pigs, and if he brews he shall give the lord 1d. worth of beer.
>
> Joan Hoby, 9 acres of freehold for which she pays 18d. per annum Also 1 messuage and 9 acres customary land which Robert, son of Hugh the Reeve held, for which she works one day a week from St. Peter's Day to Nativity of the Blessed Virgin Mary, and three days a week from then to Michaelmas. And if the corn is ripe before St. Peter Advincula, she does two days work and reaps for one day as boon service. She also mows, sows and makes hay.
>
> Renna Haderick holds land.....and if she ploughs with a full team she has 1d. at the Annunciation, and if she does not have a full team she must share that day with a neighbour. And if the Lord's corn is ripe by St. Peter's day, she must do one days boon service, but not if the corn is not ready. From the said feast to the Nativity of the Blessed Virgin Mary she must do one day's boon service each week, and, from the Nativity of the Blessed Virgin Mary to Michaelmas two days a week. If one or more feasts fall before Thursday

in the week then she is quit for one day's work, and she has the Thursday for ploughing. And if a feast falls on a Friday or Saturday, she is not quit of any work because she will carry one load for two days, and will bring in six bushells of hard corn or eight bushells of oats to a load. She will thresh three level bushells of rye or wheat, 3 heaped bushells of barley and peas, eight level bushells of oats. She shall winnow and carry them to the barn.

William Suwant holds 1 messuage.....The said William must attend the county and hundred court at his own cost for his lord and for his vill, and if the hue and cry is raised he must warn the whole vill to attend the Hundred [court], if he does not do so, he will be amerced [fined] in the Lord's court.

All tenants had to attend the Manor Court (suit of court), pay heriots, and often paid merchet for the right to marry.

There are also two agreements; one made in 1241 by which the Abbot of St. Peter's Gloucester gave over all rights in Kingstone to the Abbot of Cormeilles for 60 marks (£40), the other in 1313 when the Abbot of Cormeilles leased the manor of Kingstone for life to John Dobin for 20 marks, the rent to be paid to his bailiff at Newent Priory.

When John Dobin took over he was referred to as the Bailiff of Kingstone and assumed responsibility for goods which he, or his executors, would have to account for at the end of his term or lease. They were as follows:

Two brass pots, also two posnets, one basin, one washbasin. One wagon bound with iron, also one wagon without tyres. One wagon for dung price 2s. ploughs with iron tyres and harness, price of 4s. One iron hurdle, one pitcher, a mattock, one spade, one great vat, two medium sized harrows, one vat for the bath, four great barrels, two barrels for beer, two baskets, one bushel measure, one dry measure, four sieves, one winnowing pan, one tripod, one andiron, one tablcloth, one towel. Also two bells in the chapel.

When Edward III seized the Cormeilles lands during the Hundred Years War, the manor of Newent and advowson were given to the College of Fotheringhay in Northamptonshire including this small manor of Kingstone.

The two Cartularies of the Abbey's possessions are in the British Library, namely MSS. 15668 Edw.I and Edw.II and MSS.18461, Edw.III.
There is a microfilm of MSS.18461 in the Gloucester County Record Office.

APPENDIX II KINGSTONE VICARAGE TERRIER

A Terrier of the Tythes and yearly profits belonging to the Vicarage of Kingstone in the Deanery of Hereford, delivered into the office there the 8th day of November, 1746.

Imprimis, There is due to the Vicar annually two eggs from every Hen and three from every Cock, Two pence a piece for offerings at Easter from every married person and child exceeding sixteen years, four pence from every Servant, one penny from every cow, an half penny every calf rear'd, the tenth penny if sold, the left shoulder if killed by the owner. One penny the garden for and in lieu of tenth milk and minute Herbs.

Item, there is due the tenth of all the wool, Lamb, Hemp, Flax, Geese, Aples, Pigs, Hops and other personal possessions, tythable through the parish the tenth of the Hay and Herbage. Item, the Vicar receives £1.6s.8d. in money and 8 bushels of wheat by composition from the Rector or Impropriator of the predial Tythes, And six shillings for and in lieu of the tenth Hay of Arkson, And 6s.8d. for an Estate there known by the name of the Grange for and in lieu of the Hay.

Item, the Vicar by Custom receives the tenth of Rye, Wheat, Barley, Oates, Pulse and pease in all home Inclosures, and old ground newly broken up, wch never were plowed in mans memory, or tyth'd by the Rector or impropriator there. Item, there is no Glebe land nor Vicaridge House there, only the profit of the Churchyard containing two parts of an acre of thereabouts.

Signed Richard Vaughan, Vicar.

James Wathan
Thomas Maddox Churchwardens.

The above document is in the Hereford Record Office.

AUTHOR'S NOTE: The Rev. Mr. Vaughan's reference to 'no Glebe land' is somewhat misleading. Presumably, he means the priest had no glebe of his own to cultivate since the ancient glebe lands were farmed as part of Green Court, the tenant having the benefit of them, together with tithes which were rented from the dean and chapter. The sum of £1 6s 8d and the eight bushels of wheat, however, was still payable in addition to the tithe rental. (Lease of 1799).

APPENDIX III CENSUS FIGURES, TABLES OF MONEY AND MEASUREMENT

KINGSTONE POPULATION FIGURES

1801	**1811**	**1821**	**1831**	**1841**	**1851**	**1861**	**1871**	**1881**	**1891**
372	366	406	492	501	510	460	488	437	369

1901	**1911**	**1921**	**1931**	**1941**	**1951**	**1961**	**1971**	**1981**	**1991**
347	346	333	292	War	1161	948	890	1031	1021

OCCUPATIONS other than agriculture (farmers, shepherds, cowmen, waggoners, farm servants and labourers).

	1841		1891		
	Inhabited Houses 93		Inhabited Houses 119		
1	Cooper	3	Charwomen	2	Bootmakers
2	Publicans	1	Well Sinker	1	Doctor
1	Maltster	2	Hauliers/Carters	1	P. Meth. Minister
2	Dressmakers	11	Tailors/Outfitters	1	Governess
5	Shoemakers	2	Laundresses	1	School Master
5	Tailors	3	Blacksmiths	1	School Mistress
2	Apprentice Tailors	1	Butcher		
1	Carpenter	1	Nurse		
1	Carpenter/Wheelwright	2	Steam Eng. Drivers		
1	Clockmaker	2	Grocers		
1	Blacksmith	7	Dressmakers		
1	Grocer	6	Carpenters		
1	Primitive Methodist Min	2	Wheelwrights		
1	Mason	2	Publicans		

REFERENCES

Population figures and data for 1801 to 1851 from *Population Tables of England and Wales (West Midland Division)*. For 1861 to 1991 from *Population Census and Surveys*, HMSO.

OLD MONEY

12	pence	=	one shilling
20	shillings	=	one pound
240	pence	=	one pound
160	pence	=	one mark (13s 4d)
21	shillings	=	one guinea

The original pence were of silver until 1797.

MEASUREMENT

40	perches	=	1	rood
4	roods	=	1	acre

APPENDIX IV ROLL OF HEAD TEACHERS OF THE KINGSTONE SCHOOLS

HEAD TEACHERS OF KINGSTONE AND THRUXTON PRIMARY SCHOOL FROM 1845 TO THE PRESENT

	DATES	SERVICE
Joseph Sanders	In 1851 census	Not known
John Jarrett	?	Not known
George Baker	March 1862 to March 1864	2 years
William Draper	March 1864 to March 1865	1 year
C. Fillmore	March 1865 to June 1868	3 years 3 months
William Bennett	June 1868 to Sept. 1872	4 years 3 months
Arabella Sarrison	Oct. 1872 to Dec. 1875	3 years 2 months
Janet Breckenridge	Jan. 1876 to Dec. 1877	2 years
Louisa Polkinghorn	Dec. 1877 to Dec. 1880	3 years
Alice A. Gregory	Jan. 1881 to Nov. 1882	1 year 10 months
Ruth Liddle	Nov. 1882 to Aug. 1883	10 months
Mary Lello	Oct. 1883 to Nov. 1884	1 year 1 month
Sarah A. Loversidge	Nov. 1884 to Dec. 1884	1 month
Emma Beard	January 1885	2 weeks
M. Hawkins	Jan. 1885 to April 1885	3 months
C.E. Bullock	April 1885 to April 1926	41 years
T.R. Edwards	April 1926 to Aug. 1949	23 years 3 months
T.G. Angwin	Sept. 1950 to June 1954	3 years 9 months
B.A. Williams	Sept. 1954 to July 1968	13 years 9 months
Supply Head Teachers	1 term	
E.J. Coleman	Jan. 1969 to July 1978	9 years 6 months
Supply Head Teachers	1 term	
J. Pullen, B.A., M.Ed.	Jan. 1979 to present	

NB: All the above teachers were certificated with the exception of Joseph Sanders, Mary Lello and Emma Beard in the last century.

HEAD TEACHERS OF KINGSTONE HIGH SCHOOL FROM 1948 TO THE PRESENT

	DATES	SERVICE
T.R. Edwards	Jan. 1948 to May 1948	4 months
N.K. Tillotson	Acting supply heads from	
A.G. Snook	May 1948 to July 1950	
G.L. Hall, M.A.	Sept. 1950 to July 1954	3 years 9 months
L.B.I.M. Lawrence, B.A.	Sept. to Dec. 1955 (acting head)	4 months
J.L. Reed, B.A.	Jan. 1955 to July 1978	23 years 6 months
L.E.J. Powell, B.A.	Sept. 1978 to July 1989	11 years 9 months
G. Bedford, PhD.	Sept. 1989 to Aug. 1993	4 years
M.E. Cousins, B.A.	Sept. to Dec. 1993 (acting head)	4 months
M. Bride, B.A.	January 1994 to the present	

APPENDIX V GLOSSARY OF TERMS

ancient demesne	land held by the Crown before 1066
andirons	pair of iron trivets to support burning wood, placed on each side of the hearth
assart	to clear woodland
bandoleros	small leather covered wooden cases, each containing powder for a musket, fixed to a broad band worn over the shoulder and across the chest
bill	agricultural tool for lopping trees/hedges with long or short handle, also used as a weapon by infantry
chafing dish	small enclosed brazier containing coals or charcoal for heating food or drink
chasuble	an over vestment, nearly circular, worn by a priest
chief rent	a small feudal rent usually in respect of a freehold by which the tenant was free of any other service
cheese ring	a wringer or press, also applicable to apple pulp
coberts	the rests upon which a spit was held, sometimes called cob-irons
cordwainer	a shoemaker
dissel wayne	an ox wagon
essoins	absentees from the manor court
faggots	bundles of wood
fealty	oath to serve
frank-almoign	form of tenure whereby clergy would pray for the soul of the donor
furnace	a very large boiler or pan, often of copper, in this book connected with cider making
glebe	land belonging to the church for the support of the incumbent
hatchment	a copy of the armourial bearings of the dead, placed on their home or tomb
heling or healing	a covering, e.g. bed heling
heriot	fine payable to the lord on death of tenant, a type of death duty
hide	measurement of land, about 120 acres
honour	a grouping of lands and manors under one paramount lord
housebote	allowance of wood for house repairs and fuel
hundred	an ancient shire division
merchet	permission to marry
messuage	dwelling house with out-buildings and garden, larger than a tenement
moiety	a half, one of two equal portions
pain or payne	a fine or penalty
pike	a hay fork

pillow biers	pillow cases
pinfold	another name for a pound, small enclosed area where straying animals were confined
posnett	small pot for boiling with handle and three feet
reeve	farm bailiff
saunce	sanctus bell
sub-infeudate	sub-let
suit of court	attendance by tenant at the lord's court
terrier	document detailing lands belonging to the church
tester	ceiling of a bed, of carved wood or material
tewes	harness
thrave	a measure of straw, 12 sheaves, just over 2 cwt.
towes	chains or ropes
tram	stand on which cider barrels were stored
tunicle	small tunic worn by a priest
virgate	quarter of a hide, about 28-30 acres
voider	a large basket or tray

SOURCE MATERIAL

Hereford Cathedral Library
Kingstone and Allensmore Court Rolls.
Capes Charters.
Calendar of Cathedral Muniments.
Articles of Presentments and Visitations.
Dean and Chapter Act Books.
Parliamentary Survey 1649.

Hereford Record Office
Kingstone Parish Registers.
Kingstone Tithe Map.
Kingstone Enclosure Award.
Whitfield Archives.
Guy's Hospital Estate Archives.
Coningsby Collection.
Kingstone School Trust Deed and Plan 1845.
School Minute Books, Account Book, miscellaneous documents incl. H.M. Inspector's Reports, etc.
Census Returns 1841 to 1891.
Land Tax Assessments 1777 to 1838.
Deanery Wills.
Glebe Terriers.
Perambulation of Abbeydore Parish 1822.
Books of Inquisitions Post Mortem.
Report of Commissioners concerning Charities *c*1835.
Quarter Sessions Books.
Testa de Neville.
Notes of Thruxton and Kingstone. Rev. E. Jacson, *c*1860.
Translation of 1397 Visitation to Churches.

Hereford City Library, Reference Department
Registers of the Cantilupe Society.
Webtree Mss.
Hill Mss.

National Library of Wales, Aberystwyth
The Mynde Collection. (There is a catalogue in the H.R.O).

The British Library
Newent Cartularies MSS.18461 and 15668. Abbey of Cormeilles.

Gloucester County Record Office
Newent Cartulary. Microfilm 208. Copy of MSS.18461.
Transactions of the Bristol and Gloucester Archaelogical Society.

BIBLIOGRAPHY

C.W. ATKINS 'Evolution of Rural Settlements, Herefordshire'..Thesis. H.R.O.
W.O. AULT *Open Field Farming in Medieval England*, 1972.
A.T. BANNISTER *History of Ewyas Harold*, 1902
...*Herefordshire Place Names*, 1916
...*The Cathedral Church of Hereford*.
M. CLIVE *Caroline Clive*, 1949
S.D. COATES and D.G. TUCKER *Water Mills of the Middle Wye Valley*, 1983
R. COBBALD *Biography of a Victorian Village*, 1977
G.H. CORK *Medieval Chantries and Chantry Chapels*, 1963
J.C. COX *Royal Forests of England*, 1905
W. DUGDALE *Monasticon Anglicanum*, 1849 ed.
K. EDWARDS *English Secular Cathedrals in the Middle Ages*, 1949
R.W. EYTON *Antiquities of Shropshire*, vol.5, 1854/60
M.A.FARADAY *Herefordshire Militia Assessments of 1663*, 1972
G.E. and K.R. FUSSELL *The English Countryman*, 1981
V.H.GALBRAITH and J.TAIT, eds. *Herefordshire Domesday*, 1950
H.L.GRAY *English Field Systems*, 1959 ed.
C.GITTINGS *Death, Burial and the Individual in Early Modern England*, 1984
P.C.HAMMOND *The Parson and the Victorian Parish*, 1977
P.HORN *Labouring Life in the Victorian Countryside*, 1976
W.H. HOSKINS *The Midland Peasant*, 1957
...*Fieldwork in Local History*, 1982 ed.
...*Local History in England*, 1962 ed.
N.J. HONE *The Manor and Manorial Records*, 1906
E.M. LEATHER *Folk-Lore of Herefordshire*, 1973 ed. (reprinted 1991)
J.H. MATTHEWS *History of Herefordshire*, 1912
J.P. MALCOLM *First Impressions, or Sketches from Art and Nature*. London, 1807.
J.R.H. MOORMAN *History of the Church of England*, 1953
M. MUNTHE *Hellens*, 1957
R. PARKER *The Common Stream*, 1975
N. PEVSNER *Herefordshire*, Buildings of England series, 1963
C. PLATT *The Monastic Grange in Medieval England*, 1969
C. READE, ed. *Memorials of Old Herefordshire*, 1904
R.B. PUGH *How to write a Parish History*, 1954 ed.
C.J. ROBINSON *Mansions and Manors of Herefordshire*, 1873
F. SHARPE *Church Bells of Herefordshire*, 1969-75
F. SEEBOHM The English Village Community, 1913
B. SCUDAMORE & H.C. MOFFATT Church Plate of the County of Hereford, 1903
C. TAYLOR *Villages in the Landscape*, 1975
W.E. TATE *The Parish Chest*, 1983 ed.
F. & C. THORN, eds. *Domesday Book, Herefordshire*, 1983
J. WEST *Village Records*, 1962

D.G. WALTER 'Honours of the Earls of Hereford in the 12C', in Transactions of the Bristol and Gloucester Archaeological Society, 1960.
D.H. WILLIAMS *White Monks in Gwent and the Border*, 1976
W.G. WIGHTMAN *The Lacy Family in Herefordshire*.
Burkes Peerage and Burkes Extinct Peerage, Victoria County History, The Hereford Journal, The Hereford Times, trade directories, Transactions of the Woolhope Naturalists' Field Club, Michelin Guide to Normandy.

DEEDS perused by kind permission of the owners:
2, Lyndale Cottages; Meadow End, Dene Pool; Brook Cottage; Whitehouse Farm; Upper New Mills, Eaton Bishop; High House and the Dell; Rose Cottage (the Tin House) now demolished; Rose Cottage, adjacent to the Forge; Church House; Kingstone Mill; Yew Tree Cottage; Gladstone Villa; Stoney Cottage; Kingstone Forge; The old Orles Nursery, Smallbrook; Smallbrook Farm.

INDEX